In the Garden

Essays in Honor of Frances Hodgson Burnett

Edited by
Angelica Shirley Carpenter

THE SCARECROW PRESS, INC.
Lanham, Maryland · Toronto · Plymouth, UK
2006

SCARECROW PRESS, INC.

Published in the United States of America
by Scarecrow Press, Inc.
A wholly owned subsidiary of
The Rowman & Littlefield Publishing Group, Inc.
4501 Forbes Boulevard, Suite 200, Lanham, Maryland 20706
www.scarecrowpress.com

Estover Road
Plymouth PL6 7PY
United Kingdom

Copyright © 2006 by Angelica Shirley Carpenter

All rights reserved. No part of this publication may be reproduced, stored in a retrieval system, or transmitted in any form or by any means, electronic, mechanical, photocopying, recording, or otherwise, without the prior permission of the publisher.

British Library Cataloguing in Publication Information Available

Library of Congress Cataloging-in-Publication Data

In the garden : essays in honor of Frances Hodgson Burnett / edited by Angelica Shirley Carpenter.
   p. cm.
   Includes index.
   ISBN-13: 978-0-8108-5288-4 (pbk. : alk. paper)
   ISBN-10: 0-8108-5288-8 (pbk. : alk. paper)
   1. Burnett, Frances Hodgson, 1849–1924. I. Carpenter, Angelica Shirley.

PS1216.I5 2006
813'.4—dc22

2006017825

∞™ The paper used in this publication meets the minimum requirements of American National Standard for Information Sciences—Permanence of Paper for Printed Library Materials, ANSI/NISO Z39.48-1992.
Manufactured in the United States of America.

For Susan

Frances Hodgson Burnett as photographed by Frances Benjamin Johnston in 1895 in Washington, D.C. Reproduced by permission of The Huntington Library, San Marino, California.

Contents

	Foreword *Michael Cart*	vii
	Acknowledgments	ix
	Introduction *Angelica Shirley Carpenter*	xi
1	Not Just for Children: The Life and Legacy of Frances Hodgson Burnett *Gretchen Holbrook Gerzina*	1
2	A Biographer Looks Back *Ann Thwaite*	17
3	Rereading *Little Lord Fauntleroy*: Deconstructing the Innocent Child *Ariko Kawabata*	33
4	The Changing Mothering Roles in *Little Lord Fauntleroy*, *A Little Princess*, and *The Secret Garden* *Deborah Druley*	51
5	Rats in Black Holes and Corners: An Examination of Frances Hodgson Burnett's Portrayal of the Urban Poor *Carole Dunbar*	67
6	The Making of a Marchioness *Alison Lurie*	79
7	Lady of the Manor *Angelica Shirley Carpenter*	93

8	"A Delicate Invisible Hand": Frances Hodgson Burnett's Contributions to Theatre for Youth *Barbara Jo Maier*	113
9	The Film Adaptations of Frances Hodgson Burnett's Stories *Paul H. Frobose*	131
10	Snugness: The Robin in Its Nest *Jerry Griswold*	147
11	Cultural Work: The Critical and Commercial Reception of *The Secret Garden*, 1911–2004 *Anne Lundin*	153
12	Painting the Garden: Noel Streatfeild, the Garden as Restorative, and Pre-1950 Dramatizations of *The Secret Garden* *Sally Sims Stokes*	169
13	Dreams, Imaginations, and Shattered Illusions: Overlooked Realism in Carol Wiseman's Film Adaptation of Burnett's *A Little Princess* *Lance Weldy*	189
14	Discovering the Fiction of Frances Hodgson Burnett *Deborah Fox Bellew*	205
15	The Frances Hodgson Burnett Online Discussion Group: A Modern History *Diana Birchall*	217
16	Keeper of the Keys *Gretchen Holbrook Gerzina Interviews Penny Deupree*	223
	A Filmography of Motion Picture Adaptations of Frances Hodgson Burnett's Stories *Paul H. Frobose*	231
	Index	243
	About the Editor and Contributors	257

Foreword

Michael Cart

Though she died more than eighty years ago, Anglo-American author Frances Hodgson Burnett's reputation remains evergreen, and her work continues to inspire the interest of casual readers and critics alike.

Under the aegis of the Arne Nixon Center for the Study of Children's Literature at California State University, Fresno, these disparate folk came together for the first-ever conference on Burnett's life and work from April 25 to 27, 2003.

Among the more than two dozen distinguished presenters at this memorable gathering were Burnett's two principal biographers—Ann Thwaite and Gretchen Holbrook Gerzina—along with Pulitzer Prize-winning novelist Alison Lurie. Their international celebrity and the extraordinary diversity of topics addressed by other speakers offered evidence—if any were needed—of Burnett's enduring prominence in the world of children's literature and the capacity of her work to excite the creative efforts of those who continue to adapt her work for cinematic and theatrical presentation.

Included in this generous volume are not only essays from the Burnett Conference but also a paper generated by the thirty-first annual conference of the Children's Literature Association, held at the Nixon Center the following year.

Appropriately, all profits deriving from the sale of this book will benefit the Arne Nixon Center, which is quickly building a reputation as one of the premiere centers for the study of children's literature in the Western states.

Acknowledgments

𝒯hanks to everyone who helped with the Burnett conference: staff; student assistants; interns; sponsors; volunteers of the Arne Nixon Center; the Arne Nixon Center Advocates; the staff of the Henry Madden Library; the Friends of the Madden Library; the Fresno Area Reading Council; the California Reading and Literature Project; the Heartland Regional Library Network of the Library of California; Fresno Pacific University; and especially Provost Jeronima Echeverria; Dean Michael Gorman; Christy Hicks; Marcie Morrison; Jennifer Crow; Janet Bancroft; Maria Carrizales; Dearley Amara; Karen Dennison; Terence McArthur; Denise and Salvatore Sciandra; Laurel Ashlock; Kathleen Godfrey; Cynthia McDonald; Jo Ellen Priest Misakian; Kathie Reid; Bob Boro; Bill and Lise Van Beurden; John, Rebecca, and Katharine McGregor; Phyllis Bixler; Terry Lewis; the performers and teachers from Bullard TALENT K–8 School; and my husband Richard Carpenter.

For help with illustrations, thanks to contributors Deborah Fox Bellew, Penny Deupree, and Sally Sims Stokes, and to Robert Hirst and Peter E. Hanff of the Bancroft Library at Berkeley.

Special thanks to my assistant editor Matthew Borrego.

Introduction

Angelica Shirley Carpenter

If People magazine had existed in Frances Hodgson Burnett's lifetime, she would certainly have figured prominently in its pages. Celebrities were newsworthy, even in the late 1800s, and bestselling novelist Burnett was on the A list. Her books, plays, travels, elaborate clothes, and her unconventional personal life made front page news on both sides of the Atlantic. A Victorian "Lifestyles of the Rich and Famous" would have included her, too, as part of two social circles—the most prominent British and American writers, actors, artists, and politicians (see figure I.1).

In new times and in new media, her fame continues. A Google search for her name yields 310,000 citations. A search for the phrase "The Secret Garden" results in almost two million hits. Admittedly not all of these are related to the title of her most famous book, but many are.

Her work was featured at the British Library in 2005, in an exhibition entitled "The Writer in the Garden." Here were displayed five handwritten pages, in her sloping, hard-to-read writing, from the manuscript of *The Secret Garden*. A caption proclaimed this novel "one of the most influential books ever written" and credited Burnett with inspiring D. H. Lawrence, "whose *Lady Chatterley's Lover* also contains a great house on the Yorkshire moors, a repressed, invalided aristocrat and a warm, vital working class man who understands the ways of bird and beast . . . the echoes persist [throughout Lawrence's novel]." I wonder if Frances Hodgson Burnett would have approved of the company she is keeping in the twenty-first century!

In 2005 she was also featured at the Tate Britain (art museum) in "The Cult of Youth" exhibition. "Frances Hodgson Burnett's 'The Secret

I.1 Celebrity author Frances Hodgson Burnett tells how she based the character of Fauntleroy on her younger son, Vivian. Illustrations by Reginald Birch. Private collection of Deborah Fox Bellew.

Garden' 1911 suggested the open air could nurture a wholesome physicality," said the exhibition's introductory sign. "Childhood was the key theme at the end of the 19th century." Proclaiming *The Secret Garden* the culmination of a trend of youth-obsessed books like *Peter Pan* and *The Picture of Dorian Gray*, the Tate displayed paintings of children playing and working out of doors. "Studies of sunlight on children's faces and bodies suggest the open air was seen as nurturing and confirmed a new aesthetic of youthful athleticism and beauty," the sign continued.

More than a century later, that aesthetic still holds. Burnett's books and books about her can be found in libraries, bookstores, and children's literature courses. Her adult novels, long forgotten, are making a comeback and her most popular children's stories live on in movies, audio recordings, plays, and television programs and in contemporary books, too. Meg Cabot began *The Princess Diaries* with an epigraph from *A Little Princess*. Best-selling authors like Lois Lowry, Jane Yolen, Katherine Patterson, Kate DiCamillo, and Jacqueline Wilson, the Children's Laureate of Britain, claim Burnett as a childhood favorite and a major influence on their own writing.

I have found tributes to her work in more unlikely places, too, for example, six years ago, when I moved to Fresno, California. There I saw a large community vegetable garden. The gardeners, I learned, were Hmong immigrants, recently arrived in the United States from Laos.

I met Richard Moats, who was teaching English to a class of these Hmong men and boys. He had planned to use children's books in this effort. But the books he had selected were not needed; the class he took over had already started reading a long novel, *The Secret Garden*. Richard worried that this book might be more appropriate for female readers, and he feared also that its Yorkshire dialect might prove confusing to people who were struggling with English.

But the book came through for him. The Hmong men and boys loved *The Secret Garden*. They, like all other fans of this novel, identified with the idea of planting a garden in a strange land in order to make a new home.

The book you are reading now is an exploration of ideas, some traditional and some new, about Frances Hodgson Burnett and her work. It began at a conference, in face-to-face meetings, but developed via the Internet, which enabled contributors in four countries to work together. The title *In the Garden*, suggested by Sally Sims Stokes, was used twice by Burnett: for the last chapter of *The Secret Garden* in 1911 and as the title of her final article, published posthumously as a book in 1924.

This *In the Garden* begins with an essay by Gretchen Holbrook Gerzina, whose scholarly biography *Frances Hodgson Burnett: The Unexpected Life of the Author of* The Secret Garden is the latest to be written, and, to date, the most thorough study of our subject author. Gerzina, working with Burnett's great-granddaughter Penny Deupree, gained access to many previously unknown family documents. Gerzina's introductory essay, adapted from her book, provides us with an overview of Burnett's life and with an entertaining account of the way in which her friends conspired and argued about the best way to honor her after her death.

Published in 1974, Ann Thwaite's biography *Waiting for the Party: The Life of Frances Hodgson Burnett, 1849-1924* was the first nonfamily biography published about the author. In "A Biographer Looks Back," Thwaite, who is well-known now for her life stories of famous Victorians, tells how she came to write the first of these about Burnett. Working with Burnett's daughter-in-law and granddaughter (the granddaughter was Penny Deupree's aunt) in New York, Thwaite traveled also to Kent to do research for her book. There she interviewed people who still remembered the famous author.

In recognition of Burnett's worldwide appeal, and to give readers a flavor (or flavour) of the international scholars who study her, we have left British spelling as submitted, however, American punctuation is used throughout the book. Similarly the authors refer to Frances Hodgson Burnett as they deem appropriate, by a variety of names.

The third chapter focuses on *Little Lord Fauntleroy*, a book much beloved on both sides of the Atlantic and the Pacific (it was published in Japanese in the 1890s). Cedric Errol, the story's hero, became a role model for Victorian boys, but in more recent times he has been considered "an insufferable mollycoddle"[1] and "an odious little prig."[2] Ariko Kawabata, who first read Burnett in Japanese, offers a new theory about the two mothers in Fauntleroy—one good and one bad—and this, in turn, leads to a new, gender-based interpretation of Cedric's behavior.

Deborah Druley also discusses mothers in three books—*Little Lord Fauntleroy*, *A Little Princess*, and *The Secret Garden*. Burnett's portrayal of unconventional mothering in these stories hardly surprises, given her own nonconformist and frequently absentee approach to parenthood, but it may have seemed radical when her books were first published.

Picking essays for an anthology can be compared to choosing ingredients for a stew or any other savory dish that combines a variety of flavors. For a Burnett burgoo (well, really, it should be a Lancashire hotpot) we would need fresh garden herbs and then a little pepper and spice, which may be found in Carole Dunbar's appraisal of Burnett's portrayal of the urban poor.

In chapter 5 Alison Lurie, who wrote about Burnett in her book *Don't Tell the Grown-Ups: The Subversive Power of Children's Literature*, considers Burnett's novel *The Making of a Marchioness* as a fairy tale and its sequel as a Victorian melodrama, comparing Burnett's own life to that of the books' long-suffering heroine.

My "Lady of the Manor" chapter is a literary travelogue, historical and contemporary, about Maytham Hall, Burnett's country home in Kent. Of the many places where she lived, this was the home she loved best. The house and her life there are described in quotations from her books, which were often based on this setting and on real events.

For ten years Maytham was her home base as she traveled back and forth between England and America. In both countries she helped to produce hit plays based on her books. Barbara Jo Maier describes Burnett's considerable success as a playwright, which was unusual for a woman author of that time, and shows how Burnett helped to establish theatre for youth as a genre in America.

Maier's social history of the Victorian theatre is mirrored at a later time period by Paul Frobose's description of the growth of silent movies. Frobose offers the first filmography of movies based on Burnett's books and an interesting new analysis of her fame in the last decade of her life. Sadly, of eleven silent movies based on her books, only one has survived.

In his essay Jerry Griswold examines snugness—one of the particular pleasures of childhood—and admires Burnett's understanding of this concept and her artistry in incorporating it into *The Secret Garden* in one perfectly chosen image.

Anne Lundin examines the original and continuing success of *The Secret Garden*. Its fame and classic status came long after Burnett's death, following decades when it was ignored by experts in children's literature but still read and loved by generations of children.

In Noel Streatfeild's 1949 novel *The Painted Garden* (an abridged version is known in the United States as *Movie Shoes*), a Hollywood studio makes a movie of *The Secret Garden*. Sally Sims Stokes considers

Burnett's early and continuing influence on Streatfeild and examines historical dramatizations of *The Secret Garden* which may have inspired Streatfeild's realistic depiction of a film studio.

Lance Weldy uses Internet reviews to compare three movie versions of *A Little Princess*: Walter Lang's 1938 movie starring Shirley Temple, Carol Wiseman's 1986 version of the story, and Alfonso Cuarón's film from 1995. And the winner is . . . Carol Wiseman, who lets the dead stay dead!

Collector Deborah Fox Bellew offers up-to-date advice for finding, acquiring, and reading Burnett fiction online, despite her own penchant for acquiring books and magazines published in Burnett's lifetime.

Diana Birchall describes the Frances Hodgson Burnett online literary discussion group that she founded in 2003. As a writer, historian, and fan of Victorian fiction, she makes the perfect moderator for this group.

The discussion group offers a new forum for Burnett fans, who consider themselves a community of kindred spirits. One of them Penny Deupree—really is kindred: she is Burnett's great-granddaughter. In an interview with Gretchen Holbrook Gerzina, she describes the surprising way in which she inherited the family archive.

"I do not know," wrote Frances Hodgson Burnett, "whether many people realize how much more than is ever written there really is in a story—how many parts of it are never told—how much more really happened than there is in the book one holds in one's hand and pores over. . . . Between the lines of every story there is another story, and that is the one that is never heard and can only be guessed at by the people who are good at guessing."[3]

We hope that these articles, by people who are very good at guessing, will please the reader by offering new interpretations of Frances Hodgson Burnett's life and work.

NOTES

1. *Dictionary of American Biography*, ed. Allen Johnston (New York: Charles Scribner's Sons, 1929), 298.

2. F. J. Darton, *Children's Books in England*, 2nd ed. (Cambridge: Cambridge University Press, 1958), 239.

3. Frances Hodgson Burnett, *A Little Princess* (New York: Charles Scribner's Sons, 1928), v.

• 1 •

Not Just for Children: The Life and Legacy of Frances Hodgson Burnett

Gretchen Holbrook Gerzina

Editor's note: The material in this article was the keynote speech at a conference organized by Angelica Carpenter, "Frances Hodgson Burnett: Beyond The Secret Garden," at California State University, Fresno, in 2003. This article is adapted from The book Frances Hodgson Burnett: The Unexpected Life of the Author of *The Secret Garden. Copyright 2004 by Gretchen Holbrook Gerzina. Reprinted by permission of Rutgers University Press.*

In April of 1925, six months after Frances Hodgson Burnett died slowly and painfully of colon cancer in her house on Long Island, several of her friends met in the Manhattan apartment of the writer and magazine editor Elizabeth Garver Jordan to plan a memorial to their late friend. Jordan, a determined newspaper journalist who rose to the top in a man's world, had been the editor in chief of *Harper's Bazaar* and worked with all the big names in American letters, including Mark Twain and Henry James. She met Frances in May 1913 when they crossed the Atlantic on a steamer headed for Trieste and the two became instant friends, chatting over cigarettes in the evenings about writing, women's careers, and Europe and America. She didn't know it, but it was to be Burnett's last trip to Europe and the beginning of perhaps the most intimate friendship of the last years of her life.

Those who formed the memorial committee were united in their wish to honor the extraordinary woman they had loved. Little else bound them. Elizabeth Jordan was a brisk, capable, and outgoing woman whose efficient style clashed with the less decisive manner of the writer Marguerite Merington, whose interests were more social than professional. Merington wanted a committee that would work more slowly and include celebrities whose reputations could assist in fundraising. Kitty Hall Brownell, who had been close to Frances longer than anyone not related to her—for forty years—wanted to mull over the proposals without making quick commitments. Frederick Stokes, Frances's publisher, offered to do whatever he could to further their cause, except attend meetings. The actress Eleanor Robson Belmont, who starred in one of Burnett's most popular plays, had made a brilliant society marriage that kept her schedule full. It's not clear whether the actress Mary Pickford, who played both the mother's and child's roles in the first film version of *Little Lord Fauntleroy*, ever attended a meeting at all, even though she agreed to let them use her name.

What they and the others who joined them that day did agree upon almost immediately was the nature of the memorial. It was to be in Central Park, and to consist of something simple and natural, ideally a stone bench whose back was to be carved with the figures of her most famous characters: Cedric of *Little Lord Fauntleroy*, Sara Crewe of *A Little Princess*, and Glad of *The Dawn of a To-morrow*. All these characters were children or adolescents, as popular in their stage iterations as in the novels. Children could be read to on the bench, eat at small tables and chairs set close by, and watch birds in the accompanying birdbath or fountain. That much decided, Jordan set out immediately to interview an architect, a sculptor, and the park commissioner, and to have Frances Hodgson Burnett Memorial Committee stationery printed up with Jordan's Gramercy Park address. "Personally, I do not think the enterprise will demand much time or work," she wrote to Belmont. "As I have said, it is a modest one, and our plan is to raise the money by subscription, giving even the children a chance to subscribe.... It is certain to be popular, and it is what Frances herself would approve."[1]

At the suggestion of a committee member, Jordan met with the young German-American art deco sculptor C. Paul Jennewein, and the architect John Mead Howells, son of William Dean Howells. She found Jennewein's work to be "exquisite, rare, Greek," and reported that Howells "at once fell in love with the site we have chosen, which he thinks is ideal."[2] She took it upon herself to suggest that the birdbath should be designed after another of Burnett's books, *The Secret Garden*, which while reasonably successful when published had none of the outstanding popular recognition of the books represented on the proposed bench. Even so, she reported that "both sculptor and architect took fire at that idea."³ She was careful to let them know that the plan was entirely tentative and needed the entire committee's approval; they agreed to work up landscape and sculpture designs for a very modest fee, and to present them to the committee.

She also went to work drumming up contributors. Edward Bok, the Netherlands-born editor of *Ladies' Home Journal* and Pulitzer Prize winner, sent them $250 immediately, and the lawyer John A. Garver went in for a hundred. Then Burnett's son Vivian telephoned to offer another thousand—no doubt out of his recent and substantial inheritance from his mother. Within weeks she had pledges for a fifth of the projected cost, a location, and designers.

Somehow it all went wrong at the next committee meeting. Howells arrived, sketches in hand, and with the good news that Jennewein had decided to forego his usual $400 fee for such a drawing. As the sketches were handed around, the committee members were decidedly lukewarm in their response, "or vague, or critical, or all three." "May I be *very* frank?" Marguerite Merington interrupted, and tactlessly suggested that Reginald Birch, the famous illustrator, be asked to make a drawing for the bench because "everyone knew all about Mr. Birch."⁴ Someone else suggested that perhaps they could use the Jennewein sketch for publicity purposes, without committing to him for the actual commission. After seeing Howells out and dismissing the group, Jordan sat down and wrote scathing letters to Merington, Belmont, and Agnes Houston, tendering her resignation and that of her roommate (and likely her partner) Martha Hill Cutler. Not only had the committee been stunningly rude to Howells, she said, but there were now "two warring factions" in the group, not helped by the fact that Merington wanted to load the committee with her own supporters and take credit for originating the project.⁵ Houston attempted reconciliation, calling Jordan and leaving a message for her with Cutler, pointing out that the bench had ignored the carved figures originally called for but seeing it as an easily remedied problem, and acknowledging that Jordan's "work has been invaluable, and it would be most unfortunate for a break to cause us to lose her splendid enthusiasm, for what after all is only a personal and trivial point." Still, she believed that Jordan had acted too independently and didn't mind seeing her go.⁶ Merington, who had been present at Burnett's death, gave no credit to Jordan for the project's design and success in a 1928 article in *McCall's Magazine*.⁷

By the following February the committee boasted fifty members—many of them undoubtedly honorary and included for the value of their names—and was run by Rodman Gilder, the son of Burnett's most important editor, the late Richard Watson Gilder. Cutler and Jordan were back on the list, along with such luminaries as novelist Fannie Hurst (author of *Imitation of Life*); theatre owner and producer Daniel Frohman, whose Lyceum Theatre produced several of Burnett's plays; the actress Annie Russell, who had appeared in Burnett's play *Esmeralda*; and Reginald Birch himself, whose drawing of a woman sitting on a stone bench reading to a group of children appeared as the committee's letterhead. They contracted with sculptor Bessie Potter Vonnoh for the design, since Burnett's sister Edith Jordan and others believed that "Frances herself would have liked a woman to do the work."[8] Plans for a $35,000 memorial were submitted to the Municipal Art Commission and the diminutive Vonnoh went to work on the bronze castings of Dickon and Mary, the *Secret Garden* figures Jordan had selected for the fountain. In July they were stunned to learn that the commission had rejected the plans—which proposed to use "virtually the whole of the promontory that juts into The Pond at the southeasterly corner of Central Park"—and asked them to resubmit.[9]

They were dealt a further blow when in December a journalist publicly denounced Burnett for the "untold pain and sorrow" that *Little Lord Fauntleroy* had inflicted upon "thousands of little boys." The book for which she was most renowned, which sparked an international craze for lace collars and long curls on boys despite Burnett's protests and the fact that Cedric was a feisty and masculine little boy in her novel, made her seem an inappropriate subject for a public memorial. The park commissioner himself had to come to Burnett's defense. "Personally I am opposed to encroachments of park territory by memorials, but I cannot agree with you in your particular objection," Walter Herrick responded. "I remember reading the story of 'Little Lord Fauntleroy' when I was a youngster with a great deal of enjoyment. It is a beautiful, wholesome piece of fiction, and if hysterical parents chose to inflict upon their children the fictional costume of Fauntleroy I think the blame should be placed on them and not on Mrs. Burnett. I know my mother also read the book and she did not insist or even conceive of having me wear long curls or a velvet suit."[10]

Nevertheless the project somehow derailed. The Vonnoh sculpture spent years stored in the Grand Central Art Galleries, while a series of shifts in park management kept the memorial on hold. Finally, in April of 1937, twelve years after Burnett's death and nearly as many since the first meeting of the memorial committee, a dedication took place in the Conservatory Garden of Central Park, at Fifth Avenue and 104th Street. Walter Herrick was there, as was Mayor Fiorello LaGuardia, and a host of Burnett's friends. Her granddaughter Verity represented the family. The memorial remains there today: (see figure 1.1) the elfin reclining figure of Dickon, flute in hand, and a graceful and nubile Mary, the uplifted bowl in her hand serving as a birdbath in the lovely and life-sized fountain. Reading benches are close by, and it's all set in a wonderful garden.

The prolonged difficulties of the memorial highlight the discrepancies between private friendships and public reputations that plagued Burnett, and followed past the grave. How would she wish to be remembered? Did friends and acquaintances from one part of her life carry more weight than those from another? Who got to control the public representation of her life and work? These are, of course, questions that face a biographer no less than those preparing a different kind of memorial, and they are no less important when the biographer was a relative. Immediately after her death her son Vivian rushed to complete the first biography of his mother, hoping to circumvent the gossipmongers who might otherwise leap to publish a racier version of the way the author of *Little Lord Fauntleroy* spent her life. His wife, Constance Buel Burnett, wrote another version for young adults. Even so their children, Burnett's beloved granddaughters, grew up to be women who rarely spoke of her.

Burnett moved in an enormous and varied social sphere, beginning in 1865 when she arrived in America for the first time during the final weeks of the American Civil War when she was just fifteen, and ending with her death at seventy-four. Between those years she published fifty-two books and wrote and produced thirteen plays, married and divorced an American doctor, then married and separated from an English doctor. She was wildly successful in both America and England. That success began when she was just eighteen, and in the fifty-six years of her professional writing life, no publisher in either America or England ever turned down her work. She crossed the Atlantic no fewer than thirty-

1.1 Bessie Potter Vonnoh's statue of Dickon and Mary in Central Park. Photograph by Simon A. Gerzina.

three times, and when the ships she traveled on pulled in to the New York or Boston harbor, she was invariably met by crowds of newspaper and magazine reporters who asked about her latest play or novel, her marriages and separations, her relationship with her children, and her often fragile health.

She spent her life as neither English nor American, but reveled in straddling both countries' opportunities and attitudes. The characters in her books and plays delighted in breaking down the class and continental divisions, bringing American independence of thought and speech into the English drawing room, or Yorkshire dialect into the books read by American Southerners. Even her name differed on each side of the Atlantic. American friends knew her as Mrs. Burnett; the English called her Mrs. Hodgson Burnett. Until the last third of her life, when she left the English country house where she later set *The Secret Garden* and built her house on Long Island, she skirted the issue of whether she considered herself American or English. A British citizen for nearly all her life, she took out American citizenship only when found herself required to do so.

The two nations pulled on her in different ways throughout her life, and in 1907 she published a novel, *The Shuttle*, devoted to characters who spent their lives traversing the Atlantic, bound to both countries by marriage, work, or cultural affinity. "Fate and Life planned the weaving," she wrote on the novel's first page, "and it seemed mere circumstance which guided the Shuttle to and fro between two worlds divided by a gulf broader and deeper than the thousands of miles of salt, fierce sea."[11] The "two worlds divided" in the novel have as much to do with personal matters as with geographic ones, and so it was in her own life.

Burnett's life itself can be divided into two halves: from her birth in 1849, until 1890; and from 1890 until her death in 1924. We can look at these two halves in terms of children—those of her body and those of her imagination. She was born the third of five red-haired children to a middle-class family in Manchester, England. I've run across descriptions of her that portray her as a barefoot slum child, which was far from the truth. Her father owned a business that provided all sorts of household furnishings—from tea sets to chandeliers to gas fittings—to the thriving Manchester market, whose economy was based upon the textile industry, which in turn depended upon cotton imported from the

American South. In 1853, when Frances was not yet four, her father died of a stroke. Her mother Eliza struggled to carry on the business for a number of years, a difficult and often unrewarding task that saw the family make a series of moves to less and less affluent neighborhoods. When the supply of cotton dried up during the American Civil War, and thus the market for the business's wares, Eliza finally decided to take up her brother William Boond's offer to have the family join him in Tennessee where he had a series of money-making businesses and schemes, some of them more successful than others, some apparently more legitimate than others. Frances's oldest brother, Herbert, went on ahead, purportedly serving for a time as a Confederate spy, and the rest of the family joined him several months later in 1865, in the closing days of the war. Thus it was that at the age of fifteen Frances became both English and American; she would later become both Southerner and Northerner.

They lived for a time in tiny New Market, Tennessee, in a log cabin, but moved after a year into Clinton Pike, a Knoxville suburb, and later into Knoxville itself. There Eliza Hodgson died, leaving the young people to fend for themselves in a house they called Vagabondia, a house that became full of courtship, striving, and playfulness. Frances had long taken up with young Swan Burnett, a doctor's son in Knoxville; her brother Herbert married Swan's sister Ann; their two sisters Edith and Edwina married musical young men who were, like them, originally from England.

Before moving into Knoxville, Frances had continued to do what she'd done all her life: create stories for her family and school friends, and write them down in the ledger books of the family business. When one looks at this juvenilia, one can see—amidst the drawings of her done by her little sisters, and the moony "Swan Burnetts" scattered across the pages—the origins of her gift. She wrote endlessly, and her stories went on for too long, full of sentimental description breathlessly put down in often illegible pencil. In desperate need for money she sent a story to a magazine; it came back with questions but no check, so she sent it out again to another, and the rest, as they say, is history. She was never rejected by a publisher and became the best-known and best-paid woman author of her lifetime. She came to believe, as did many who knew her, that her stories simply materialized from some unnamed and powerful force. She rarely revised and stories and novels were sent off to the publishers virtually as they emerged from her pen.

She rather reluctantly married Swan Burnett in 1873—although mysteriously her marriage certificate says 1874—and they had two sons; after a year's sojourn in Paris they moved to Washington, D.C., where Swan set up a medical practice as an ophthalmologist. Her sisters had by now moved with their husbands and four children to California, their brother Herbert remarried after Ann's death and moved to Virginia; another brother remained in Knoxville. With stories published in most of the American magazines, and her first novel, *That Lass o' Lowrie's*, published in 1877, Frances found herself a popular and successful writer. She began to travel, making important new friends in New England. Her early serials were shamelessly pirated, and for years she would be involved in matters of copyright and intellectual property, later winning a landmark case in London. She began to produce her stories as plays, and felt driven to make money to support not only herself and her rather expensive tastes, but to provide for her sons a future in which they would become gentlemen. In the early 1880s she began to suffer from debilitating illnesses referred to as "nervous exhaustion," really a form of depression and nervous breakdown, brought on by years of hard work.

She loved telling stories to her sons Lionel and Vivian, sometimes turning them into stories she published in *St. Nicholas Magazine*. In 1885–1886 she published the story that changed her life: *Little Lord Fauntleroy* was her eighteenth published book, but it put her on the map as a writer. She became the J. K. Rowling of her time, and although it was not necessarily viewed as a book only for children, *Fauntleroy*—her first book that could possibly be viewed as a children's book—established her once and for all as a children's writer in the eyes of the future.

Her relationship with her own children was similarly ambiguous. She loved them fiercely. She delighted in being a mother. Yet at the same time, she spent increasingly long periods away from them. Her illnesses kept her away and secluded. Her work on novels and plays kept her busy. Yet even this was not as simple as it seems; she insisted later that she had a grand plan for their upbringing and development that only money could provide. She had an understandable reticence about talking to them about the eventually unbridgeable gulf between her and their father and undoubtedly saw that although Swan couldn't offer her what she needed, he could provide a stable home for their sons while she wandered. Yet her love for them was never in question.

From 1888 to 1890 she was away from her family, usually in London, more than she was with them; thus it was that when she fell ill in Europe after an accident, and her sons grew increasingly depressed in Washington without her, she thought she could encourage them by letters. It soon became apparent that Lionel, her elder son, was seriously ill with tuberculosis. Frances rushed home and took the boys to Europe, from spa to spa, finally settling with Lionel in Paris after Swan fetched Vivian home. In December 1890 Lionel died in her arms.

That is the end of the first half of her life, and much of what followed in the second half was a response to it. Her drive to support herself and make a future for Vivian kept her working endlessly, but she was also well-off and extremely well-known on both sides of the Atlantic. She traveled back and forth between Europe and America every year or so. She gave endless interviews, and began to support endless philanthropic causes, many of them to do with children. She took young people to live in her London houses, including the son of her sister Edith, whom she educated. She was, as they say, an easy mark, for her sympathy, and grief led her to support people and causes without questioning them. There is no doubt that some of this stemmed from her guilt at having been separated from her own children. She supported whole families: Edith and her husband lived with her or in her houses for the rest of their lives; Vivian went to Harvard and never became fully self-supporting; she sent money to her sister Edwina's family in California; she helped to support her brother Herbert, his second wife, and their nine children in Virginia; she supported her Manchester relatives. As she told someone who wrote to ask her to contribute to a charity in 1914, "Please *do* understand I do not carry mere single persons I carry whole families and they are on both sides of the Atlantic. I have been a fortunate woman but I am far from a rich one absolutely because I have *always* done this thing and also because there seems to be no charity or kindly plan of help on earth which does not—as it sometimes seems—appeal to me."

There are two other hugely important facts about the second half of her life: a divorce from Swan and a disastrous marriage to Stephen Townesend, an English doctor turned actor with whom she had a ten-year affair; and the taking of Maytham Hall, the home of her heart which she later used as the setting for *The Secret Garden*. Stephen nearly broke her spirit: he was a man of tempers and moods, and verbally if not necessarily physically abusive. She had sworn never to marry again but by bullying and blackmail he talked her into it. She finally escaped this nightmare, but at the expense of her already fragile health. Maytham Hall, in Kent—especially after Stephen moved out—was her Eden. She filled it with friends, and became a serious gardener, especially of roses. It was hers for nine years and she left it, weeping, when the owner decided to sell and Frances decided to build a house in America, on Long Island, near her remaining son and his family. There her gardens became legend, as they did at her house in Bermuda, where she and Edith spent many of their winters.

Throughout her life Frances was known for four things: her unrelenting literary production, which often drove her to illness; her love of beautiful clothes and domestic surroundings; her inability to remain settled in any one place, or even in one country; and her wonderful gardens. To these traits a modern biographer would add several others: border-crossings of all kinds, and transformations through self-determination and nature; a fierce independence, coupled with a sometimes disastrous sympathy for others; a tendency to romanticize herself and her life, equally matched by a warmth and generosity for others; a refusal to read newspapers, but a temper that rose up against wrongdoers and led her to conduct battles in public. She was, for example, named in a lengthy lawsuit by Edith's daughter-in-law, after Frances rose to Edith's defense in a family squabble. She was a passionate and loving person who inspired the devotion of nearly all who knew her. She delighted in her friendships and loves, and was utterly committed to those she loved, and to decent and philanthropic behavior. Because of this many who met her thought she lived a fairy tale existence, but shortly after her death her son said that "one of the most surprising things" that people would learn about his mother was "the fact that her life was not a happy one." He told an audience in Knoxville that "Frances Hodgson Burnett had a great deal of physical and mental suffering, and many sorrows that the world did not know about." In her final hours she told him "that she had never wanted to add more sorrow to the load that people carried. She wanted to bring real joy into the lives of other people. She was a real romanticist."[12]

Elizabeth Jordan, probably her closest friend in the last years of her life, recalled that "as soon as her success made it possible she transformed her life into a sort of fairy-tale, deliberately shutting out the sordid, the sad, and the unlovely. Nevertheless, when life called on her to face tragic realities she always did it with high courage."[13]

During the last twenty years or so of her life she wrote increasing numbers of short children's books, often for the Christmas market, sometimes to help Vivian in his magazine publishing career, sometimes as a break from her long, long novels, but also because they gave her imaginative joy. Still, she would be astounded to learn that today she is considered entirely a writer of children's books. Her novels often dealt with very mature subjects: unhappy marriages and marital infidelity, illegitimate births, spousal abuse, women who refused to be limited by societal dictates, crossings of class lines. *The Secret Garden*, which regularly tops lists of most influential books, passed nearly unnoticed by critics and readers when it appeared, and she discusses it in none of her letters the way she did with her other works. Elizabeth Jordan's shifting of the memorial's focus to Dickon and Mary was, therefore, eerily prescient. Few visitors to the bronze figures in Central Park can know that when first cast it would have been far less recognizable to those who saw it than Fauntleroy, Sara, and Glad.

Indeed, leaving aside *Fauntleroy*, *The Secret Garden* and the many versions of *A Little Princess* (story, play, and expanded novel), her contemporaries might well have cited several other books as bearing the Frances Hodgson Burnett hallmark. The first would be *Through One Administration*, her 1883 novel about the social life behind the political life in Washington. As a friend of President Garfield and his family, and as someone in great demand socially, Frances knew well the dangers and backstabbing that went on in Washington circles. It deals with a woman—very much Frances—who is married to a weak man—based loosely, but not completely, on Swan—and falsely rumored to be having an affair with a family friend—based on her friend Charlie Rice. In the book Bertha manages to recover her reputation and finds joy in her children, but it wouldn't be long before Frances herself became the subject of persistent and noxious newspaper and magazine gossip. As an indication of the wide audience for her work, I ran across a diary entry of my great-uncle, who was reading *Through One Administration* while serving as the manager of a western mine.

They might also cite *The Making of a Marchioness* and its sequel *The Methods of Lady Walderhurst*, two distinctly unsentimental novels. If marriage was ever to be looked upon as a financial and social arrangement rather than as a love match, that is made clear in these pages. Perhaps they would cite *The Shuttle*, a scathing look at transatlantic marriages and very much based upon her own disastrous situation with Stephen Townesend, or its sequel—and my personal favorite—*T. Tembarom*, about a feckless but street-smart young American man who inherits English wealth, a sort of adult and savvy *Fauntleroy* for the Jazz Age.

Undoubtedly they would cite *A Lady of Quality*, a book that for all its nods to love and marriage and sentiment is a clear sign of her growing feminism in its gender-bending heroine. It sold like hotcakes, and critics be damned; it went on the stage in England and America with its swashbuckling female protagonist a favorite role of actresses; like several of her novels it was made into a film.

Frances herself would no doubt name *The Dawn of a To-morrow*, which pulled together her uniquely formed religious beliefs of New Thought, optimism, and hope, all of which—as her journals kept after Lionel's death show—had to do with an almost childlike insistence on a glorious life after death.

For her biographers, the greatest task involves opening out the life and legacy of an important woman whose work today rests on such narrow ground. Fortunately, new material in the form of early writings, journals, and letters has come to light which puts her life and her work into a much wider context of love and loss, a growing feminist sensibility that led her to participate in the women's suffrage parades, a much stronger and more extended family context, and even a surprising and willful naivety. Kitty Hall Brownell recalled taking Frances to her first vaudeville show—something which quickly became a favorite pastime—and watching Frances's deep pity for a performer which an enormous hairy mole on his face. Gradually the laughter around her awakened her to the fact that this was part of his make-up. "Is it possible that that horror has been stuck on as being *funny*?" she asked. Another time, in bed with a terrible cold, she was warned to keep warm. She looked down mournfully at her already extravagant nightgown and sighed, "Yes, I must have more lace."

Frances Hodgson Burnett's life reminds us that before our time there were women struggling to combine work and family, and that just as it does today, enormous and public success often carries with it a private price. In her final book, *In the Garden*, she declared that "I love it all. I love to dig. I love to kneel down in the grass at the edge of a flower bed and pull out the weeds fiercely and throw them into a heap by my side. I love to fight with those who can spring up again almost in a night and taunt me. I tear them up by the roots again and again, and when at last after many days, perhaps, it seems as if I had beaten them for a time at least, I go away feeling like an army with banners."[14]

The image of the triumphant gardener wrestling with life itself and emerging victorious has inspired legions of girls on both sides of the Atlantic to believe that they could discover secret gardens and rejuvenate and order the chaos of adolescent loneliness. As she wrote hopefully from her deathbed in October 1924, one month away from her seventy-fifth birthday, "As long as one has a garden, one has a future; and as long as one has a future one is alive."[15] It is fitting that a memorial exists in one of the best-known gardens in the world, and that it represents in its design another whose name has become a universal phrase for the unseen and the redemptive.

At the dedication ceremony for the Central Park memorial, Brownell spoke of a story Frances narrated but never wrote. "It began with a description of a garden in May—a garden so full of wonders of color and form and fragrance, of wings and glitter, shadows and shine, music of birds and insects, that the impression was of something so precious as to seem outside of our workaday world, to suggest some elaborate and superlative garden of exclusive royalty," Brownell told the audience. "And then . . . the story was to lead one very gradually to understand that such a place was accessible to us, she had herself found it—amazingly!—in the plot of this very Park named the Ramble. There it stood . . . but the secret of seeing it lay with the eyes that looked."[16]

Understanding her requires us to look at her life and work and to see a woman who worked within and against the restrictions of Victorian life to develop her own code of spiritual and moral behavior; who wrote love stories but ardently believed in a woman's right to independence; and who not only became one of the most revered writers of her time but the only one whose name and work lives on all over the world, in nearly all languages, passed on from generation to generation.

NOTES

1. Elizabeth Jordan to Mrs. August Belmont, April 21, 1925. Columbia University Libraries, Special Collections, Spec Ms Coll. Belmont.
2. Elizabeth Jordan to Mrs. Belmont, June 3, 1925. Columbia University Libraries, Special Collections, Spec Ms Coll. Belmont.
3. Elizabeth Jordan to Mrs. Belmont, June 3, 1925. Columbia University Libraries, Special Collections, Spec Ms Coll. Belmont.
4. Elizabeth Jordan to Marguerite Merington, June 11, 1925. Columbia University Libraries, Special Collections, Spec Ms Coll. Belmont.
5. Extracts from Miss Jordan's letter to Mrs. Houston, June 11th [1925] and Elizabeth Jordan to Mrs. Belmont, June 14, 1925, both in Columbia University Libraries, Special Collections, Spec Ms Coll. Belmont.
6. Agnes Houston to Eleanor Robson Belmont, n.d., and June 11, 1925. Columbia University Libraries, Special Collections, Spec Ms Coll. Belmont.
7. Marguerite Merington, "The Garden of the Children's Story Teller," *McCall's Magazine*, April 1928, 71 and 106.
8. Marguerite Merington to Eleanor Robson Belmont, June 17, 1925. Columbia University Libraries, Special Collections, Spec Ms Coll. Belmont.
9. "Plans of Fauntleroy Memorial in Central Park Rejected by Board, but May Be Resubmitted," *New York Times*, July 16, 1926.
10. "Park Commissioner Defends 'Fauntleroy,' Tells Objector to the Burnett Memorials That It Was Wholesome Fiction," *New York Times*, December 23, 1927.
11. Frances Hodgson Burnett, *The Shuttle* (New York: Frederick A. Stokes Company, 1907), 1.
12. "Claim Vivian Burnett Was the 'Lord Fauntleroy'; Son Does Not Admit It," unidentified newspaper clipping in the McClung Historical Collection, Knoxville, Tennessee.
13. Elizabeth Jordan, *Three Rousing Cheers: An Autobiography* (New York and London: D. Appleton Century, 1938), 327.
14. Frances Hodgson Burnett, *In the Garden* (Boston and New York: The Medici Society of America, 1925), 20.
15. Burnett, *In the Garden*, 30.
16. Gertrude Hall Brownell, untitled and unpublished dedication, University of Georgia, Hargrett Rare Book and Manuscript Collection, MA 210, Box 4, Folder 10, 4.

• 2 •

A Biographer Looks Back

Ann Thwaite

Editor's note: The material in this article was originally presented as an informal talk at a conference organized by Angelica Carpenter, "Frances Hodgson Burnett: Beyond the Secret Garden," at California State University, Fresno, in 2003.

When I started out as a biographer, after years of writing for children, it was the late sixties. In those days there were, of course, no computers. There were no search engines or Google or computerised records of where letters are located. It was all rather hard work and it was easy to miss things. But I hope I did convey the flavour of the period and, indeed, the personality of Frances Hodgson Burnett, in spite of all the problems and obstacles.

I want to tell you how I came to write *Waiting for the Party: The Life of Frances Hodgson Burnett*. It was my first biography so it is extremely important to me. I came from the background of children's literature. My first children's book was published in 1958 when I was very young. I had written many children's books by the late 1960s when I started thinking about doing something else. It's not something to be proud of, but it's quite interesting, I think. I decided to write a biography because I was so tired of going to literary parties, which I did a great deal (provided I could get a babysitter), because my husband was successively a features producer at the BBC, literary editor of *The Listener*, and then literary editor of the *New Statesman* and we were always being asked to these parties. People would say to me, "Oh, what do you do?" as people do at parties, only slightly more subtly sometimes, and I would say I write children's books and they said, "Oh, under what name?" or they would simply change the conversation completely. People were not interested. It was worse than that. It was as if, as Joan Aiken (a children's novelist I admire) once said, they expected one to be skipping around and seeing fairies at the bottom of the garden. This was a problem for me because I had (and I see some parallels with Frances Hodgson there) the idea of being equal in some way to the man in my life.

I have always been amazed that the women's movement didn't take Frances Hodgson Burnett up earlier because she was the most extraordinary figure in her time. She was not only earning a living but actually the breadwinner of the family when Swan was studying in Paris. In the late 1960s, ninety years later, I had these feminist feelings. I had done the same degree at Oxford as my husband, and I couldn't see why he couldn't work six months on *The Listener* and I could work the other six months and we could swap over, you know. But life didn't work like that and there I was, stuck at home with the children and writing children's books and going to these parties where nobody seemed to think children's books were very important and I thought, well, I'll show them that I can write a book that adults will read.

And I suppose I thought at that point that I might try to be an adult novelist because I had written a number of children's novels. One of my first children's novels was published by Harcourt Brace and Margaret McElderry was my editor. Some of you will remember this very distinguished woman editor. My book was picked out in the New York Public Library list of the best books of the year. I had a lot of early success in the children's book field and, of course, I do actually believe children's books are more important than adult books. I want to assure you of that, even though I felt the need to write an adult book at that stage in my life, I didn't think I could write an adult novel that I would want to read, whereas I thought I could write an adult biography that I would want to read. I thought that if I wrote a novel it would turn out to be a rather inferior Margaret Drabble or Iris Murdoch, adult woman novelists at that time whom I admired. I didn't think that I could write a novel that I would admire. So I decided that I was going to write a biography and the question was to find a subject, a good subject.

I had just published with Macmillan a book called *The Camelthorn Papers*, which was actually never published in America partly because I had foolishly not included any American children in this group of children who were living in North Africa. There was an Egyptian boy and two English girls. There were plenty of American oilmen there in Libya at that time. I could so easily have thrown in an American child and then I certainly would have had an American publisher. But, anyway, the editor of this book at Macmillan in England was Marni Hodgkin, an extremely successful and important children's editor in the 1960s. *The Camelthorn Papers* was published by Macmillan. Marni Hodgkin, who was the editor, was an American, and by an extraordinary chance she had a family connection with Frances Hodgson Burnett.

I was talking to her one day. She was a good friend of mine and still is; she's still alive and in her eighties. She told me that her mother was a de Kay; some of you will know that Helena de Kay was married to Richard Gilder who was Mrs. Burnett's editor at the *Century* magazine and that the de Kay family are supposed to be the children behind *Racketty-Packetty House*. Marni was taken to visit Frances Hodgson Burnett at Plandome [her home on Long Island]. She was, she told me herself, at that time a sensible stolid commonsensical sort of a child, not a child who was subject to wild flights of the imagination. The elderly author was actually in bed—enduring what proved to be her final illness. It must have been 1924. But she pointed out to the child, who was nine or so, this cupboard, which I saw many years later in her daughter-in-law Constance Burnett's house in Boston.

This was a marvellous Jacobean cupboard (see figure 2.1), which Frances Hodgson Burnett had converted into a doll's house for the children who came to visit her. She told Marni to open the doors of the doll's house, which from the outside looked like a perfectly ordinary cupboard. (Indeed, when I saw it the shelves were empty; it was no longer a doll's house.) Marni opened the doors and there were the dolls sitting, not moving, just sitting in their seats or standing, and still. But then when she closed the doors, Frances Hodgson Burnett said to her, "Now, of course, they'll come alive again." And for a moment, Marni said, as a child, her reason tottered: she *really believed* Frances Hodgson Burnett.

That was rather an inspiring story. Mrs. Rous, Marni's mother, was still alive at that stage, and I visited her in New York and had some long conversations with her. She knew Frances Hodgson Burnett very well, had heard her read *The Secret Garden* aloud. She gave me a copy of *The Romantick Lady*, the only existing biography, by her son Vivian Burnett. That was the beginning of my real interest in Frances Hodgson Burnett.

2.1 Frances Hodgson Burnett's Jacobean cupboard, used as a dollhouse. Ladies' Home Journal *(April 1915)*.

I knew nothing about her, really. Other triggers at the same time, that made me want to write about her, included Marghanita Laski's 1950 book about *Mrs. Molesworth, Mrs. Ewing and Mrs. Hodgson Burnett* and the comments on that book by John Rowe Townsend. Some of you may not realise just how neglected *The Secret Garden* and Frances Hodgson Burnett were at this point, by critics if not by readers. What put me on to this fact was a book, which I commend to you in its various editions, called *Written for Children*, by John Rowe Townsend, published in 1965. I'm going to give you an extract from that book which also refers to Marghanita Laski:

> Frances Hodgson Burnett was a more powerful, and I believe a more important, writer than Miss Yonge or Mrs. Ewing or Mrs. Molesworth. On the strength of only three books . . . I believe she must be acknowledged as standing far above every other woman writer for children except E. Nesbit; and there are depths in Mrs. Hodgson Burnett that Nesbit never tried to plumb. It is hard to account for her neglect (neglect by critics, that is; she has not been neglected by readers). I do not know of any modern study of her work beyond an eighteen page chapter in a book by Marghanita Laski. . . . True, Mrs. Hodgson Burnett's personal character was flamboyant and unappealing; in the years of her success she suffered a gross inflation of the ego; and Miss Laski justly says she emerges from the pages of her son's book The Romantick Lady as "aggressively domineering, offensively whimsical and abominably self-centred and conceited." But if we were to judge writers by their personal qualities rather than their work—a mistake which Miss Laski does not make—the map of English literature would be a very odd one. I think myself that a large part of the explanation lies in the notoriety of Little Lord Fauntleroy. Instead of adding to its author's reputation, as it should, this book hangs albatross-wise around her neck.[1]

Until I read this I had no idea Frances Hodgson Burnett was considered to be flamboyant and unappealing. And I couldn't believe that she could be! Could the author of The Secret Garden really be so self-centred and unattractive?

In my introduction to *Waiting for the Party* I go on to say how important *The Secret Garden* was to me as a child. I also acknowledged my debt to Vivian Burnett's work. If his mother emerges from that book as "domineering, whimsical and abominably self-centred," it was certainly not because her son saw her like that. His book is an act of filial piety; he was a devoted son. His style is unbearably fey, but he is surprisingly frank and there was a great deal to arouse my curiosity and to make me want to find out what she was really like. *The Romantick Lady* had not been published in England and had long been out of print in America (see figure 2.2). So few people had read it and very few people, of course, had read Marghanita Laski's little book either. Frances Hodgson Burnett's life was a very unknown field and people were interested.

It was quite surprising when I went to these literary parties and people said, "Oh, what do you do? What are you working on?" and I said, "I'm working on a biography of Frances Hodgson Burnett, author of *The Secret Garden.*" People were immediately interested. And my stock went

2.2   An idealized Frances on the dust jacket of her son's 1927 biography, surrounded by characters from her novels. Hageboom illustration for the dust jacket of Vivian Burnett's The Romantick Lady (Frances Hodgson Burnett): The Life Story of an Imagination *(New York: Charles Scribner's Sons, 1927).*

up considerably. But it was only when I came to write *A. A. Milne* that my children were able to say, "Thank goodness, at last Mum is writing about someone you don't have to explain!" The name "Frances Hodgson Burnett" remains surprisingly unfamiliar. Again and again people admit their ignorance, but everyone has heard of *The Secret Garden*.

A lot of people, I found, not only didn't know that she'd written any adult books, but they didn't know that the same person had written *Little Lord Fauntleroy* and *The Secret Garden*. People were very surprised about that fact, that they knew the titles of both books but had no idea that the same person had written them.

You may remember I quoted John Rowe Townsend saying that *Little Lord Fauntleroy* hung albatross-wise around her neck. But I have to say that I have read it extremely successfully with children of the right age, which I consider to be seven or eight, my own children and at least one grandchild, with only making the most minor cuts (amounting to two pages) perhaps, in the whole book just of some of those slightly nauseating descriptions of the beauty of the child and the beauty of the relationship between the child and the mother. Very, very few cuts make it totally acceptable to a modern child.

A Little Princess, the book published nearly twenty years after *Fauntleroy*, works marvellously without any cuts and some readers like it best of all the books. We all want our own children, I think, and children we know, to enjoy the same pleasures that we had. We like to pass on our own experience of particular books and it sometimes doesn't work. But one way that I found that often works very well is to read a couple of chapters and to get the child into the book and then leave it for them to finish. I have read aloud the whole of *Little Lord Fauntleroy* several times, and it is a tremendous story for a child listener wanting to know that happens next, more so than *The Secret Garden*, actually. *The Secret Garden* is a much greater book, but it doesn't have quite the same narrative force as *Little Lord Fauntleroy*. The plot has some preposterous coincidences, but children don't mind that. Many people read mainly to substantiate their day dreams and the Fauntleroy story is the perfect day dream. It was a huge bestseller. But one of the things that I often wonder about Frances Hodgson Burnett, because I admire enormously her early adult books, is what sort of writer she would have been, what sort of reputation she would have had, it she hadn't written *Little Lord Fauntleroy*. I did actually publish an edition of *That Lass o' Lowrie's* years ago, which sank without trace, I'm sorry to say. It is a moving and impressive book, but I think the problem there is dialect. I haven't really worked out why the dialect, the way that Dickon talks in *The Secret Garden*, doesn't seem to worry people at all but in *That Lass o' Lowrie's* it was a real stumbling block.

Now I'm going to get on to the whole process of writing my biography, how I started, in a rather amateurish way, without any sort of technology. I am still technology free. I still write my biographies by hand and have nothing to do with computers or the Internet, but when I started I had no idea how biographies were written. I had a friend in Richmond, in outer London, living near me. I had this acquaintance, Janet Dunbar, who'd written a rather good biography of J. M. Barrie, and I simply went and asked her what method she used and I have used the same method from that day to this.

But it is quite interesting. I may be the last person to write a biography in this old-fashioned way. I'm going to give my working papers to one of our two big children's literature collections in England, I haven't quite decided, either Roehampton or Newcastle, because it is a totally outdated method. Let me explain it to you and you'll be amazed that I could even manage to finish a book with these methods.

What I have and what I still use, even with my most recent book *Glimpses of the Wonderful: The Life of Philip Henry Gosse*, is numerous files. I have a card file of names, themes, titles. I have one on cats, one on servants, one on religion, one on every single person who crops up in a story, and every book title and every play title and so on, cards, in alphabetical order, in a file, in a box. You end up with maybe only a couple of cards on one particular person or theme, but it might be twenty or thirty.

With the Burnett biography, there were a great many cards for Henry James. The Henry James relationship is an extremely interesting one, and I spent a good deal of time investigating that. I don't actually think that James admired Frances Hodgson Burnett as she would like to have thought he did. Between the 1974 hardback and the Faber 1994 paperback I was able to read the new edition of James's letters with two crucial references to Mrs. Burnett and to add them to my book, the only additions I made. James was adept at "the mere twaddle of graciousness,"[2] his own phrase for those marvellous letters that he wrote to his "Noblest of Neighbours and Most Heavenly of Women."[3] Mrs. Burnett certainly thought he was her close friend. When she was having a terrible time at Maytham with Stephen Townesend, her second husband, she wrote to her sister that she would not let him cut her off from her family and friends, that she would call on a few of her men friends to confront him—and one of the men she named was Henry James. Obviously she felt she knew him intimately, to ask such a thing of him. But, equally obviously, she did not know him. James would have hated being involved in such a situation.

But I'm trying to tell you about my method, so I'll get back to that now and I'll get on to Maytham later. I have file cards, as I said, but also file pages, each one with the dates on top and lots and lots of cross references between the two. Then any letter that I wanted to have actually in front of me when I was writing the book, I would photocopy and put in its date sequence but, as you know, letters don't always refer to just what is going on at that particular moment and there would be very often memories of an earlier time and then, of course, that reference would have to go on the page referring to that year. The cards and pages multiply as I work. With Mrs. Burnett the amount of material was manageable, which was not so with my second subject, Edmund Gosse. He was a good friend of Frances Hodgson Burnett, and I was fascinated by the fact that they were born in the same year. They died only four years apart too, so I got this really strong feeling of what that particular time was like. I really felt I got to know the nineteenth century at that point. All five of my biographical subjects were born in the nineteenth century, A. A. Milne last of all, in 1882. So even he grew up as a Victorian.

I developed this strong feeling for Victorian England, but I can see that *Waiting for the Party* may drive any subsequent scholar absolutely mad because with this book, unlike my later ones, I don't give direct sources. I simply say that most of the letters came from either the family or from the Scribner Archives at Princeton. I don't give specific references, which must be extremely irritating.

I have a friend called John Gross, who wrote a rather marvellous book called *The Rise and Fall of the Man of Letters* and in that book, which in fact gave me the idea to write about Edmund Gosse (because he said there was room for a biography), he actually said, "Every quotation doesn't need a reference as if it were applying for a job,"[4] which I thought was an absolutely marvellous excuse not to be as scholarly as I have subsequently had to become.

I don't know how many of you realise, but in England nearly all biographers are writers—freelance writers, not academics. Very, very few English biographers work within a university system, whereas in America, I think, it's totally the reverse; nearly all biographers do work within universities. Although I had to become more scholarly, I still always had my eye mainly on the general reader and that was particularly so when I was writing my first biography about Frances Hodgson Burnett.

I remember Elizabeth Jane Howard, who is a rather interesting English novelist, when she reviewed the book, saying that I should be "congratulated upon finding somebody so extraordinary and so neglected to write about,"[5] but it was luck in a way, really. I got interested in her, as I explained, from feeling that there were things about her that nobody knew. But I had no idea at the beginning how extraordinary her life was. It was not until I came to read *The Romantick Lady*, and that was after I was already committed to writing the book. I felt I had to have a contract before I made two longish visits to America for research. They were so difficult to organise, you can imagine, with family life, with young children. It was only when I was given *The Romantick Lady* in New York that I discovered just what a remarkable life she had had.

I actually had signed a contract without consulting the Burnett family, and I did this very deliberately because I really thought if they don't want it I shall manage without their help. I wanted their help, of course, but I realised—as was the case with Christopher Milne writing about A. A. Milne, and was certainly the case with Vivian Burnett writing about his mother—one of the reasons that sons (or daughters) write about their parents is to stop other people doing it. I thought there was a chance that the family might not want me to write my book because in some ways this story was quite a scandalous and difficult one for a family at that period, much less so now, I think.

I can't remember now how I got in touch with Dorinda Le Clair, Mrs. Burnett's granddaughter. I think it was probably through her mother, Vivian's widow, who had published a brief children's biography of her mother-in-law called *Happily Ever After*, a title which, she agreed, was not really appropriate. I was glad to be able to tell them I had a contract. If I hadn't already had one, they might indeed have been able to discourage me from writing.

I was extraordinarily lucky. Macmillan wanted to do the book. Macmillan was my children's book publisher, where Marni Hodgkin worked. They wanted to do it and they kept on telling me that I had to write a proposal. And I really knew so little at that point that I kept putting it off. You see, I hadn't yet read *The Romantick Lady* and I knew very, very little. I just knew that I was curious and I wanted to do it and Macmillan wouldn't give me a contract without a proposal, and at one of those literary parties I was mentioning I was talking to a friend who was by then editorial director of Secker and Warburg, one of the best publishers in London, and he said, "What have you been doing, what are you . . ."

And I said, "I want to write a biography of Frances Hodgson Burnett, the author of *The Secret Garden*," and then I told him a bit about her. "But Macmillan won't give me a contract unless I write a proposal."

And he said, "Oh, I'll give you a contract without a proposal." Just like that! Mind you, I think he had read one or two of my children's books and some of my reviews. He had read me and he knew that I could write and finish books, but that was incredibly lucky. Then I was able to write to the family and say, "I have a contract to write a biography of Frances Hodgson Burnett," and that made a huge difference.

I think that was in 1969, and my book was not published until 1974. It does help to take a long time. All biographers know that— you must take a really long time writing a biography. The longer you take, the more people get to trust you and share things with you. I had a particularly vivid experience of this with *A. A. Milne*. Nobody would tell me anything at first, or, if they did tell me things, people would say to me, "No, you can't put that in." And then after two or three years, they accepted that I would eventually find everything out. It was the same with the Le Clairs, with Dorinda Le Clair, Frances's granddaughter. It was only after we had known each other for a couple of years that they entrusted me with letters that Vivian had not used in his book, and very intimate and revealing letters they were. Right from the beginning they were very hospitable in Boston. They took me to meet Vivian's widow, Constance, who was still living on Beacon Hill and who had this cupboard in her house, the cupboard that came in Marni's story that I told you and we had some long conversations. I asked them what papers they had and they were a little vague. They told me about Scribner's. I already realised that the Scribner Archives would be something that I should look at. I can't remember what they said at that first meeting, but over the years, as I got to know them, they came to the point of letting me see absolutely everything they had, though I now realise there were other letters that Dorinda's sister Verity had, which I did not see and which Gretchen Gerzina was later able to use.

The only letters, that Vivian Burnett had not used at all in *The Romantick Lady*, which is in many ways extraordinarily frank, were the ones from the time of the second marriage, about Stephen Townesend.

I had some contact with Stephen's family, who gave me some very interesting information, but who had had no idea of the disastrous nature of that marriage, and it was an awful shock then to discover what I had discovered and I felt bad about it because they had been so proud of their relationship with the famous author of *The Secret Garden*. Stephen Townesend had no children; these were great-nieces and nephews. They were very shocked and saddened and couldn't believe things were as bad as I said they were. They said they believed that he paid for his own board and lodging, in order not to seem to be a "toy boy" or whatever phrase one might have used then. He was ten years younger than she was, and it caused so many scandalous stories, which were totally inaccurate, in the newspapers. The stories exaggerated the difference in their ages even more. But they had been proud of the fact that their great-uncle had been married to Frances Hodgson Burnett, and it was hard for them to discover his true nature.

Angelica Carpenter in her book says that I suggested that Stephen blackmailed Frances into marrying him. It was Frances herself who used the word: "He talks about my 'duties as a wife' as if I had married him of my own accord—as if I had not been forced and blackguarded and blackmailed into it."[6]

There is no question that he did threaten her, that he married her, really, against her will. It is an extraordinary story.

Maytham Hall at Rolvenden in Kent was the setting for much of that marriage, and it has often been suggested that it is also the setting for *The Secret Garden*. But fictional settings, as any novelist would tell you, very rarely come from one particular place. Certainly the rose garden at Maytham is crucial but Maytham, the house, is totally unlike Misselthwaite Manor. Of course there are no moors and Kent is totally different from Yorkshire. It is interesting that Frances Hodgson Burnett hardly knew Yorkshire. She only visited once, I think, when she stayed in Lord Crewe's grand house in Yorkshire, Fryston Hall. The moors, it would seem, came from *Wuthering Heights*.

You can see a plaque in Rolvenden Church in Kent, commemorating Mrs. Burnett's association with the village. But, sadly for anyone who wants to go and see it, the house that exists there now bears no resemblance to the house she rented. Only the rose garden—the walled garden—remains as a reminder of Maytham's connection with the author of *The Secret Garden*.

Rolvenden was very important to her. Her role as lady of the manor meant a great deal to her, and I was delighted to find when I made my enquiries before going down to Rolvenden, through the current vicar, to find that four people were still alive who remembered her, which was rather amazing as she had visited Rolvenden for the last time in 1907.

Over sixty years later I went down and was able to speak to the four people who remembered her. One of them, still living all those years later, in a cottage without a bathroom, remembered the writer leaving a gold sovereign in her new baby's fist. Another had been the stable boy at Maytham. He was in his eighties when I talked to him. Now many people had asked him about *The Secret Garden* and he had a rehearsed speech—it was obviously something that he had said on many, many occasions—saying how she wasn't a real gardener, which, of course, we all know she was. "All my life," she wrote in her last book, "I have been a passionate gardener";[7] she *was* a real gardener. Anyone who could talk about weeds the way she did was a real gardener. But Harry Millum, as he was called, this old man I met in Rolvenden, had his own story. You know the children's game Chinese Whispers, the way that things change with repeated telling; he had this story that he liked to give whenever anyone asked him about *The Secret Garden*.

But no one had ever asked him about Stephen Townesend before. No one knew about Stephen Townesend and when I asked him about her husband at that time, when she was living at Great Maytham, he said that he cared for his horses more than he cared for his wife. That was his actual phrase and I'm absolutely sure that was an accurate memory. The stable lad had noticed that he was more concerned about his horses than he was about his wife; that was a genuine memory. It is quite difficult to get genuine memories from people who have often been asked about famous people they've met.

The other people who remembered her were interesting too. There was the vicar's daughter and another woman. They had both been children at the time. They remembered her generosity, her kindness, her giving them lifts in her carriage. If they were in the village street and she was just going down to the other end of it, then she'd let them climb up and ride with her. She really loved children, in a way that we know, for instance, that Beatrix Potter didn't. You know those stories about Beatrix Potter turning children out of her hayfield and things like that, something that Frances would never have done. She was extremely fond of children.

And years later, one of her friends went to Rolvenden in the early 1920s—long after Frances's last visit to England—and wrote to her and said they will remember you in Rolvenden, and she was extremely pleased about this. That was in the 1920s and then I went in 1970 and found there were still people who remembered her. I think that really is a tremendous compliment to her. There exists, too, the servants' letter when she finally left, regretting her departure and hoping to have "the Pleasure of Serving you again."[8] For a biographer, the survival of letters like that one is very important.

Letters and diaries written at the time, occasional references in letters between friends and acquaintances (so difficult to find unless the letters—like those of Henry James—are eventually published), newspaper interviews, all these things have to be weighed and interpreted and seen in context by the biographer. It is also very important for a biographer to look at the children's books in context and at the relationship between adult and children's books at that time. *The Secret Garden* was first published in the *American Magazine*, a magazine for adults, though its writer saw it as "a child's story."[9] Now we are familiar with "crossover" books, with *Harry Potter*, for instance, being issued in different editions for adults and children. In the nineteenth century many books were seen as family stories. There were no separate children's editors at publishers; there were no separate children's review pages. The best-sellers of the year were ones, very often, that we would call children's books. In my biography I gave a list of the best sellers around the time of *Little Lord Fauntleroy*, and the only one that was specifically an adult book was *War and Peace*, appearing then in translation for the first time. All the others were ones that we would think of as children's books, which were then family books.

Anyone who thinks that Frances Hodgson Burnett was oversentimental and whimsical only needs to look at some of the other things written at the same time to see why her books have survived and others have not.

I would like to end by reminding you of the fact that Frances Hodgson Burnett, before she wrote *Little Lord Fauntleroy*, was regarded as one of the leading writers in America—a leading writer for adults. An article in the July 1883 issue of *Century*, called "The Native Element in American Fiction" (so she was already being treated completely as an American), listed Frances as one of those "who hold the front rank today in general estimation" and "had their visible beginnings in the five years following 1870." The others were William Dean Howells, Henry James, George Washington Cable, and Constance Fenimore Woolson.[10]

Henry James, of course, is the only one of those who is still read today. It is interesting to speculate whether, if it had not been for the huge success of Fauntleroy, she might herself be no longer read. Or might she rather, as I tend to think, have gone on to have a reputation comparable with that of Elizabeth Gaskell, whose novels *Mary Barton*, *North and South*, and even *Cranford* have much in common with Mrs. Burnett's early writing for adults, and they are never out of print. Fauntleroy changed her life, not just her reputation. But *The Secret Garden* keeps her "in the front rank today in general estimation" in the history of children's literature.

NOTES

1. John Rowe Townsend, *Written for Children* (London: Bodley Head, 1990), 71–72.
2. Ann Thwaite, *Waiting for the Party: The Life of Frances Hodgson Burnett, 1849–1924* (London: Secker & Warburg, 1974), 154.
3. Thwaite, *Waiting for the Party*, 184.
4. John Gross, *The Rise and Fall of the Man of Letters* (London: Weidenfeld and Nicolson, 1969), 298.
5. Elizabeth Jane Howard, review of *Waiting for the Party* (London: *Times*, May 1974, exact date not available), personal collection of Ann Thwaite.
6. Frances Hodgson Burnett to Edith Jordan, May 1900; Thwaite, *Waiting for the Party*, 191–92.
7. Frances Hodgson Burnett, *In the Garden* (Boston and New York: The Medici Society of America, 1925), 9.
8. Thwaite, *Waiting for the Party*, 216.
9. Thwaite, *Waiting for the Party*, 222.
10. James Herbert Morse, "The Native Element in American Fiction," *The Century* (July 1883): 362–76.

• 3 •

Rereading *Little Lord Fauntleroy*: Deconstructing the Innocent Child

Ariko Kawabata

Editor's note: The material in this article was originally a part of the PhD thesis "The Border Crossings of Frances Hodgson Burnett: Children's Literature and Romance in Fin de Siècle Britain," submitted to Roehampton University in 2004.

British Prime Minister William Gladstone was a friend of Frances Hodgson Burnett's and a fan of her book *Little Lord Fauntleroy*. She said, "He told me he believed the book would have great effect in bringing about added good feeling between the two nations and making them understand each other."[1] Burnett's greatest contribution to Anglo-American relations may have been her creation of Cedric; her monstrously successful book about him connects the prevailing concern about the relationship between newly rising America and fatherland England with the myth of the redemptive child. *Little Lord Fauntleroy* is the representative example of the cult of "the Beautiful Child," which was prevalent in nineteenth-century cultural ethos.

Largely influenced by the theory of Jean Jacques Rousseau (1712–1778), this new concept of the child, with Wordsworthian clouds of glory trailing behind him, represents a perfect vision, untouched by the vice of civilization. As the innocent redeemer, the child is sentimentalized, beautified, and idolized in many nineteenth-century novels for adults and for children. Charles Dickens's *The Old Curiosity Shop* (1840–1841) and George Eliot's *Silas Marner* (1861) are famous examples. In children's literature, many evangelical writers used this convention to promote Christian knowledge, describing innocent, angel-like children telling adults about heavenly bliss.

In a more secular context, Florence Montgomery's *Transformed* (1886), Lewis Carroll's *Alice*, Mrs. Molesworth's *Carrots*, and Barrie's *Peter Pan* are all variations of the ideal, or sentimentalized, child, though with important deviations in each case. The Beautiful Child cult was widely prevalent from the middle of the century to the beginning of World War I, continuing through A. A. Milne's *Winnie-the-Pooh* (1926), and it may still shape the cultural unconscious today. The cult, however, culminated in the publication and dramatization of *Little Lord Fauntleroy* in 1886.

This story is about a boy, who, living with his widowed mother in a humble house in America, is, in fact, the sole remaining heir to the title and estate of an ancient aristocratic family in England. Cedric's grandfather, who hates America and Americans, had disapproved of his younger son's marriage to an American girl. As all other possible inheritors, including Cedric's father and uncle, have died, the old Earl is forced to invite his American grandson, Cedric Errol, and Cedric's American mother to come to England to live. Cedric is an attractive, loving child and under his influence, the old Earl gradually opens his mind and changes his attitudes. The conclusion of the story proved satisfactory to both English and American readers, adults and children, and the book was a smash hit.

During its serialization in 1885, *Little Lord Fauntleroy* was favourably received by readers of all ages and both genders. When it came out as a book in the following year, it quickly engendered an enthusiastic sensation all over America. The book became one of the best sellers of 1886 together with *King Solomon's Mines* and *War and Peace*, and one of the biggest sellers of all time.[2] Gretchen Holbrook Gerzina says that following the play's success, "there would be no one from the smallest Midwestern American town to the streets of Paris who had not heard of Cedric."[3] Enthusiasm for the book, called the "Fauntleroy Craze," spread all over Europe, and even to Japan.[4] By 1974 it had sold more than one million copies in English, and had been translated in to at least twelve other languages.[5] Its readers ranged from preschool children, who had the book read aloud to them, to famous intellectuals, including Louisa May Alcott, James Russell Lowell, and Mr. Gladstone, mentioned earlier, and his wife.

One important reason for Burnett's success is that she used the familiar plot of the Beautiful Child who redeems the old man. Cedric, with his innate goodness, innocent faith, and lovely childishness, eventually wins the heart of his stern English grandfather, and thereby domesticates and civilizes the intolerant old patriarch. In the end, the Earl of Dorincourt repents of his dislike for anything American, admits the virtuous influence of Mrs. Errol, and is reconciled with her. Now the fatherless child and the widowed mother, having been alienated from the father's land across the Atlantic through misunderstandings, national prejudice, and false pride, are integrated with the fatherland. In the process, an old, desolate and stagnant community in Britain is healed at the hands of the transatlantic mother and son, and a seemingly perfect reunion between America and Britain is at last achieved.

Jerry Griswold argues that at the time of *Fauntleroy*'s publication, America "called for a revised myth that defined America not in terms of its youthful antagonism toward Europe, but as a mature nation-state taking its place among the 'family of nations.'"[6] According to him, *Little Lord Fauntleroy* is the very myth desired. Its hero, Cedric, is an ideal hybrid who inherits the merits of both his fatherland and motherland. In other words, after the turmoil of the Civil War, America needed to assert its new national identity, and in order to do that, it wanted to reestablish an amiable Anglo-American bond. It is important, however, for my argument, to follow Griswold's theory:

> Over the course of the novel, Cedric's peacemaking mission succeeds. He wins his grandfather's affection and love, and through him, hostility within the family is brought to an end. This rapprochement is made all the easier by an opportunity that is provided for the earl to discharge his hostility upon the false claimants. The American woman and her son who dishonestly claim to be the earl's heirs [see figure 3.1] are just the kind of ill-bred and avaricious Americans the earl first expected to meet in Cedric and his mother, and their false claim allows the earl an opportunity to vent his paternal anger outside the family, upon these doubles, in a safe and justifiable way.[7]

It is worthy of notice that Griswold describes this false mother and son as "doubles." Minna and Tom, shadowy doubles of the ideal pair of Mrs. Errol and Cedric, turn out to be the wife and son of Ben, brother of Dick, who was Cedric's dear friend in his American days. This conveniently contrived plot is often criticized as one of the biggest flaws in the story. Nevertheless it must be considered closely, especially the false mother Minna, because she is the only figure who cannot join the

"SHE WAS TOLD BY THE FOOTMAN AT THE DOOR THAT THE EARL WOULD NOT SEE HER."

3.1 Minna and her son, the false claimants in Little Lord Fauntleroy, are shown the door. Illustration by Reginald Birch for Little Lord Fauntleroy, St. Nicholas XIII, no. 11, (September 1886): 823.

complete reconciliation at the end of the book. She is rejected as the scapegoat, with everyone's faults attached to her existence. In other words, she is forced to assume what I might call the dangerous aspect of the American woman, the threat they offer to patriarchy, which must be hidden in order to forge transatlantic bonds. Careful division of American women into two types, angelic Mrs. Errol and evil Minna, is the key necessary for the satisfactory conclusion of the story.

In other words, the ultimate Other in *Little Lord Fauntleroy* is Minna, who exposes the fact that the bond is the homo-social relationship between fathers and husbands, dependent on the shared misogyny. She seems to be a trifling figure in the story's main plot, but this antiheroine is in fact the central plotter, in both senses of the word: a conspirator and a plot-mover. Her existence makes it safe to position the American wife and son in the context of the traditional aristocratic world of Britain. The detailed analysis of her image will eventually lead us to awareness of the process of constructing the cultural myths of the ideal Anglo-American bond and also the cult of the Beautiful Child.

Reconstructing the life of Minna is nothing but deconstructing the story from the "Other's" point of view, turning its positives into negatives, and vice versa. Unlike Cedric's history, her story is only fragmentary, related at first by the lawyer, Mr. Havisham. She is then referred to as a "hefty 'un" in Dick's recollection, and from the rambling points of view of servants and the Earl. When these scattered pieces of the picture are pieced into a whole, the story of Minna's life emerges as an exact negative version of Cedric's mother's story.

According to her ex-husband Ben, "[Minna's] father is a respectable sort of man, though he's low down in the world. Her mother was just like herself. She's dead, but he's alive, and he's honest enough to be ashamed of her."[8] Dick refers to her marital life with Ben when he talks to Mr. Hobbs about his own boyhood. Dick says she was beautiful but "a regular tiger-cat,"[9] who gave birth to a son, but one day, in a temper, she threw a dish at the baby, scarring his face. After that she is said to have disappeared with her son, being tired of her husband's poverty. We are told about her reappearance in Britain by Mr. Havisham. While working as a nurse, she was loved by Bevis, the elder son of the Earl, and married him, but shortly after divorced and left him. She makes a false claim that her son Tom was fathered by Bevis, and that she is the true Lady Fauntleroy. In this way, she enters the Earl's castle with her son as the true Lord Fauntleroy. However, her identity is revealed by Dick, owing to her picture that appears in an American newspaper. Dick and Ben come to Britain to expose the true identity of the woman, using as evidence the scar on the child's face. After this "she gave [Mr. Havisham] one savage look and dashed past him."[10] About forty pages after her first entrance into the text, she disappears from our sight and is never referred to again.

Evidence of a scar or a birthmark is a cliché of family romances in which orphans or lost heroes are identified. The archetypal example is found in Homer's *Odyssey*, in which the long-lost protagonist is identified by a servant who finds a scar on his master's foot. However, in this case, the recognition is reversed and parodied as negative evidence for the false hero. In the same way, Minna's life, as it is reconstructed above, clearly repeats Mrs. Errol's but as a parody. They share the same pattern in that they are both American women who married English noblemen. Both have sons and on the death of their husbands (according to Minna's claim), both unexpectedly become mothers of heirs to English aristocrats.

We know very little about Mrs. Errol's life, which is, in fact, more obscure than Minna's. Mrs. Errol is an orphan and her background is not told in the story; merely that before her marriage she was working as a companion to a rich old lady. The similarity between Minna and Mrs. Errol suggests that the former can be a negative shadow of the latter, and that Minna is Mrs. Errol as she might have been. Because of their shared quality, the difference between the two is much more striking; as the Earl says to Mrs. Errol, "After seeing that repulsive woman who calls herself the wife of my son Bevis, I actually felt it would be a relief to look at you."[11]

In the case of Mrs. Errol, being born an orphan does not mean ambiguous lineage as in the case of Minna, but rather it demonstrates her innocence and purity, and conveniently deprives her of relatives who could be an obstacle to her linkage to the English aristocracy. To explain this difference, the contrast between these two heroines must be explored more closely. It is widely accepted that nineteenth-century heroines in English novels appear in "terms of pairs of opposites" as positive/negative stereotypes: benign mother/terrible enchantress, pure virgin/fallen whore, angel in the house/woman of the street.[12] When we regard Mrs. Errol and Minna in this light, they precisely fit these dual female types that were separated under the Victorian patriarchal system. It is even more suggestive that the figures of these two women are described mostly by the representative of traditional male authority:

Mr. Havisham, who endeavours to protect and maintain the continuity of the establishment itself. It is therefore profitable to examine how Mrs. Errol, the angelic woman, is depicted: "She looked in the simple black dress, fitting closely to her slender figure, more like a young girl than the mother of a boy of seven. She had a pretty, sorrowful young face, and a very tender, innocent look in her large brown eyes."[13] Phrases such as "like a young girl," "pretty," and "innocent" are indispensable to her portrait, expressing her angel-like purity. She is the very picture of the ideal Victorian woman, always pure and beautiful, morally right, and selflessly generous. Her love is, as Mrs. Sarah Ellis puts it in her famous book of conduct, *The Women of England: Their Social Duties and Domestic Habits* (1839), trustworthy like a child's, affectionate like a sister's, and watchful like a mother's. Her first name is never referred to in the text, because as a mother she is called only "Dearest," and as a wife, "Mrs. Errol." She is thus entirely without independent identity, perfectly suited to her traditional gender role. Although it was an impossible ideal of the time for a woman to be a mother and at the same time a virgin, in the figure of Mrs. Errol, the ideal is apparently realized in this girl-like widow. In other words, her description suggests her lack of sexuality, which is the greatest difference between her and Minna. As for Minna, Mr. Havisham reports, "She is absolutely uneducated and openly mercenary. She cares for nothing but the money. She is very handsome in a coarse way, but . . ."[14] It is repeatedly stated that she is very beautiful but in a passionate, "vulgar" way. In particular her black, abundant hair is remarkable. For example, Dick focuses on her attractiveness as follows: "She was a daisy-lookin' gal, too, when she was dressed up 'n' not mad. She'd big black eyes 'n' black hair down to her knees; she'd make it into a rope as big as your arm, and twist it 'round 'n' round her head; 'n' I tell you her eyes'd snap!"[15] Her black hair and eyes signify her passionate character, the outward sign of her excessive sexuality and whore-like nature.[16]

If Mrs. Errol suits one conventional type of angelic pure beauty, and Minna its negative version of the fallen woman, the latter can be read as a personification of the suppressed desire of the former as in the case of Jane Eyre and Bertha Mason. That is, in order for Mrs. Errol to play the role of an ideal mother figure concealing her first name, her own sexuality must be expelled into the figure of Minna, who soon disappears from the text. It is noticeable that Minna is never called by her family name, neither her father's nor her husband's. She has no legitimate position in the patriarchal order.

There is another reason why Minna is depicted as a whore and rejected from the story. In nineteenth-century Britain, a whore or a fallen woman was a very ambiguous term. In its extreme, a woman might be called *fallen* and treated as a harlot, if she had a relationship with more than one man. Since Minna commits bigamy, she is categorised as a fallen woman, which strikes a clear contrast with the virtuous widow, Mrs. Errol. It is also important that these fallen women were regarded as a detestable source of social evil. On the one hand, there was a new awareness of the dangers of venereal diseases, but on the other hand, it is pointed out that those women were fatally dangerous to the continuity of the patriarchal society since they constituted a destructive element that lurked within the institution. Upper- and middle-class men were constantly anxious about the possibility of revenge by these working-class women. Moreover, they feared these women's excessive sexuality seduced sons of respectable lineage and contaminated their noble blood. Their fears were given expression in the Contagious Disease Acts of the 1860s. This is exactly the case of Minna and Bevis. I would like to emphasize again that Minna inherits her ambiguous blood from the side of her mother, not her father. It is clear now why the misogynous Earl, who wants a legitimate pure heir to his family, hates and avoids Minna as an abominable being. If all faults and vices are attributed to this woman outside the family, Mrs. Errol as a pure American wife and mother is proved harmless. In this way the Earl can accept her without any obstacles.

It is necessary, however, to look into this legitimate Anglo-American lineage more closely, for the potential danger of Minna's sexuality is ascribed to her non-Anglo-American heritage. Let us reconsider Griswold's phrases quoted before. When the authenticy of the Anglo-American is established, who are the "Others" between America and Britain? They are, evidently, non-Anglo-Saxon immigrants. Minna's maternal ethnicity remains obscure, but Latina heritage is suggested by the stereotypical description of sensual exoticism, including "bold-faced, black-eyed thing"[17] and "passionate temper."[18] In fact, Dick wonders if she is "part Itali-un,"[19] and newspapers report she is a gypsy, or a Spaniard.[20] To place her within a Latina nationality or one of the nomadic minorities who were discriminated against is an indispensable factor in the process of making her a scapegoat. It reflects the anxiety shared by both nations that those "foul" races might menace the purity of their Anglo-Saxon blood.[21]

So far as I have mentioned, the signs of Minna's "Otherness" are not always substantial facts, but negative shadows of the ideal womanhood created by men, and reflecting the fears of Anglo-American patriarchal legitimacy. We can therefore say that they are the Earl's "return of the repressed," as well as the dark double of the angelic Mrs. Errol.

What is the Earl's secret self-portrait, which has been concealed even from himself? The key words to this problem are "money" and "power." Minna plays the role of a mercenary American exactly as the Earl has expected. But further consideration of this matter reveals that her desire for money and power mirrors that of the Earl himself. Being self-centred and irritable, he lacks love for his own children, but wants to buy Cedric's affection with money. He has been exposed to worldly experiences with the result that he has become mercenary. Morality in Victorian society, however, regarded obsessions with money and worldly power as dirty and impure. Desire for money and power is exactly the negative self of the Earl, which he represses and conceals. Stuck between his desire and his need to maintain a respectable household, he projects all the negative images of his own character upon the sacrificial sheep: Minna. Notice the words when he swears Minna is "exactly the kind of person I should have expected my son Bevis to choose."[22] He regards her as the perfect match for his debauched son, who has in fact inherited the father's faults. Moreover, his other son, Maurice, had already died and although the reason for his death remains untold, it might be from his decadent life abroad, implying the declining fate of the old aristocratic household. It is especially interesting that Rome is chosen as the place of his death as this adds something to Minna's image of being a foreign whore. As I have repeatedly suggested, her "Otherness" is inscribed through level after level of the story.

Hitherto I have not referred to the boy protagonist of the book, but it is time to turn our eyes to the innocent child figure who has been so famous, or notorious, for more than a century. What kind of relationship does Cedric have with Minna? This must be the most crucial problem in constructing the cultural myths around the child as an innocent redeemer and as an ideal Anglo-American hybrid. The answer to this question is none. Cedric never meets this woman and never even once refers to her. That is because she represents exactly the existence that must be concealed from him, and discarded before he notices her, in order to establish the cultural myths. She cannot have any relationship with him; that is, she is exactly what adults around Cedric want him not to see. If the innocence of childhood is defined as knowing no vices or sins, these vices or sins are nothing but adults' desire for sexuality and money, which are all projected upon Minna.

At the very opening of the novel, we are told that "Cedric himself knew nothing whatever about it."[23] This expression is characteristic of the description of Cedric as an innocent. Similar phrases that suggest he knows nothing are repeated some sixteen times throughout the text. Moreover, it might be argued that his innocence is exploited as a means to purify adults' experiences.

The Earl suddenly conceives a charity plan to improve the poorest parts of his estate, though he so far has had scant concern for the poor tenants living there. It is of course a ploy to conceal his real ugliness from "innocent" Cedric, and then in turn, the Earl can keep his respectability and is redeemed, with his experiences purified by Cedric's innocent influence. These two quotations confirm my point:

> To see each of his ugly, selfish motives changed into a good and generous one by the simplicity of a child was a singular experience.[24]
>
> Sometimes in secret he actually found himself wishing that his own past life had been a better one, and that there had been less in it than this pure, childish heart would shrink from if it knew the truth. It was not agreeable to think how the beautiful innocent face would look if its owner should be made by any chance to understand that his grandfather had been called for many a year 'the wicked Earl of Dorincourt.' The thought even made him feel a trifle nervous. He did not wish the boy to find it out.[25]

Above all, however, the most important fact that Cedric knows nothing about is the Earl's hatred for Mrs. Errol. Mrs. Errol especially entreats him to keep this secret from her son: "I should prefer he should not be told," she said to Mr. Havisham. "He would not really understand; he would only be shocked and hurt; and I feel sure that his feeling for the Earl will be a more natural and affectionate one if he does not know that his grandfather dislikes me so bitterly."[26]

Thus protected and sheltered from the ugly reality, the "dark side" and "shadow" are shut out from his presence. Cedric is kept ignorant of the feud in the family, and "without knowing," prepares his mother's acceptance into the earldom. Though it seems the mother cherishes her son very dearly, it might be possible that his mother and grandfather would collude to keep him ignorant for their own sakes respectively. Is Mrs. Errol really as selfless as the author wants readers to believe? More than once, she plays on her son's influence very slyly to change his grandfather's mind. Though she justifies herself, as is seen in the quotation below, this innocent mother is not so childish and pure as she first appears: "And a bold thought came into her wise little mother-heart. Gradually she had begun to see, as had others, that it had been her boy's good fortune to please the Earl very much, and that he would scarcely be likely to be denied anything for which he expressed a desire. 'The Earl would give him everything,' she said to Mr. Mordaunt. 'He would indulge his every whim. Why should not that indulgence be used for the good of others? It is for me to see that this shall come to pass.'"[27]

In her strategy to exploit her child, a striking similarity shared by Mrs. Errol and Minna has emerged again, in that it is noteworthy that on one occasion Mrs. Errol actually confesses the affinity between herself and Minna in order to shield Minna from the Earl's anger. She says, referring to their shared maternal love, "Perhaps she [Minna] cares for [Tom] as much as I care for Cedric, my Lord."[28] Now we have come full circle, recognising Minna as the alter ego of Mrs. Errol.

In 1886, when this work was published, submissive Victorian heroines were gradually losing popularity. Why, then, was an old-fashioned, selfless wife-mother like Mrs. Errol so popular and praised? One suggestion found in Reynolds and Humble's *Victorian Heroines* is that morality in children's literature is rather more conservative than that in novels for adults, and the former tends to maintain old-fashioned values.[29] The other reason may be that Mrs. Errol is more than anything the mother of the Beautiful Child. As Anna Wilson argues, the power of the self-made American hero is "hard to reconcile with a female, domestic model," but female readers can seek "an alternative means to virtue" through the figure of Cedric.[30] So they, on both sides of the Atlantic, wished to have such a beautiful son, and perhaps saw that they could exercise their power through that innocent child. I quite agree with Wilson when she states that "Fauntleroy is his mother's creation"[31] on several levels. Moreover we recognise, as Jacqueline Rose argues, that children's innocence is the result of adults' colonisation, for they exploit the influence of the ideal redeemers.[32]

While Minna outwardly makes her son a false inheritor and exploits him as a mean to rise within the social order, Mrs. Errol, repeating "his father would wish it to be so"[33] and pretending everything is for the sake of Cedric, perfectly plays the role of the ideal woman. But when we remember her words quoted before, she seems much closer to Minna as a strategist. Mrs. Errol is the true romantic heroine of this story, for she is a Cinderella-with-a-child who succeeds in marrying above her station, while Minna's version fails.

After Minna is expelled from the mansion, the Earl visits Mrs. Errol for the first time (see figure 3.2). The conversation between them is

"'ARE YOU QUITE SURE YOU WANT ME?' SAID MRS. ERROL."

3.2   The Earl invites Fauntleroy's mother to come live in the castle. Illustration by Reginald Birch for Little Lord Fauntleroy, St. Nicholas XIII, no. 12, (October 1886): 886.

worthy of notice: "'Where,' he said, 'is Lord Fauntleroy?' Mrs. Errol came forward, a flush rising to her cheek. 'Is it Lord Fauntleroy?' she asked. 'Is it indeed?' The Earl put out his hand and grasped hers. 'Yes,' he answered, 'it is.'"[34] As this quotation suggests, for a long time what Mrs. Errol has set her heart on is discovering whether her son is a legitimate heir to the title or not. Though the Earl declares that Cedric is his grandson whether or not he is Lord Fauntleroy, Mrs. Errol here betrays her true ambition; wanting to be the mother of the next earl.

It is strange that Mrs. Errol and Cedric never mention Minna's disappearance, though they always insist they must consider everyone's welfare. In a way, however, it is most probable for them to remain silent on the subject because their achieving the status of being ideal depends on the summons and expulsion of this foul "double."

Phyllis Bixler says that the episode of the false mother and son is "the greatest stain on credibility" of the text.[35] Nevertheless, the existence of Minna, or rather, the process of summoning her up only to expel her, is crucial to the very structure of *Little Lord Fauntleroy*, and to the making of the myths it evokes. To add one thing to the analysis made by Griswold, the episode of Minna's purgation can be regarded as an allegory of the fear and avoidance of Anglo-Americans toward non-Anglo-Saxon immigrants who were increasing at the end of the nineteenth century. At the cost of Minna, Cedric can claim his Anglo-American identity. As for the Cult of Beautiful Child, to keep the child pure and free of sin, and for him to be a redemptive innocent, again, Minna must be a scapegoat. Though her son Tom is saved and adopted by Ben, his honest, real father, Minna is the "Other" from the beginning to the end. She is forced to serve everyone's happiness and then buried in the darkness, expelled from the text. Thus the dangerous side of the American woman must be sacrificed to restore the ideal order between Anglo-American men, and the innocent child maintains his innocence in order to revive the old hierarchy.

NOTES

1. Frances Hodgson Burnett to Kitty Hall Brownell. Ann Thwaite, *Waiting for the Party: The Life of Frances Hodgson Burnett, 1849–1924* (London: Faber and Faber, 1994), 107–8.

WISHES

BY FLORENCE E. PRATT.

A REGINALD BIRCH little boy
   Met the sweetest of Greenaway girls;
She, dressed all in Puritan brown,
   He, with cavalier ruffles and curls.

Her eyes were of solemnest brown,
   Her hair was cropped close to her head.
His curls were a riot of gold,
   His cheeks were of healthiest red.

They looked at each other awhile,
   Gay gallant and Puritan maid;
Then the Reginald Birch little boy
   Slowly and solemnly said:

"I wish *you* wore rufflety clothes!
   I wish that *my* hair was cut short!

3.3   Reginald Birch illustrated this poem for Florence E. Pratt's Wishes, St. Nicholas, *23, Part 1 (February 1896): 332.*

WISHES.   333

'Cause the boys call me 'missy' and 'girl,'
And it interferes so with my sport."

Said she, "Oh, I like pretty clothes,
And I *do* wish they 'd let my hair curl!
I wish *you* were a Greenaway boy,
And I was a Fauntleroy girl!"

LITTLE MR. BY-AND-BY.

LITTLE Mr. By-and-By,
You will mark him by his cry,
And the way he loiters when
Called again and yet again,
Glum if he must leave his play
Though all time be holiday.

Little Mr. By-and-By,
Eyes cast down and mouth awry!
In the mountains of the moon

He is known as Pretty Soon;
And he 's cousin to Don't Care,
As no doubt you 're well aware.

Little Mr. By-and-By
Always has a fretful "Why?"
When he 's asked to come or go,
Like his sister — Susan Slow.
Hope we 'll never — you nor I —
Be like Mr. By-and-By.

Clinton Scollard.

2. Thwaite, *Waiting for the Party*, 94–95.

3. Gretchen Holbrook Gerzina, *Frances Hodgson Burnett: The Unexpected Life of the Author of* The Secret Garden (New Brunswick, NJ: Rutgers University Press, 2004), 110.

4. It was translated by Sizuko Wakamatsu, a Christian writer, and serialized in *Jogaku-Zasshi* between 1890 and 1892. This translation was an innovative one for its use of vernacular form and the Christian message that the translator wanted to convey in those still feudal days in the Meiji period.

5. Thwaite, *Waiting for the Party*, 94.

6. Jerry Griswold, *Audacious Kids: Coming of Age in America's Classic Children's Books* (Oxford: Oxford University Press, 1992), 96.

7. Griswold, *Audacious Kids*, 99–100.

8. Frances Hodgson Burnett, *Little Lord Fauntleroy* (London: Puffin, 1994), 225.

9. Burnett, *Little Lord Fauntleroy*, 187.

10. Burnett, *Little Lord Fauntleroy*, 226.

11. Burnett, *Little Lord Fauntleroy*, 212.

12. Kimberley Reynolds and Nicki Humble, *Victorian Heroines: Representations of Femininity in Nineteenth-Century Literature and Art* (New York: New York University Press, 1993), 1.

13. Burnett, *Little Lord Fauntleroy*, 23–24.

14. Burnett, *Little Lord Fauntleroy*, 184.

15. Burnett, *Little Lord Fauntleroy*, 197.

16. Look, for example, at the contemporary female portraits by pre-Raphaelite painters. Serpentine long hair is a typical attribute of those femmes fatales.

17. Burnett, *Little Lord Fauntleroy*, 203.

18. Burnett, *Little Lord Fauntleroy*, 207.

19. Burnett, *Little Lord Fauntleroy*, 197.

20. Burnett, *Little Lord Fauntleroy*, 215.

21. Remember the anti-miscegenation laws of the United States at that time—if Minna were Mexican, for example, she may not have been legally allowed to marry a "white" man.

22. Burnett, *Little Lord Fauntleroy*, 209.

23. Burnett, *Little Lord Fauntleroy*, 1.

24. Burnett, *Little Lord Fauntleroy*, 123.

25. Burnett, *Little Lord Fauntleroy*, 152–53.

26. Burnett, *Little Lord Fauntleroy*, 152.

27. Burnett, *Little Lord Fauntleroy*, 162.

28. Burnett, *Little Lord Fauntleroy*, 210.

29. Reynolds and Humble, *Victorian Heroines*, 9.

30. Anna Wilson, "*Little Lord Fauntleroy*: The Darling of Mothers and the Abomination of a Generation," *American Literary History* 8, no. 2 (1996): 239.
31. Wilson, "*Little Lord Fauntleroy*: The Darling of Mothers and the Abomination of a Generation," 240.
32. Jacqueline Rose, *The Case of Peter Pan: or the Impossibility of Children's Literature* (Philadelphia: University of Pennsylvania Press, revised edition 1994).
33. Burnett, *Little Lord Fauntleroy*, 66.
34. Burnett, *Little Lord Fauntleroy*, 227.
35. Phyllis Bixler, "*Little Lord Fauntleroy*: Continuity and Change in Popular Entertainment." In *Children's Novels and the Movies*, edited by Douglas Street (New York: Frederick Ungar. 1983), 74.

· 4 ·

The Changing Mothering Roles in *Little Lord Fauntleroy*, *A Little Princess*, and *The Secret Garden*

Deborah Druley

Editor's note: The material in this article was originally presented at a conference organized by Angelica Carpenter, "Frances Hodgson Burnett: Beyond the Secret Garden," at California State University, Fresno, in 2003.

Although much has been written on how female authors addressed the issue of Victorian repression through adult literature, little research has been devoted to examining these same issues in children's literature. In fact, it has only been recently that children's literature has received extensive, serious literary study. Like women's literature, children's literature has been marginalized in part due to its emphasis on domesticity. In her article, "Feminine Language and the Politics of Children's Literature," Deborah Thacker discusses this marginalization: "The proximity of children's literature to the domestic, nurturing, maternal, and thus, the feminine sphere can be seen as a contributing factor in the marginalization of the subject in academic discourses. However, it is [this] notion of the silencing of the 'Other,' whether it be women, children, or those who are racially different, that enriches what it is possible to say about children's texts and that has led to the process of change currently taking place."[1]

Another contributing factor to this marginalization is that children's literature has been seen as reinforcing the dominant discourse through traditional role bias. Nonetheless, there were writers during the Victorian period who challenged these gender-biased assumptions, and who sought to subvert the patriarchal discourse through their narratives. One such writer is Frances Hodgson Burnett. Phyllis Bixler writes, "Burnett's popular adult fiction is of interest also because of her treatment of certain social themes.... Popular adult fiction and much of children's fiction serve both to pass on traditional values and to help society accommodate change."[2]

Burnett's fiction can be read as vehicles to effect change in the culture. Although most of her fiction is set within the traditionally private and domestic female sphere, she does offer challenges to the Victorian idea of the mothering role in three of her most popular stories for children: *Little Lord Fauntleroy*, *A Little Princess*, and *The Secret Garden*. While at first glance these stories appear to endorse sentimental gender roles, a close examination reveals that Burnett's ideas of mothering evolve with each story from the traditional female role to a more gender-neutral role. In these three narratives, Burnett elevates the place of the mother in society. She demonstrates how the mothering role is one of great value, a role that people of all ages and of both genders should value and take part in. Taken together, these three novels, especially *The Secret Garden*, can be seen as an invitation for men and boys to participate with women and girls in the work, joys, and responsibilities of mothering. These stories suggest that the role of mothering is a conscious role, not confined to women by nature or biology. Instead, mothering is a role that a person can choose to embrace, regardless of gender. In presenting mothering in such a manner, Burnett seeks to "accommodate change" in society as Bixler suggests. By elevating the mothering role, Burnett subverts patriarchal Victorian norms that essentialize and devalue the role of the mother even while appearing to idolize it.

In her book, *A Literature of Their Own*, Elaine Showalter describes Victorian society's ideal mother: "The middle-class ideology of the proper sphere of womanhood, which developed in post-industrial England and America, prescribed a woman who would be a Perfect Lady, an Angel in the House, contentedly submissive to men, but strong in her inner purity and religiosity, queen in her own realm of the Home."[3]

In *Little Lord Fauntleroy*, published in 1886, the reader is introduced to the ideal Victorian mother, Mrs. Errol. Mrs. Errol's almost perfect nature is revealed as she is described as a beautiful, patient, moral, loyal, accepting, and industrious woman. Moreover, she absolutely places her child's needs and future before her own happiness and convenience. When asked to move to England in order to give up her only child to the Earl, and to live apart from Cedric, she neither cries nor protests. Instead, she says, "My husband would wish it.... It would be best for my little boy."[4] She submits to her husband's imagined will even though she is a widow making her own decisions. By Victorian standards, Mrs. Errol is properly dependent upon the men in her family for financial and emotional support. Additionally, Cedric happily assumes the task of caring for his mother though he is just a little boy. Modeling after his father, Cedric knows that caring for his mother is his proper male role. He takes care to shelter her from emotional pain. Burnett writes that "since his papa's death, Cedric had found out that it was best not to talk to his mamma about him."[5] "He [Cedric] was so much of a companion for his mother that she scarcely cared for any other."[6]

Additionally, Cedric considers it his responsibility to care for her financially. When Cedric tells the Earl that he misses his mother, Cedric explains that his mother is his closest friend. He says, "My father left her to me to take care of her, and when I am a man I am going to work and earn money for her."[7]

In addition to being dependent, Mrs. Errol is ideal in her purity. Although at first the Earl hates her, Mrs. Errol remains loyal to both Cedric and her husband's memory. Therefore, she never speaks ill of the Earl to her son, but trusts that the Earl will be good to him. She believes that Cedric and the Earl will love each other. Mrs. Errol's trusting nature is too pure to suspect any evil motive in the Earl. Burnett writes, "His [the Earl's] motives were far from being good, and if he had been dealing with a nature less affectionate and warm-hearted than Little Lord Fauntleroy's, great harm might have been done. And Cedric's mother was too gentle to suspect any harm. She thought that perhaps this meant that a lonely, unhappy man, whose children were dead, wished to be kind to her little boy, and win his love and confidence."[8] Unsoiled by the world's wickedness, Mrs. Errol cannot fathom anything but the best, even from someone as selfish as the Earl.

Like all good mothers, Mrs. Errol is in charge of her son's moral development. When Mr. Havisham reveals Cedric's power and position as future earl, Mrs. Errol realizes that it is her responsibility to teach Cedric how to use his position justly. "'Oh,' cried his mother. 'And he is such a little boy—a very little boy. How can I teach him to use it well? It makes me half afraid. My pretty little Cedric.'"[9]

Mrs. Errol represents the ideal, but Burnett endows her character with more independence and agency than typical for a Victorian wife and mother. During the time that Mrs. Errol lives apart from Cedric, she tends to the poor on the estate. Though helping and teaching the poor are well within the scope of the traditional mother, Mrs. Errol violates this role when she exercises more than traditional agency. Through her relationship with Cedric, she has the Earl finance the tearing down and rebuilding of a dilapidated village on the estate. When she first sees the condition of the tenants living at Erlesboro, she is appalled. Seeing the poor children's condition, she compares their situation to her son's privileged life. She decides to teach Cedric to use his position for good:

> And as she looked at the squalid, uncared-for children growing up in the midst of vice and brutal indifference, she thought of her own little boy spending his days in the great, splendid castle, guarded and served like a young prince, having no wish ungratified, and knowing nothing but luxury and ease and beauty. And a bold thought came into her wise little mother-heart. Gradually, she had begun to see, as had others, that it had been her boy's good fortune to please the Earl very much, and that he would scarcely be likely to be denied anything for which he expressed a desire. "The Earl would give him anything.... He would indulge his every whim. Why should not that indulgence be used for the good of others? It is for me to see that this shall come to pass."[10]

When she tells her son about the conditions of the tenants, Cedric responds by asking his grandfather to improve the state of affairs at Erlesboro. While still remaining within her submissive role, Mrs. Errol finds a way to exercise her own will to improve life for the poor. Though Mrs. Errol acts in a manipulative manner to meet her goals, still her actions break with the patriarchal culture in her exercise of independent judgment and agency. She finds an active role for herself to effect change within the Victorian framework. It is through the creation of Mrs. Errol's character that Burnett takes a step toward expanding the role of the mother from passive to active.

In *A Little Princess*, published in book form in 1905, the role of mothering continues to evolve and progress. In this story a young, motherless English girl is brought from India to England in order to receive a proper education. The story is, in a way, typical of Victorian children's literature: it is the tale of a "dispossessed heiress" who suffers patiently, and is "ultimately rewarded with the restoration of her fortunes—after, of course, the requisite sojourn in the kitchen."[11]

In this narrative, Burnett extends the role of mothering to include not just women, but girls as well. Although raising girls to be mothers was in line with Victorian principles, Burnett takes this role even further as Sara's desire to mother extends to mothering her own father. As the story progresses, however, Sara's role deviates from tradition in that she experiences emotions that are not in line with the prescribed passivity required for girls. More like a traditional boy than girl, Sara has a difficult time controlling her anger. Additionally, in contrast to the Victorian middle-class idea that women should be financially supported and not work outside the home, Sara violates the traditional role in that she desires to work to support herself.

Similar to Cedric's relationship with his mother, Sara is in charge of caring for, or the "mothering" of, her own father, though here the mothering role is taken to an extreme. Like Cedric and Mrs. Errol, Sara and her father have an unusually close relationship. At times their relationship is so close as to seem inappropriate, and some passages are disturbing. In many ways, their relationship reflects that of a married couple. Yet, in the context of Victorian society, Sara's relationship with her father is considered proper, as Sara is simply fulfilling the nurturing and mothering role dictated by her culture. One passage that may at first seem disturbing takes place at the beginning of the story. Sara is brought to the school in London where she will, for the first time, live apart from her father. Sara has never known her mother, as her mother died when she was born, and she has no other relatives. Burnett writes, "Her young, handsome, rich, petting father seemed to be the only relation she had in the world. They had always played together and been fond of each other."[12] Sara's main concern in being separated from her father is that she will no longer be able to take care of him. Captain Crewe assures her that she will soon learn enough to be able to come home to India and resume taking care of him. Sara dreams of being reunited with her father after completing her education: "She had liked to think of that. To keep the house for her father; to ride with him, and sit at the head of his table when he had dinner parties; to talk to him and read his books—that would be what she would like the most in the world, and if one must go away to 'the place' in England to attain it, she must make up her mind to go."[13]

Captain Crewe finds nothing odd in her desire to look after him. He delights in her old womanly mannerisms, often referring to her as his "Little Missus." Thus both Sara and her father consider her nurturing role as entirely proper within Victorian society. In light of their culture, there is nothing abnormal about their close relationship.

Just as Sara mothers her father, her mothering role extends to many of the girls at her school. Elisabeth Gruner addresses Sara's mothering role in her article, "Cinderella, Marie Antoinette, and Sara: Roles and Role Models in *A Little Princess*." Claiming that *A Little Princess* is loosely based on the story of "Cinderella," Gruner explores the various roles that Sara assumes. Among these roles are the "Princess," the "Storyteller," the "Teacher," the "Worker," and the "Mother." Gruner argues that most of the roles Sara plays involve both teaching and mothering, with mothering being her primary role. She claims that Sara's storytelling (see figure 4.1) serves the function of teaching and mothering the girls at the school, as well as mothering herself. Gruner writes, "By narrating her own and her companions' stories, imaginatively embellished, Sara learns about oppression and injustice, and 'mothers' herself and her orphaned companions into a more vital and fulfilling adolescence than the school otherwise provides. Storytelling supplies the absent mother to some of the students at the school, including Sara herself. . . . Orphaned Sara can not be expected to know much about mothering, but in fact it is her primary talent, her original skill."[14]

How Sara knows how to mother is somewhat of a mystery, considering that she has never had a mother herself. In any event, Sara's ability to tell stories, and, therefore, to mother was valued by the Victorians. Gruner writes, "Narrative, within the novel and perhaps of the novel itself, allows for sympathetic identification and even for moral growth. And the Victorian mother's primary task was, of course, moral teaching."[15] Sara's skills at storytelling and mothering seem to come naturally to her, and were considered by the Victorians as the proper role for even young girls.

However, Sara's character differs from the traditional role in that she is active, not passive. In many places in the story, she fights to control her temper, and she has a difficult time taking continual verbal abuse from Miss Minchin. Sara believes that anger and emotional outbursts are inappropriate for a girl, so she makes up stories to help reign in her strong emotions. Her favorite story is that of being a princess, which she uses as an ideal to live up to. Early on in the narrative, when Lavinia teases her about her princess fantasy, Burnett writes, "[Sara's] trick of

"SHE PLUNGED INTO THE GORY RECORDS OF THE FRENCH REVOLUTION."

4.1   Sara tells Ermengarde a story of the French Revolution. Illustration by Harold Piffard for A Little Princess (London: Frederick Warne and Co., 1905), facing page 214.

pretending things was the joy of her life. She never spoke of it to girls she was not fond of. Her new 'pretend' about being a princess was very near to her heart, and she was shy and sensitive about it.... 'It's true,' she said. 'Sometimes I do pretend I am a princess, so that I can try and behave like one.'"[16]

Throughout the novel, Sara makes up stories to strengthen her resolve to be good and moral, so that she could fulfill the prescribed Victorian female role. In her society, girls were taught to be passive, compliant, and without agency. Anger was considered a more masculine trait. Believing that anger is morally wrong and unsuitable for a lady, Sara attempts to reign in her strong emotions by providing herself with traditional female role models, especially that of being a princess.

However, there are times when Sara does speak up and express her true thoughts. After Miss Minchin tells Sara that she is destitute, she does not allow the child even a moment to grieve. Instead, she informs Sara that while she will have a home, it will be only as a servant. She demands that Sara be grateful for her generosity. Instead of passively accepting Miss Minchin's abuse, Sara tells her what she thinks: "'You are not kind,' she said. 'You are *not* kind, and it is *not* a home.'"[17] Sara is not passive, thus violating traditional norms. She does not passively allow others to abuse her.

Sara also differs from the traditional role in her enthusiasm for work. When Miss Minchin first tells Sara of her impoverished state, informing her that, like Becky, "she must work for your living,"[18] Sara responds by exclaiming, "Can I work? ... If I work it will not matter so much [that she has lost her father and her position]. What can I do?"[19] Sara is both excited and empowered by the ability to work to support herself.

With Sara's character, Burnett explores the boundaries of the mothering role. Although Sara upholds many Victorian feminine values, she also violates and challenges them through her exercise of agency and free thought. Sara's ability to act, to make choices within her environment, and to speak out on occasion go against the grain of traditional Victorian norms for girls.

In *The Secret Garden*, published in 1911, the role of mothering takes the most drastic change in course. In the story, mothering extends to and includes both genders and all ages, and includes being in touch with the procreative and nurturing power of Mother Nature. All three children in the story nurture the garden, and, in effect, exhibit a motherly attitude toward the earth. The garden, in turn, has a nurturing effect on Mary, Dickon, and Colin. Colin, especially, is healed through the life of the garden.

There are several mothers in the story, but none who seem to fit the Victorian society's ideal mother. None of the mothers exhibit behaviors consistent with Showalter's definition of the perfect Victorian mother: "A Perfect Lady, an Angel in the House, contentedly submissive to men, but strong in her inner purity and religiosity."[20] Although not in line with this ideal, Burnett describes three literal mothers, and readers are invited to make comparisons among them. These mothers include Mrs. Lennox, a birth mother who rejects the maternal role; Mrs. Craven, a mother who is involuntarily absent from her child; and Mrs. Sowerby, the ideal mother in the story. Additionally, Burnett surprises the reader with an unexpected mother, Dickon, who represents a mother from the opposite gender who voluntarily embraces the maternal role. The first mother, Mrs. Lennox, represents a biological mother who rejects the maternal role. While living with her husband in India, she has a child named Mary. Although it was customary for women of Mrs. Lennox's status to have servants care for their children, it was also common for the mothers to spend some time with them. However, Burnett makes it clear that Mrs. Lennox had no interest in personally caring for and nurturing her little girl. She is not interested in the real work of mothering. Burnett writes that Mary's mother "had been a great beauty who cared only to go to parties and amuse herself with gay people. She had not wanted a little girl at all, and when Mary was born she handed her over to the care of an Ayah, who was made to understand that if she wished to please the Mem Sahib she must keep the child out of sight as much as possible."[21] Mrs. Lennox feels no attachment toward her daughter; she rejects, in no uncertain terms, the maternal role. In some sense, Mary is an orphan even before her mother and father die.

Because Mary is rarely allowed in her mother's presence, she is always intrigued when afforded an opportunity to see her, even though Mary feels no connection with her. Burnett writes that Mary liked to look at her mother "from a distance and she had thought her very pretty, but as she knew very little of her she could scarcely have been expected to love her or to miss her when she was gone."[22] As a result of this lack of mothering, Mary becomes a selfish, self-absorbed, and contrary child.

In contrast, the second mother in the story would have willingly accepted the maternal role had she lived. Mrs. Craven represents those mothers who would embrace mothering. Unfortunately for her little boy, Mrs. Craven dies from injuries she receives in the garden. Consequently, Colin is also motherless. Unlike Mary, however, he has never seen or known his mother. In contrast to Mrs. Lennox, Mrs. Craven does not voluntarily leave her child. If she had lived, she would have cared for her son. Even after her death, her spirit watches over her child and calls to her husband through the garden. Mrs. Craven, the originator of the Secret Garden, loves her roses, and sends her spirit into the garden to watch over her child.

Although she comes from a lower class, Susan Sowerby is the ideal mother in this story. She places children's needs and well-being before cultural norms. Mary tells Colin that "she knows all about children. . . . She has twelve. She knows."[23] Through experience, Mrs. Sowerby knows that children need fresh air and freedom to order to become healthy adults. She purchases a rope for Mary to use outside: "Nothin' will do her more good than skippin' rope. It's th' sensiblest toy a child can have. Let her play out in th' fresh air skippin' an' it'll stretch her legs an' arms an' give her some strength in 'em."[24]

Mrs. Sowerby does not consider her financial state when it comes to mothering. Dickon tells his mother that Colin and Mary have found a way into the Secret Garden, and that all three of them are bringing it back to life. As they tend the garden, Mary and Colin become healthier. As this newly found health increases their appetites, Mrs. Sowerby provides them with food, even though she is a poor woman barely able to feed her own children.

Mrs. Sowerby values the work of mothering, and is not hesitant to speak up on behalf of a child even if she must defy class convention. At least twice in the story, she confronts Mr. Craven. While he walks on the moor one day, she boldly informs him of her concerns for Mary. She tells him that he should see Mary and make certain Mary gets enough exercise, freedom, and fresh air.[25] Because Mr. Craven respects her ability to mother, he takes her advice though he thinks she is "rather bold to stop me on the moor."[26] The second time Mrs. Sowerby "makes bold" is when she writes to Mr. Craven while he is in the Austrian Tyrol. She suggests he come home, though she does not tell him it is so he can see his son's progress. She writes, "I think you would be glad to come and—

if you will excuse me, sir—I think your lady would ask you to come if she was here."[27] When Mr. Craven returns home, he is able to see that the garden has healed Colin. It is through Mrs. Sowerby's concern for the child that Colin and Mr. Craven are reunited as father and son.

At this point, the story shifts from literal mothers to an unexpected one. Dickon, who is a healthy, wise, and strong boy, is also very maternal in his relationship with the earth and with others. (See figure 4.2.) He demonstrates that tending the earth and being involved in its life cycles can heal and restore both children and adults. By understanding the healing properties of the earth, he becomes the ultimate mother. Though very much a boy, Dickon is aware that he chooses to be different from other boys by caring for animals. When Mary asks him if he can keep a secret, he says, "I'm keeping secrets all th' time.... If I couldn't keep secrets from th' other lads, secrets about foxes' cubs, an' birds' nests, an' wild things' holes, there'd be naught safe on th' moor. Aye, I can keep secrets."[28] Like a mother, Dickon protects and nurtures the young.

Dickon first meets Colin when Colin is ill and bedridden. Dickon brings a newborn, motherless lamb to Colin and shows him how to feed it: "He walked over to Colin's sofa and put the new-born lamb quietly on his lap, and immediately the little creature turned to the warm velvet dressing-gown and began to nuzzle and nuzzle into its folds and butt its tight-curled head with soft impatience against his side. 'What is it doing?' cried Colin. 'What does it want?' 'It wants its mother,' said Dickon, smiling more and more. 'I brought it to thee a bit hungry because I knowed tha'd like to see it feed.'"[29]

Dickon teaches Colin how to nurse the lamb, thereby beginning his lessons on mothering the earth. Throughout the story, he teaches Colin and Mary how to care for flowers and animals, and both children are healed through caring for the garden. It is by being outside in the fresh air and discovering the Secret Garden that Mary increases her appetite, gets fatter, and grows prettier. Likewise, it is through Colin's mother's garden that he gains an appetite, grows stronger, puts on weight, and learns to walk and run. Burnett writes that "while the secret garden was coming alive" the two children were coming alive with it.[30]

In the story, mothering is a chosen role. While Mary's mother rejects the work of mothering, Mrs. Sowerby values her role as mother, caring for Colin and Mary while they are motherless. Dickon also

"IT SEEMED SCARCELY BEARABLE TO LEAVE SUCH DELIGHTFULNESS"—*Page 231*

4.2 Mary and Dickon in the garden. Illustration by Maria L. Kirk for The Secret Garden *(New York: Frederick A. Stokes, 1911), frontispiece.*

chooses the work of mothering, discovering a great deal of joy from the work. He mothers the earth, and, through the earth, he mothers both Colin and Mary back to health.

In contrast to those who voluntarily assume the maternal role, Mr. Craven, in his grief, rejects both the mothering and fathering role. While he has cared for Colin physically, he has virtually abandoned his son's emotional needs. Mr. Craven had given Colin "doctors and nurses and luxuries, but he had shrunk from the mere thought of the boy and had buried himself in his own misery."[31] While in Austria, Mr. Craven becomes aware that "he had forgotten and deserted his home and duties."[32] It is in the mountains that both the spirit of Colin's mother and the letter from Mrs. Sowerby remind him of his duties. When he returns to the garden, he finds his son healthy and thriving. By asking Colin to take him into his deceased wife's garden, Mr. Craven accepts both his wife's death and her spirit that remains there. Through this act, he shows that he is willing to take on the duties of being both mother and father to his son. "'Take me into the garden, my boy,' he said at last. 'And tell me all about it.'"[33]

Other critics have considered the genderless role of mothering in this novel. Anna Silver argues that *The Secret Garden* is "at heart a novel about mothering: motherless Mary and Colin are restored to health, 'mothered,' by the nurturant power of a garden."[34] She goes on to say, "Burnett undermines nineteenth-century constructions of gender and maternity throughout the novel. Her conception of maternity is non-gendered; both women and men can mother."[35]

Although I agree with Silver, I would add that the significance of this vision is in its progress in Burnett's stories from the mothering role as primarily feminine to a role that either gender can assume. In her book *Maternal Thinking: Toward a Politics of Peace*, Sara Ruddick argues that mothering is a practice or work that one agrees to assume or reject. Mothering is not determined "by fixed biological or legal relationships to children but by the work [individuals] set out to do."[36] She further asserts that there is a difference between those who give birth and those who do the work of mothering. She writes, "Anyone who commits her or himself to responding to children's demands, and makes the work of response [to children] a considerable part of her or his life, is a mother."[37] Although mothering is done primarily by women, "it is not difficult to imagine men taking up mothering as easily and successfully as women—or conversely, women as easily declining to mother as well as men."[38]

In these three children's novels, Burnett presents the reader with all types of mothers, including the ideal Victorian mother; women mothers who decline the work of mothering; and men and women, boys and girls who all choose to assume the role and work of mothering. Culminating especially in *The Secret Garden*, all are invited to participate in the valuable work of mothering.

NOTES

1. Deborah Thacker, "Feminine Language and the Politics of Children's Literature," *The Lion and the Unicorn* 25, no. 1 (2001): 3.
2. Phyllis Bixler, *Frances Hodgson Burnett* (Boston: Twayne, 1984), ii.
3. Elaine Showalter, *A Literature of Their Own* (New Jersey: Princeton, 1999), 14.
4. Frances Hodgson Burnett, *Little Lord Fauntleroy* (London: Puffin, 1981), 26–27.
5. Burnett, *Little Lord Fauntleroy*, 1.
6. Burnett, *Little Lord Fauntleroy*, 8.
7. Burnett, *Little Lord Fauntleroy*, 97.
8. Burnett, *Little Lord Fauntleroy*, 42.
9. Burnett, *Little Lord Fauntleroy*, 43.
10. Burnett, *Little Lord Fauntleroy*, 162.
11. Elisabeth R. Gruner, "Cinderella, Marie Antoinette, and Sara: Roles and Role Models in *A Little Princess*," *The Lion and the Unicorn* 22, no. 2 (1998): 168.
12. Frances Hodgson Burnett, *A Little Princess* (New York: Harper Collins, 1963), 3.
13. Burnett, *A Little Princess*, 4.
14. Gruner, "Cinderella, Marie Antoinette, and Sara," 171, 176.
15. Gruner, "Cinderella, Marie Antoinette, and Sara," 176.
16. Burnett, *A Little Princess*, 75–76.
17. Burnett, *A Little Princess*, 111.
18. Burnett, *A Little Princess*, 110.
19. Burnett, *A Little Princess*, 110.
20. Showalter, *A Literature of Their Own*, 14.
21. Frances Hodgson Burnett, *The Secret Garden* (New York: Random House, 1987), 3.
22. Burnett, *The Secret Garden*, 9.

23. Burnett, *The Secret Garden*, 107.
24. Burnett, *The Secret Garden*, 67.
25. Burnett, *The Secret Garden*, 197.
26. Burnett, *The Secret Garden*, 8.
27. Burnett, *The Secret Garden*, 263.
28. Burnett, *The Secret Garden*, 92.
29. Burnett, *The Secret Garden*, 184.
30. Burnett, *The Secret Garden*, 258.
31. Burnett, *The Secret Garden*, 264.
32. Burnett, *The Secret Garden*, 259.
33. Burnett, *The Secret Garden*, 270.
34. Anna K. Silver, "Domesticating Bronte's Moors: Motherhood in *The Secret Garden*," *The Lion and the Unicorn* 21, no. 2 (1997): 193.
35. Silver, "Domesticating Bronte's Moors," 193.
36. Sara Ruddick, *Maternal Thinking: Toward a Politics of Peace*, ix.
37. Ruddick, *Maternal Thinking*, xii.
38. Ruddick, *Maternal Thinking*, xii.

• 5 •

Rats in Black Holes and Corners: An Examination of Frances Hodgson Burnett's Portrayal of the Urban Poor

Carole Dunbar

Editor's note: The material in this article was originally presented at a conference organized by Angelica Carpenter, "Frances Hodgson Burnett: Beyond the Secret Garden," at California State University, Fresno, in 2003.

We are told by Engels, writing of Manchester, Hodgson Burnett's native city, four years before her birth, of the peculiarity of the city's layout. He writes, not without a degree of irony, that "the finest part of the arrangement is this, that the members of this money aristocracy can take the shortest road through the middle of the labouring districts to their places of business, without ever seeing that they are in the midst of the grimy misery that lurks to the right and the left. . . . I have never seen so systematic a shutting out of the working class from the thoroughfares, so tender a concealment of everything which might affront the eye and the nerves of the bourgeois, as in Manchester."[1]

The perceived necessity for the division of the social classes inherent in the city's planning is seemingly subverted by the young Frances Hodgson who tells us in her autobiographical work, *The One I Knew the Best of All*, in which she refers to herself when young in the third person, that she "adored Street children. She adored above all things the dialect they spoke, and the queer things they said. To stray into a forbidden back street and lure a dirty little factory child into conversation was a delight."[2] Unlike the middle-class child protagonists who could not understand the Manchester dialect in *The Carved Lions*, written by Hodgson Burnett's contemporary and fellow Mancunian Mrs. Molesworth, Frances is, we are told, "fluent."[3] The very use of the word, however, suggests that the language, the use of which is so described, is one other than the speaker's own, that it is a foreign tongue. This impression is supported by the use of the adjective "queer," describing either what was said or the manner of its articulation. It gives a sense of the abnormal, the strange, the exotic, which feeds into the notion of the "forbidden" territory from which it emanates, with its overtones of danger and menace. When linked to the term "lure," these proscribed, these unexplored regions suggest images of the jungle, consistent with both the nineteenth-century designation for inner city slums and the images used to describe street children (see figure 5.1), the most common of which, "savage," Hodgson Burnett uses of Ann in *A Little Princess*. Although "delightful" the conversations between the young Frances and the working-class children she encountered are not recorded. The abiding impression the reader is given is of her own youthful daring in undertaking a foray into the regions Disraeli saw as another nation, and which the Salvationist General Booth, alluding to Africa, describes as "Darkest England." It was an experience outside the constraints of her middle-class childhood.

In essence, Hodgson Burnett's experience emphasises the gulf between the classes by stressing the otherness of the urban poor, and also suggests the fear of the urban proletariat endemic in the middle classes in nineteenth-century England. With the memory of social revolution still reverberating around Europe, public demonstrations of working-class vexation unnerved the English upper classes, even at the highest level. On August 17, 1842, Lord Melbourne sent a grim report to Queen Victoria in which he writes, "Lord Melbourne hopes that these tumults in the manufacturing districts are subsiding, but he cannot conceal from your majesty that he views them with great alarm—much greater than he generally thinks it prudent to express."[4] The largest of the "manufacturing districts" was Manchester.

Manchester was at the centre of the Industrial Revolution—its sobriquet Cottonopolis suggesting its prominence and fame—and was renowned for its working-class political radicalism and civil unrest. The city enjoyed, the historian Asa Briggs tells us, "an unenviable notoriety on account of its rioting propensities."[5] Whilst the factory system in the area was based on an almost feudal regime, the amassing of working people both in places of employment and in high-density living conditions encouraged amongst the poor a pooling of discontent manifested in widespread militancy, engendering in the middle classes, the so-called fear of the mob. According to J. R. Clynes, an erstwhile child

5.1 "The little starving London savage." Illustration by Reginald Birch for Sara Crewe, or, What Happened at Miss Minchin's *(New York: Charles Scribner's Sons, 1888), 41.*

worker in the mills in Oldham, eight miles from Manchester, who rose to become Lord Privy Seal, the threat of revolution did not dissipate completely until the end of the nineteenth century.[6]

Hodgson Burnett's work, "The Boy who Became a Socialist," although set in America, in a sense harks back to the fears of middle-class Mancunians, and to the personal insecurities that result from the author's father's death and the financial constraints that dogged her childhood. In "The Boy Who Became a Socialist," Hodgson Burnett, purportedly, discusses the emergence of her son's social conscience. The amused and softly mocking tone, a tone often found in her work for children, is itself significant. The foundation for much of the humour resides in the Socialist's youth and lack of experience, and the perception that social issues are not the concern of the young. The reader perceives that if the eponymous boy was old enough to be called a man, and therefore to be taken seriously, his mother's concern would be significant. As he is only a child, his questioning of social structures is merely an occasion for amusement, just as Cedric Errol's choice of friends is in *Little Lord Fauntleroy*. "Smiling a little," the author attempts to equate socialism with young gentlemanly behaviour: "If you are a good socialist, you will hang up your hat and not leave your bat in the hall or your racket on the piano."[7] This is a far cry from such tenets as that all property is theft. Hodgson Burnett does not share her son's sorrow occasioned by the discrepancy between his own comfort and affluence and the hardship endured by his friend, Sam, a child bootblack. While she concedes the poverty of the young worker, she sees it as character building, a veritable foundation for adult life: "He has a good heart and kind feelings and it did them no harm that he was ragged and bare-footed and even sometimes hungry, and think how much he must have learned about business and self-dependence."[8]

To illustrate the fact that middle-class and working-class boys inhabit different spheres, she catalogues a sample of her son's experiences, contrasting them with those of his friend. While "Sam sold papers at the inaugurations," Vivian witnesses the royal panoply at Queen Victoria's Jubilee. The working-class child employs the "language of the boys," while "[Vivian] can speak French and understand Italian." The bootblack talks to "keen, clever American politicians," while the Socialist is familiar with "world renowned English statesmen."[9] Sam's achievements are seen as modest and parochial.

This is no mere list of the Socialist's experiences, however, but a celebration of advantages, a glorying in privilege, her son's, her own, and those of her class, privileges she does not wish to share with Sam nor his associates. The piece suggests that Hodgson Burnett has no desire to relinquish her position and manifests no guilt concerning it. This upholding of the status quo is a thread running through her writing for children. It is, after all, Cedric, the middle-class son of an aristocrat who becomes Lord Fauntleroy and not one of his working-class friends, nor the plebeian young impostor. Despite Laski's assertion that *Little Lord Fauntleroy* "is the best version of the Cinderella story in modern idiom,"[10] it is no tale of rags to riches.

Karl Marx and Friedrich Engel's *The Communist Manifesto*, published in 1848, ends with the declaration that communist aims "can be attained only by the forcible overthrow of all existing social conditions."[11] In the preface to the English edition published in 1888, Engels explains that the adjective "communist" was used in preference to "socialist" because at the time the work was written, socialism was identified with middle-class radicalism, while communism was restricted to working-class politics.[12] In the light of a threat of class revolt, which had middle-class support being given expression in widely available published form, and given the persistence of Hodgson Burnett's childhood fears of financial ruin and social demotion, her use of the term "Socialist" to identify her son is more than an amused mother's teasing. She takes the subject seriously enough to write about it, and after the gentle mocking of what she perceives to be the innocence and naiveté of her offspring, catalogues firmly the advantages to him of retaining the status quo. This whiff of class rebellion from within at a time—1892—when Hodgson Burnett had attained both wealth and celebrity raised the same spectre that had bedevilled her since childhood, that she might lose her status and the money and the privileges that underpinned it.

In her fiction this seemingly ever-present anxiety manifests itself most strongly in the portrayal of the urban working classes, "the rabble," as they are described in *The Lost Prince*. The association of "the rabble" with the ubiquitous term "the mob," connoting unrest and class strife in towns and cities, is unmistakable. In this novel Marcus Loristan lives in poverty with his father, later to be crowned king of Samavia, in a back street lodging-house in London. But throughout their period of depravation and upheavals the superior quality of the protagonist's class is maintained. Marco and his father, although dressed in ragged, patched, clothing, are emblems of aristocracy, their eminence being easily detected in the graciousness of their manners and the magnificence of their bearing. To hide his true identity while wandering in Europe disguised as a beggar, Marco has to learn to "shuffle a little and slouch as if he were of the common people."[13]

The real slouchers and shufflers, the working-class boys who make up the "Squad," are seen as a collective. While two of them are named, there is no further attempt to distinguish individuals. Like the pit-girls in Hodgson Burnett's first published novel for adults, *That Lass o' Lowrie's* (1877), they are merely disembodied voices, a kind of proletarian Greek chorus, their cockney accents accentuating their working-class status. This group of inner London lads is being drilled by The Rat (see figure 5.2), their physically disabled leader, who is, significantly, "a gentleman's son," albeit a disgraced gentleman. Although he has reduced himself and his son to the squalor of the slums, his superior breeding is reflected in the leadership qualities inherited by his offspring. Even given the boy's physical disability (a grave disadvantage in an aspiring military man, one would think) it is The Rat who is the "general" and the lower-class boys who make up the "rabble."

The metaphor of the army reflects perfectly Hodgson Burnett's portrayal of class, with, figuratively speaking, its concept of officers and men. The officers lead by virtue of their inherent authority, which emanates from upper-class roots, while the socially inferior men loyally and unquestioningly follow. Significantly, while the lives of both Marcus and The Rat embody military ideals, "the Squad is only playing,"[14] seeing behavioural rigour as nothing but a game. The boy soldiers are variously seen as "fools," "swine," "riff-raff," and "a rough lot." There is a sense that such a collection of the inner-city young needs discipline imposed on them from their social superiors in order to be kept within society's control. (It is no coincidence that Hodgson Burnett was supportive of a London Boys' Club, which ministered to inner-city youths.)

The difficulty of imposing conformity on the working classes is inherent in Hodgson Burnett's depiction of the urban poor. The only individual working-class adult to be featured in *The Lost Prince* is the Loristans' landlady, Mrs. Beedle. She is seen to emerge and "shuffle down" to her "subterranean" cellar-kitchen, like an animal in a burrow, sniffing the air for the scent of money, demanding that her rent be paid. She is contrasted with the visiting courtiers, attended by footmen immaculate in "dark brown and gold liveries." Humiliated by her treatment

"MARCO SLIPPED INTO LINE WITH THE SQUAD, AND THE RAT BEGAN HIS DRILL: 'SQUAD! 'TENTION!'"

5.2   The Rat drills his Squad. Illustration by Maurice Lincoln Bower for The Lost Prince, St. Nicholas XLII, no. 3 (January 1915): 215.

at the hands of her social superiors, the landlady prepares to return to her hole, "as if she were not any longer a person at all."[15]

This dehumanisation of the urban poor in Hodgson Burnett's fiction is often accomplished by the use of animal images, and urban landscapes are characterised by narrowness and darkness, symbolic of the morals and mentality of their inhabitants. In *The Land of the Blue Flower*, the "forlorn little children," who help populate the gloomy Victorian Hades that is the slum area of King Amor's capital city, like Mrs. Beedle, "scud away like rats into their holes as he drew near."[16] The image of the rat is used to describe the adults later in the text, adults who inhabit "black holes and corners."[17] Rats are perceived as odious and dangerous creatures associated with plague, and therefore not merely disparaged but feared, seen as a threat to existence in a literal sense, but, metaphorically, when applied to the working classes, they are seen to endanger the continuity of the middle classes.

The threat from this "evil, ill-tempered lot of worthless malcontents and thieves"[18] is averted by the scent of the Blue Flower. Corrupted city dwellers are brought back to nature, to a force that civilises, reversing the insidious perversion of urban society, and returning humanity to the innocence and happiness of Eden.

In the short tale "The Quite True Story of an Old Hawthorn Tree," it is industrialisation that is portrayed as destroying nature, and thereby precipitating immorality. Hodgson Burnett depicts it as a "great hungry dragon which swallowed up everything beautiful that came its way,"[19] almost a rapist, it destroys the aesthetically pleasing, the simple and natural. Not only does the smoke deflower the hawthorn tree, robbing it of its "pink, innocent blossom,"[20] but the "fresh, rosy children and their games and laughter"[21] are also violated. Children's features are perverted until they are "pale, cunning little faces,"[22] symbolising the loss of both youth and purity and the perpetuating of urban corruption.

Hodgson Burnett, having been exposed to the insecurities of middle-class Manchester, represents the proletariat as criminal, immoral, or as rats, a device, according to Freud, which projects the user's "own internal impulses of hostility on to the extended world, to ascribe them, that is, to the objects which (s)he feels to be disagreeable."[23] These hostilities, when ascribed to a character in her adult fiction, find their strongest expression in the depiction of Dan Lowrie (see figure 5.3), from the novel *That Lass o' Lowrie's*, who is portrayed as little more

5.3 As a child, Frances Hodgson Burnett saw a drunken father berating his daughter. Later she used the characters in That Lass o' Lowrie's. Illustration by Reginald Birch for The One I Knew the Best of All (New York: Charles Scribner's Sons, 1893), 83.

than the personification of brutishness. It is Dan's animalistic qualities, his lack of human personality, complexity, or individuality that embody Hodgson Burnett's fears. His attributes are those that were popularly seen to characterise "the mob"; he, like it, will not be civilised. Unlike the urban poor in Hodgson Burnett's children's novels, Dan's sub-human qualities are not amenable to discipline from the upper classes, nor amelioration from the influences of nature. Dan is the symbol of the author's childhood fear of the working classes, bestial power undiluted by the trappings of deference, human sympathy, or social responsibility. He emanates from the North of England, is an industrial worker, and although living in a village, nevertheless personifies what is seen as the immorality of the urban masses. Significantly, his discontent and disaffection are made manifest in violence and the attempted destruction of his social superiors. With his anonymous associates he forms a threatening presence, made all the more unnatural by its association with the dark. The suggestions of the Gothic in Lowrie's portrayal are consistent with his almost vampire-like threat, the notion of sucking civilisation dry, destroying the health and strength of the English class system and replacing it by a foreign European philosophy, Communism, or, as Engels dubbed it, Socialism, which has at its heart the threat of a workers' revolution and the overthrow of the existing social system, a system, Hodgson Burnett tries to convince her son in 'The Boy who Became a Socialist,' which serves them, if not the poor, well.

In Hodgson Burnett's books for children, we have mere echoes of Dan Lowrie and what he symbolises. Transforming the urban working class into rodents obviates the need to address the social unrest she fears. Reality, which her biographer, Ann Thwaite, maintains, "shook" Hodgson Burnett "cruelly," need not be faced.[24] With the scuttling of rats into their holes, and the regression of urbanisation by the magic of nature, industrialisation and the urban working classes that it spawned, can be negated. Like Sara Crewe, Hodgson Burnett can then dispense her fictional largess amongst her grateful, acquiescent rural characters.

NOTES

1. Feiedrich Engels, *The Conditions of the Working Class in England* (Harmondsworth: Penguin, 1987), 86–87.
2. Frances Hodgson Burnett, *The One I Knew the Best of All* (London: Warne, 1974), 65.
3. Burnett, *The One I Knew the Best of All*, 66.
4. David Newsome, *The Victorian World Picture* (London: Fontana, 1977), 44.
5. Asa Briggs, *Victorian Cities* (London: Penguin Books, 1990), 92.
6. J. R. Clynes, *Memoirs—1869–1924* (London: Hutchinson, 1937), 86.
7. Frances Hodgson Burnett, "The Boy Who Became a Socialist," in *Children I Have Known and Giovani and the Other* (London: J. R. Osgood, 1892), 125.
8. Burnett, "The Boy Who Became a Socialist," 123.
9. Burnett, "The Boy Who Became a Socialist," 124.
10. Marghanita Laski, *Mrs. Ewing, Mrs. Molesworth, and Mrs. Hodgson Burnett* (London: Arthur Baker, 1950), 83.

11. Karl Marx and Freidrich Engels, *The Communist Manifesto* (Harmondsworth: Pelican, 1982), 120.
12. Marx and Engels, *The Communist Manifesto*, 62.
13. Frances Hodgson Burnett, *The Lost Prince* (Harmondsworth: Puffin, 1971), 183.
14. Burnett, *The Lost Prince*, 90.
15. Burnett, *The Lost Prince*, 307.
16. Frances Hodgson Burnett, *The Land of the Blue Flower* (Tiburon: H. J. Kramer Inc./Starseed Press, 1993), 26.
17. Burnett, *The Land of the Blue Flower*, 30.
18. Burnett, *The Land of the Blue Flower*, 28.
19. Frances Hodgson Burnett, "The Quite True Story of an Old Hawthorn Tree," in *Children I Have Known and Giovani and the Other* (London: J. R. Osgood, 1892), 26.
20. Burnett, "The Quite True Story of an Old Hawthorn Tree," 223.
21. Burnett, "The Quite True Story of an Old Hawthorn Tree," 224.
22. Burnett, "The Quite True Story of an Old Hawthorn Tree," 226.
23. Sigmund Freud, *On Sexuality* (Harmondsworth: Penguin, 1991), 273.
24. Ann Thwaite, *Waiting for the Party: The Life of Frances Hodgson Burnett, 1849–1924* (London: Secker & Warburg, 1974), 247.

· 6 ·

The Making of a Marchioness

Alison Lurie

Editor's note: The material in this article was originally presented at a conference organized by Angelica Carpenter, "Frances Hodgson Burnett: Beyond the Secret Garden," at California State University, Fresno, in 2003.

The Making of a Marchioness (see figure 6.1) has been often been called Frances Hodgson Burnett's best novel for grownups. While most of her other adult fiction has faded into obscurity, this story has been reprinted many times, most recently only two years ago. It has often been praised for its charm, but it is not always taken seriously. One reason for this may be that Burnett herself spoke of the book as if it were a lovable trifle. "This is such a dear thing, I can't tell you how I enjoyed writing it," she said.[1] The novel may also have been treated casually because it was written so fast and so easily—Part I [published as *The Making of a Marchioness*] took only two weeks in January of 1901.

I've always thought that *The Making of a Marchioness* is interesting as well as enjoyable. I'd like to look at it in several different ways: as a modern fairy story; as an updated Victorian melodrama, as reflection of Frances Hodgson Burnett's own life and experiences; and as a realistic novel of upper-class society in late nineteenth-century England.

Burnett knew from the start that *The Making of a Marchioness* was a kind of fairy tale. But it is a fairy tale with a difference. As its author said, the heroine "is a sort of Cinderella—a solid, kind, unselfish creature—with big feet instead of little ones."[2]

When she first appears in the book, Emily Fox-Seton is nice looking without being pretty or beautiful. She is also too old and rather too large for a fairy-tale heroine: "thirty-four and a well set-up creature,

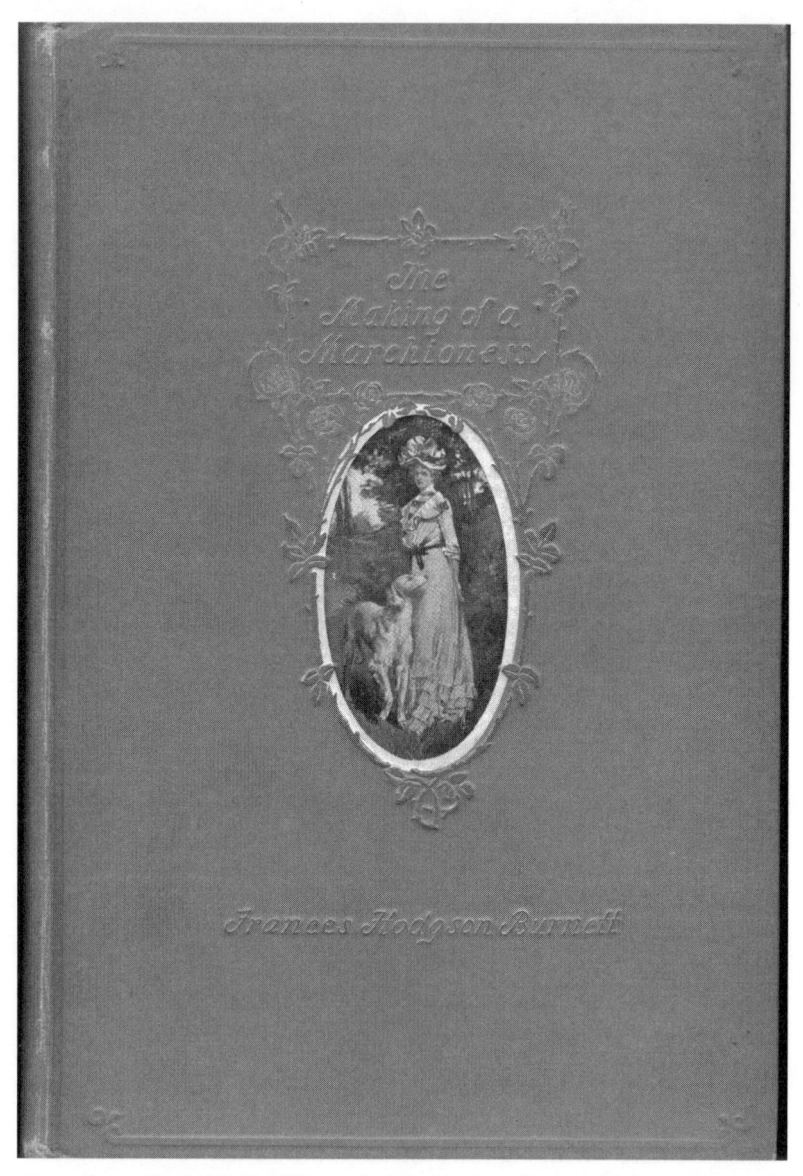

6.1   Illustration by C. D. Williams for The Making of a Marchioness, *(New York: Frederick A. Stokes, 1901).*

with fine square shoulders and a long small waist and good hips."³ One of the author's favorite words for her is "nice": "She had nice round fresh cheeks and nice big honest eyes, plenty of mouse-brown hair and a short straight nose."⁴

One thing that makes Emily a fairy-tale heroine is her simplicity and goodness. It has often been observed that it is very difficult for an author to create a truly good character who is interesting and convincing. The most common solution is to make the good person either very young, or, like Emily Fox-Seton, somewhat simple minded. As early as page 4 of the book we learn that Emily is "a simple normal-minded creature" with a "good-natured childlike smile."⁵ "It was not only her smile which was childlike," Burnett writes, "her face itself was childlike for a woman of her age and size."⁶ Again and again Emily is described as "childlike," an adjective that some people who have known and raised kids may find only partly appropriate. Unlike most children, she has no sense of humor. She is not irrational or impulsive or demanding, as most kids are at least part of the time, but she has a child's innocence and enjoyment of the world—as Burnett puts it, "She had an ingenuous appreciation of the simplest material joys. . . . She got so much more out of life than most people, though she was not aware of it."⁷

A favorite plot device of Frances Hodgson Burnett throughout her life, and the moving force in her most successful fiction, is the sudden reversal of fortune. This, of course, is also the plot of many fairy tales. "Once upon a time there was a poor woodcutter who had only one daughter, and when he died she was all alone in the world. . . ." When we hear this, we know that this girl is going to end up a princess. When we meet Emily she too is an orphan, all alone in the world—mainly because her rich relatives are not interested in helping her. As one of the other characters says, she is "perfectly well born and as penniless as a charwoman . . . at the beck and call of any one who will give her an odd job to earn a meal with."⁸

Like the classic fairy-tale heroine, Emily is kind, modest, and hardworking. She is also (like Cinderella) overworked and exploited by others. She is always willing to help out, never expecting consideration or special treatment. At the beginning of the book she is a part-time secretary and factotum for several well-to-do women, one of whom, Lady Maria Bayne, combines the roles of wicked stepmother and fairy godmother. Lady Maria is a shrewd, worldly aristocrat whom Burnett describes as "an absolutely selfish and inconsiderate old woman,"[9] largely concerned with her own comfort and amusement. Though she lacks both the supernatural powers and the goodwill of a fairy godmother, Lady Maria does in fact bring about Emily's happy ending. Because Emily is so good-natured, and never complains about the amount of work that is loaded on her, Lady Maria takes her to her country estate to help out with a big house party she is giving.

The most important guest at this house party is Lady Maria's cousin, the Marquis of Walderhurst, who eventually turns out to be Emily's Prince Charming, although he is almost totally without personal charm. Lord Walderhurst is even less of a conventional fairy-tale figure than Emily is. He is fifty-four years old, "a rigid, self-encased, and conventional elderly nobleman" with grayish-brown hair, whom Burnett describes as neither distinguished nor aristocratic looking.[10] He has come to Lady Maria's house largely in order to find a wife who can provide him with an heir. For him this is a duty, and not an enjoyable one. There are three obvious candidates: a pretty nouveau-riche American heiress; a clever, talkative literary lady; and a beautiful and wellborn but desperately poor English aristocrat, Lady Agatha, who is in love with another, younger man whom she believes she has lost.

While the other guests enjoy themselves, Emily runs errands and manages the annual village treat for over a hundred children and their families. (See figure 6.2.) "It was so easy, without the least sense of ill-feeling, to give her all the drudgery to do," Lady Maria thinks.[11] It never occurs to her that Emily might need a rest the next day; instead, though she is quite worn out, Lady Maria asks her to walk four miles to a village where there is a good fishmonger, and carry the fish for that night's grand dinner party home in a basket. It is a very hot day and the basket is heavy. I figure that since there will be a dozen or more people to dinner, there must be at least four pounds of fish. When she is part way home, Emily, who has had no lunch, is overcome with exhaustion. She sits down at the side of the road on a pile of heather and weeps. She has just discovered that her landlady in London, who has become a friend, is moving. For her, this is a disaster: "When she left Mallowe—lovely luxurious Mallowe—she would not go back to her little room . . . she would be obliged to huddle into any poor place she could find."[12]

She is found sitting on the heather with her basket of fish, by Lord Walderhurst, who has discovered her absence and come in search of her.

LORD FAUNTLEROY MAKES A SPEECH TO THE TENANTS.

6.2 Fauntleroy entertains his grandfather's tenants at a garden party that resembles the party for villagers in The Making of a Marchioness. Illustration by Reginald Birch for Little Lord Fauntleroy, St. Nicholas XIII, no. 12 (October 1886): 889.

He gets out of his carriage and almost instantly proposes. Emily is stunned. "The brilliance of the thing which had happened to her was so unheard of and so undeserved . . . that she felt she was only part of a dream," Burnett tells us.[13]

Lord Walderhurst's explanation for this sudden act is less than flattering: "'I am not a marrying man,' said his lordship, 'but I must marry, and I like you better than any woman I have ever known. I do not generally like women. I am a selfish man and I want an unselfish woman.'"[14]

Emily's reaction to this speech, however, is that of a fairy-tale heroine. His words, Burnett says, "so moved her soul that she quaked with joy."[15] Presently, on the way home, he presents her with a fairy-tale heirloom ring that contains "a ruby the size of a trouser-button."[16]

Originally, *The Making of a Marchioness* ended soon after Lord Walderhurst's proposal. Over a year later, at the urging of her publisher, who wanted a full-length novel, Burnett began working on part II [published as *The Methods of Lady Walderhurst*], which would be nearly three times as long. It, too, took off from a popular genre, as its author realized. "[In] the first story, wildly romantic things happened to unromantic persons," she explained. "[In] the second, wildly melodramatic things will happen to undramatic persons."[17] She was as good as her word: part II of *The Making of a Marchioness* contains many of the stock characters and events of the typical Victorian melodrama. It begins with the story of Emily's grand wedding and happy arrival in the most ancient and beautiful of Lord Walderhurst's three country estates. One of the rules of melodrama, of course, is that the better things are at the start of a story, the worse they will soon become, and this is what happens here. Lord Walderhurst leaves for India on business, and very soon Emily finds herself surrounded by enemies, and eventually in danger of her life.

Every melodrama needs at least one villain, and Frances Hodgson Burnett provides three, in the shape of Colonel Alec Osborn, his temperamental half-Indian wife, Hester; and Hester's sinister native servant, Ameerah, who worships strange gods and casts spells. Ameerah, too, is a stock figure of melodrama, combining the standard roles of sinister foreigner and untrustworthy servant.

Colonel Alec Osborn is a dyed-in-the-wool cad, though he has, as Burnett puts it, "a good swaggering military figure to which uniform was becoming, and a kind of animal good looks."[18] He is also Lord Walderhurst's heir, and he hates Emily because she stands between him and the inheritance of a title and great wealth. When Emily becomes pregnant, he goes into overdrive and begins to stop her letters to and from her husband, and eventually plots her murder. Emily's obvious goodness and generosity have no effect on him. But it does finally get to his wife, Hester, who begins by hating Emily, progresses to thinking her "so good that she was almost silly," and ends up revealing Colonel Osborn's plots and advising her to flee the house.[19]

The development of Hester's character is one of the best things in the book, and the scene in which, feeling "small and young and hopelessly evil," she walks in the garden at night and decides to warn Emily is exceptionally well done.[20]

The remainder of the story brings in several more classic melodrama characters and themes: the loyal servant (Emily's devoted maid, Jane Cupp) who saves the heroine's life, the flight from the murderous villain, the concealment of the heroine in a secret hideout, the birth of an heir, the last-minute reunion of heroine and hero, the final defeat and ignominious death of the villain. There is also, as in many Victorian melodramas, a suggestion that supernatural forces are at work. Hester as well as her maid believes in charms and spells.

A sort of miracle of psychological conversion, not uncommon in melodrama, occurs when Lord Walderhurst returns to London to find his wife apparently dying after having given birth to his son and heir. As Burnett puts it, "The wrench and shock were so unnatural that they reached that part of his being where human feeling was buried under self and inhuman conventionality. He spoke—and actually thought—of Emily first."[21]

Presently, in an episode that prefigures the final chapters of *The Secret Garden*, Lord Walderhurst summons Emily back from the very edge of death by calling her name over and over as, finally realizing her true worth, he kneels by her bedside. In *The Secret Garden*, of course, the summons is clearly supernatural, since it is Colin's dead mother who calls her husband back home; but the doctor who watches Emily come back to life speaks here of "powers more subtle than science."[22]

Romantic and melodramatic as it is, *The Making of a Marchioness* also has close connections to Frances Hodgson Burnett's own life. She spoke of it as "a study of a type, and in an atmosphere I know so well."[23] This is true both of Emily's early impoverished situation and of her movement into a world of wealth and luxury.

Though she spent most of her early life in near poverty, by the time Burnett came to write this story she was famous and rich. Her own prosperity gave her great pleasure, and she was willing to work extremely hard to provide herself with the kind of life she had dreamt of as a young girl. As she says in *The Making of a Marchioness*, "Respectability doesn't only mean food and a home—it means pretty, graceful things."[24] Mrs. Burnett once memorably declared that every human being deserves a life of natural splendid happiness. By the time she wrote this novel, Burnett was fifty-one, and she had come to think of servants, expensive clothes, trips abroad, and luxurious accommodations as the necessities of a splendid, happy life. She knew many people who were famous or rich or both. She had leased both a town house in London and a country estate in Kent, Maytham Hall, where, like Lady Maria, she organized treats for the village children. She gloried in the role of Lady of the Manor that Emily fits into so naturally, and managed to make herself both loved and admired by her tenants, just as Emily does.

In a way, Emily can be seen as a younger and less intelligent version of Burnett herself. Like her creator, she is not exactly beautiful. She is somewhat stocky, with a square face, a full figure, and big, well-rounded white arms. She is also deeply concerned with clothes—both because at first it is a financial struggle for her to look well dressed, and because the subject interests her deeply, just as it did Burnett. Burnett's son Vivian said that his mother loved clothes, favoring lace and gauze and "clinging, trailing chiffon things."[25] We are often told what Emily has on, and also what the principal contender for Lord Walderhurst's hand and title, Lady Agatha, is wearing. Emily believes that a young woman who wants to be admired must have a different outfit for every day—a belief that persisted at least until my years at college. After she has made friends with Lady Agatha, she asks if Lady Agatha has "anything *quite* different for" subsequent nights of the house party, remarking that "the things you wear really matter."[26]

Like Emily, Frances Hodgson Burnett was naturally generous and thoughtful. She enjoyed helping other people and making them happy. Her charity was often not only liberal but inventive. When, on her return to her native Manchester, she discovered that two of her former teachers were living in very reduced circumstances, she rented a large, elegant London house; furnished it from Liberty's; and arranged for them to run it—thus making them comfortable and financially independent. Emily, when she learns that Hester is expecting a baby, goes to London and buys it a lavish layette: at the end of the book, after Colonel Osborn is dead, she invites Hester to live with her in England.

Also, like Emily, Mrs. Burnett was a poor judge of character, at least in men. Unwilling to believe ill of others, she allowed Stephen Townesend, who later became her second husband, to move into her life and nearly ruin it; she later spoke of him as "a liar, a bully, and a coward."[27] At the same time, she had many close and loyal women friends, including her sister Edith.

For Emily, as for her creator, the life of the English aristocracy is the ideal. They share the conviction that the most wonderful destiny in the world for a woman is to be the wife of an English nobleman with a large country estate, a beautiful garden, and devoted tenants. Emily earns her reward through goodness and pure dumb luck, because she is, in spite of her large feet, a fairy-tale heroine. Burnett acquired her English country estate in a slower and more practical way—by telling stories like Emily's to readers who shared her fantasies of sudden happy reversals of fortune—but she never managed to find the nobleman to go with it. Both her husbands were commoners, and, though strikingly good-looking, they were poor providers.

Though its author saw it as a kind of fairy story followed by a kind of melodrama, *The Making of a Marchioness* can also be seen as a realistic novel—Marghanita Laski thought that Burnett "could never have supposed its realism to be as harsh as we now perceive it to be."[28] I am not sure that Laski was right about this: I think Frances Hodgson Burnett knew exactly how harsh it was.

In portraying Emily as a woman without money or supportive relatives, Mrs. Burnett does not soften her situation, which in late nineteenth-century Britain was often a desperate one. Emily is not clever or well educated enough to be a governess, or a writer like her creator. She makes a meager living by selling the only assets she has: her good birth and her cheerful willingness to do what she is told. She remakes her clothes, walks miles to save a few pence on stockings, and sometimes goes hungry in order to pay her rent on time. She has no hopes or expectations of an improvement in her circumstances—she knows that she is "too poor, too entirely unsupported by social surroundings, and not sufficiently radiant to catch the roving eye."[29] Instead, she is desperately afraid of becoming old and ill and unable to earn her living, and perhaps ending up in the workhouse.

There were many women like Emily in England at this time, shut out of higher education and most respectable occupations and dependent on the occasional kindness of acquaintances. In some ways, Emily is worse off at the start of the book than the woman from whom she rents a room, who is not a lady and can make ends meet by taking in lodgers.

Emily's world is one in which the only possible career for most poor but aristocratic girls is marriage. But the competition is fierce. All through the nineteenth century, Britain's wars and the maintenance of its colonial empire depleted the pool of available men in England. This lack was recognized, and many young women who were better off than Emily were sent out to India in what was known as the "fishing fleet" to find husbands. Emily accepts the social necessity of marriage without question. When one of her fellow house guests suggests that half a dozen women are determined to marry Lord Walderhurst, she remarks amiably, "Well, he would be a great match for any girl. He is so rich, you know. He is very rich."[30] The idea that a girl might prefer a younger and more agreeable man doesn't apparently cross her mind. Love is not necessary for marriage; money is.

Lady Agatha, who is in love with Sir Bruce Norman and thinks she has lost him, realizes that it will be her duty to marry Lord Walderhurst if she can, for the sake of her five younger sisters, all of whom are just as poor as she and will soon be equally in need of rich husbands. They cannot marry as they please; as Lady Maria says, "Most men can't afford them, and they can't afford most men. As soon as Agatha begins to go off a little, she will have to step aside."[31] In the late nineteenth century, society beauties like Lady Agatha were in some ways the equivalent of today's film stars—their lives were chronicled in the papers, and their pictures sold in shops. At one point Lady Maria coldly remarks, "Agatha has had the advertising of the illustrated papers this season, and she has gone well. In these days a new beauty is advertised like a new soap. But Agatha has not had any special offer, and I know both she and her mother are a little frightened."[32] Lady Agatha confides in Emily that if she does not marry she will be sent into the remote country to "fade out of existence in prosaic and narrowed dullness."[33]

Mrs. Burnett provides Agatha with a happy ending—the young man she loves, who is also very rich, returns from India and asks to marry her. Her wedding is later described as "a sort of fairy-tale pageant"—Emily's, by contrast, as "dignified and distinguished, but not radiant."[34] Still, they are both far more fortunate than they had expected. But this was not often the fate of beautiful and penniless young women, as both Emily's and Agatha's surprise and delight clearly show. Mrs. Burnett rescues them, but she makes it clear that they are the exception. Other novels of the period, like Edith Wharton's *The House of Mirth*, give graphic accounts of what can happen to the poor but wellborn young woman who does not find a rich husband soon enough.

There were many dangers for a woman alone besides illness and poverty. To be single and unprotected was to be vulnerable to less than respectable approaches. When Lord Walderhurst first asks Emily to marry him, what he actually says is "I came here, in fact, to ask you—if you will come and live with me?"[35] At first Emily thinks he wishes to make her his mistress, and is shocked and horrified. "London was so full of ugly stories about things done by men of his rank," she thinks. "The lives of wellborn struggling women were so hard. Sometimes such nice ones went under because temptation was so great."[36]

When she finally realizes that he is proposing marriage, she is overwhelmed. She never in fact says yes—her agreement is apparently taken for granted by both parties. For the rest of the novel, she remains tremendously grateful for her good fortune, and anxious to please Lord Walderhurst in every way possible, even at the cost of her own health and life. As Lady Maria says to him, "Emily cares a great deal more about your pleasure than her own."[37]

Marghanita Laski remarked that the theme of all Mrs. Hodgson Burnett's successful books was entry into the upper classes. This is true, of course, of both *Little Lord Fauntleroy* and *A Little Princess*, though not of *The Secret Garden*. But it is also one of the central subjects of *The Making of a Marchioness*. Emily Fox-Seton is well-born, but she is not born an aristocrat—she has to become one. She rises to the occasion, but it is not easy for her. Her wedding day is a real strain. "She seemed for hours the center of a surging, changing crowd, and her one thought was to bear herself with an outward semblance of composure."[38] When she goes to change into her traveling clothes she has to lie down and ask her maid to put eau de cologne on her face.

Once she gets to Lord Walderhurst's country estate, things begin to go easier for Emily, though she makes two serious mistakes. First, by befriending Colonel Osborn and his wife and arranging for them to live in a house that Lord Walderhurst owns nearby, she puts them in a position to plot her death. Second, when she becomes pregnant, she does not write to ask Lord Walderhurst to come home, not wanting to trouble him or interfere with his business in India.

The late nineteenth century world in which Emily lives is one of great economic inequality. Someone like Lord Walderhurst is hundreds of times richer than the ordinary working man. There are few taxes on great wealth, and no social safety net: no unemployment insurance, health insurance, or welfare system. The poor depend largely on private charity. They are expected to show immense gratitude for small gifts, and proper respect for their "betters"—that is, people who have much more money than they do.

When I first read *The Making of a Marchioness*, over thirty years ago, I would pause occasionally to congratulate myself on how far we had come since those times. Most colleges and careers were now open to women, and it was not necessary to marry someone you did not love for money. Also there was no longer such a gap between rich and poor: most people in America, I had read, defined themselves as middle class. Today I am beginning to think that I was only partly right. It is true that women can now enter almost all occupations and do not have to marry. But it is also true that many of them have to work even if they are the mothers of small children, and that often their lives, whether they are married or single, are as full of anxiety and fear of the future as Emily's was at the start of her story.

Meanwhile, in this country, the gap between rich and poor is widening again, and the social safety net is shrinking. As public support declines and private charity becomes more necessary, we are even beginning to speak in almost Victorian terms of the deserving and grateful and the undeserving and ungrateful poor. In Key West, where I have just spent the winter, homeless people are being turned out of the shacks they have built in the salt marshes near the airport and occupied in some cases for many years while working as day laborers. It is said that these people dress badly, do not wash regularly, and are sometimes rude to officials, as if this excused their eviction.

We are also now encouraged by the media to admire men and women for their wealth and beauty and power rather than for their accomplishments and character. Frances Hodgson Burnett's idea that most people deserve a natural splendid happiness begins to seem ridiculous. Natural splendid happiness is now reserved for the rich and famous. The rest of us must enjoy it vicariously by reading *People* magazine, or make do with the crumbs that fall from the tables of the wealthy. I think that if Mrs. Burnett were alive today, she would say that we have not come as far as she might have hoped.

NOTES

1. Marghanita Laski, *Mrs. Ewing, Mrs. Molesworth, and Mrs. Hodgson Burnett* (New York: Oxford University Press, 1951), 80.
2. Laski, *Mrs. Ewing, Mrs. Molesworth, and Mrs. Hodgson Burnett*, 80.
3. Frances Hodgson Burnett, *The Making of a Marchioness* (London: Persephone Books, 2001), 4.
4. Burnett, *The Making of a Marchioness*, 4.
5. Burnett, *The Making of a Marchioness*, 4.
6. Burnett, *The Making of a Marchioness*, 4.
7. Burnett, *The Making of a Marchioness*, 15.
8. Burnett, *The Making of a Marchioness*, 39.
9. Burnett, *The Making of a Marchioness*, 50.
10. Burnett, *The Making of a Marchioness*, 25.
11. Burnett, *The Making of a Marchioness*, 49–50.
12. Burnett, *The Making of a Marchioness*, 79–80.
13. Burnett, *The Making of a Marchioness*, 85.
14. Burnett, *The Making of a Marchioness*, 85.
15. Burnett, *The Making of a Marchioness*, 85.
16. Burnett, *The Making of a Marchioness*, 86.
17. Ann Thwaite, *Waiting for the Party: The Life of Frances Hodgson Burnett, 1849–1924* (New York: Charles Scribner's Sons, 1974), 198.
18. Burnett, *The Making of a Marchioness*, 111.
19. Burnett, *The Making of a Marchioness*, 226.
20. Burnett, *The Making of a Marchioness*, 227.
21. Burnett, *The Making of a Marchioness*, 280.
22. Burnett, *The Making of a Marchioness*, 284.
23. Laski, *Mrs. Ewing, Mrs. Molesworth, and Mrs. Hodgson Burnett*, 80.
24. Burnett, *The Making of a Marchioness*, personal collection of Alison Lurie.
25. Thwaite, *Waiting for the Party*, 212.
26. Burnett, *The Making of a Marchioness*, 53.
27. Frances Hodgson Burnett to Edith Jordan, Thwaite, *Waiting for the Party*, 193.
28. Thwaite, *Waiting for the Party*, 198.
29. Burnett, *The Making of a Marchioness*, 43.
30. Burnett, *The Making of a Marchioness*, 24.
31. Burnett, *The Making of a Marchioness*, 31.
32. Burnett, *The Making of a Marchioness*, 31.
33. Burnett, *The Making of a Marchioness*, 43.
34. Burnett, *The Making of a Marchioness*, 122–23.
35. Burnett, *The Making of a Marchioness*, 83.

36. Burnett, *The Making of a Marchioness*, 83.
37. Burnett, *The Making of a Marchioness*, 154.
38. Burnett, *The Making of a Marchioness*, 124.

· 7 ·

Lady of the Manor

Angelica Shirley Carpenter

In 1898 Frances Hodgson Burnett leased a country house in Kent. "It is a charming place," she wrote to her son Vivian, who was a senior at Harvard, "with a nicely timbered park and a beautiful old walled kitchen garden."[1] At Maytham Hall Frances got her first chance to live a lifestyle she had long idealized, as lady of the manor, and her first opportunity to create a garden. Her experiences at Maytham, good and bad, inspired several books, including *The Secret Garden*. A century later, the walled garden at Maytham still works a kind of literary magic on the people who live there and on Burnett fans who visit from around the world.

When she came to Maytham, the famous author was forty-eight years old and newly divorced. "The rotund little Muse,"[2] as Henry James had once called her, was nicknamed "Fluffy" for her frilly, ornate clothes and curly bangs. Her rouge and her dyed hair, described as hennaed or golden, were shocking for the time, as was her habit of smoking cigarettes, but her blue eyes and animated manner of talking were considered attractive. Her health was poor; she had a weak heart.

Frances was accompanied to Maytham by her sister Edith Jordan and by Stephen Townesend, a handsome British doctor ten years her junior. Frances and Stephen had lived together on and off for a decade. In 1890 he had lovingly cared for her elder son, Lionel, as the teenager died of tuberculosis. Stephen had always been stagestruck and after Lionel's death Frances had taken it upon herself to help him, writing and producing several plays for him. Despite his good notices, the shows always flopped.

By the time Frances leased Maytham, Stephen had given up medicine to become her business manager and partner for many projects.

Stephen, whose name had figured in some accounts of the divorce, kept his own rooms in London but spent weekends at Maytham. Though he and Frances had certainly been lovers, their romance was over by this time, at least from Frances's point of view.

"Uncle Stephen takes care of my business," Frances had written to Vivian in 1891, "and is very particular about things of that sort, but as for the rest, I feel as if I was the one who had to take care of him. He is so delicate and nervous and irritable, poor boy." Even then, she complained about his temper: "There was one thing we never had at our house," she wrote, "and that was tempers. It makes a great difference in the atmosphere."3

For years the atmosphere and Stephen's motives had worried people who cared about Frances. "She is a fatally deluded little woman," Henry James wrote to a friend, before Frances's divorce, "and I'm afraid cunning hands are plucking her of her downy plumage. I wish she would gather up her few remaining feathers while yet there is time and flutter them westward, where she has, after all, a husband and a child."4

But Frances had shed her American husband instead and moved from her expensive London townhouse to the more affordable Maytham, two hours from town by train. The thought of a new life with country distractions pleased her immensely.

She recalled her arrival in *The Shuttle* (see figure 7.1), a novel begun at Maytham in 1900. In this book a young American bride travels by carriage from the train station to her husband's country home in England: "Sometimes she saw the sweet wooded, rolling lands made lovelier by the homely farmhouses and cottages enclosed and sheltered by thick hedges and trees; once or twice they drove past a park enfolding a great house guarded by its huge sentinel oaks and beeches; once the carriage passed through an adorable little village, where children played on the green and a square-towered grey church seemed to watch over the steep-roofed cottages and creeper-covered vicarage."5

In the twenty-first century automobiles have replaced carriages, but otherwise this scene remains much the same. In Rolvenden, the real village that stands outside Maytham's gates, there is just such a square-towered church, St. Mary's, dating from the twelfth century. In Frances's time it had separate pews for gentry and servants.

Maytham itself was built from 1721 to 1763. Cellars and a tunnel survive from this era, when the proprietor used them to store brandy

7.1   Illustration by Clarence F. Underwood for The Shuttle (New York: Frederick A. Stokes, 1907).

smuggled in from France. By 1898 the building had grown to three stories with mock Tudor, half-timbered trim (see figure 7.2).

"The house is excellent—" Frances wrote to Vivian, "paneled, square hall, library, billiard room, morning room, stables, two entrance lodges, and a square tower on the roof, from which we can see the English Channel."[6]

Behind the house was a very large walled garden, "a lovesome, mystic place," Frances wrote, "shut in partly by old red brick walls against which fruit trees were trained and partly by a laurel hedge with a wood behind it."[7] The walls were original, dating from the 1700s.

Frances recalled the garden's unkempt first impression in *The Shuttle*. The book's heroine, who is the bride's younger sister, arrives at Stornham Court as Frances arrived at Maytham, in the spring: "Paths and beds were alike overgrown with weeds, but some strong, early-blooming things were fighting for life, refusing to be strangled. Against the beautiful old red walls, over which age had stolen with a wonderful grey bloom, venerable fruit trees were spread and nailed, and here and there showed their bloom; clumps of low-growing

7.2 Maytham as photographed in 1906 by Frances Benjamin Johnston. Reproduced by permission of The Huntington Library, San Marino, California.

tinges sturdily advanced their yellowness or whiteness, as if defying neglect."[8]

At Maytham, Frances had the garden cleared and then planted with grass. Though she employed gardeners, she enjoyed doing some of the work herself. As news of her project spread, friends offered plants from their own gardens or greenhouses. David Murray, the landscape painter, visited in the summer, and later arranged to send her three hundred Laurette Messimy roses. This pink flower has a long blooming period, sometimes lasting into December.[9]

Murray also helped Frances to establish the Maytham tradition of the "merry-leaf," a good example of the way in which her friends (and readers) sometimes had to endure rather too much twaddle about fairies and magic. At Maytham she decided that a five-trunked tree on the grounds had magical properties. "A Merry Leaf carried in one's pocket will make every one happy and everything go well," she wrote. "If you carry one you cannot help being adorable and you cannot help doing your work well."[10] Murray claimed that the leaf had worked for him.

"The calm here is good for me,"[11] Frances wrote to Vivian at summer's end. As winter approached, she studied seed catalogues. In her second spring at Maytham she started a herbaceous border for the garden and planted roses to grow up walls and tree trunks. In *The Secret Garden*, we see her vision realized as Mary first enters the garden: "There were ... trees in the garden, and one of the things which made the place look strangest and loveliest was that climbing roses had run all over them and swung down long tendrils which made light swaying curtains, and here and there they had caught at each other or at a far-reaching branch and had crept from one tree to another and made lovely bridges of themselves."[12]

Frances's pleasure in her garden was infectious; sometimes even her houseguests pitched in. "The lambs are big and ferocious now," Frances wrote to her friend Rosamond Campbell. "They fight like lions over their milk. I am disappointed in their characters. A ferocious lamb is as bad as a blood-thirsty dove.... Stephen sends his kind regards and feels as I do that in your absence the garden may become a ruin, as our best 'hand' is gone. You will be pleased to hear that the Rose Garden has now a thin, little green beard of grass."[13]

But Frances's delight in country life was overshadowed by her growing unhappiness. "Stephen was proving exceedingly hard to handle,"

Vivian wrote later, about this time in her life. "He was taking a position with regard to their association that had in it a suggestion of domineering ownership she did not understand. It frightened her."[14]

The title *The Shuttle* refers to steamships that sail back and forth across the Atlantic, weaving American and British cultures together. The novel tells of an unhappy marriage between a rich, innocent American girl and a nasty, older, impoverished British lord. Though Frances was older than Stephen and hardly innocent, the book offers many insights into their relationship.

In *The Shuttle* Frances describes Sir Nigel Anstruthers as "a man with a good figure and a good voice, [who] but for a heaviness of feature the result of objectionable living, might have given the impression of being better looking than he really was."[15] These are the kindest words she ever says about him in a book of 512 pages.

The book begins in New York, where Sir Nigel behaves himself just long enough to win the hand of young Rosalie Vanderpoel. As their ship steams away from the dock, he reveals his true colors. "'What a deuce of a row Americans make,' he said even before they were out of hearing of the voices. 'It will be a positive rest to be in a country where the women do not cackle and shriek with laughter.'"[16]

Rosalie soon realizes that her marriage is a mistake. On her carriage ride to Sir Nigel's country house in England, she thinks, "New York, good-tempered, lenient, free New York, was millions of miles away and Nigel was so loathly near and—and so ugly. She had never known before that he was so ugly, that his face was so heavy, his skin so thick and coarse and his expression so evilly ill-tempered. . . . Her self-reproach was as great as her terror."[17]

The Shuttle describes "a manor house reigning over an old English village,"[18] and the village, where "the men touched their foreheads as the carriage passed, and the children made bobbing curtsies."[19] Frances's carriage, with her coachman and footman in top hats, caused a similar stir in Rolvenden. Frances, who remembered her own impoverished youth, sometimes stopped to give the children rides.

In *The Shuttle*, Rosalie helps the poor villagers, who are her husband's tenants. "I suppose it gratifies your vanity to play the Lady Bountiful,"[20] sneers Sir Nigel, but Rosalie's good deeds console her and in real life, Frances took pride in the role.

"Maytham was 'The Hall' of the little Village of Rolvenden," wrote Vivian. "It, and the people in it, by virtue of history and custom dating back hundreds of years, belonged to the people of Rolvenden; that is, with something like the feeling of feudal days, 'The Hall' was looked to in all cases of sickness, misfortune, or sudden death."[21]

"Just you give me time to make them adore me,"[22] Frances wrote of the people in Rolvenden. She held fêtes for the children and helped the other local gentry to host an annual dinner for villagers. At Christmas she delivered clothes, dolls, and stockings filled with toys. Like Rosalie in *The Shuttle* she visited "small families or large ones, newly born infants or newly buried ones, old women with 'bad legs' and old men who needed comforts."[23]

While Frances ingratiated herself into the community, Stephen came and went. There was plenty of business to manage, involving several plays and books. Their personal life was stormy; with Frances he was moody and demanding.

He behaved better in the presence of company. With or without him, Maytham attracted dozens of distinguished house guests and neighbors. British and American celebrities signed the guest book with clever sayings and drawings. Often they joined in local celebrations, like a "treat" described in *The Making of a Marchioness*, another Burnett novel that borrows Maytham for a setting:

> At two o'clock a procession of village children and their friends and parents, headed by the village band, marched up the avenue and passed before the house on their way to their special part of the park. Lady Maria and her guests stood upon the broad steps and welcomed the jocund crowd as it moved by. . . . As the villagers gathered in the park, the house-party joined them by way of the gardens. A conjurer from London gave an entertainment under a huge tree, and children found white rabbits taken from their pockets, and oranges from their caps, with squeals of joy and shouts of laughter.[24]

Frances's house parties became famous. Her guests took tea on the lawn, strolled under parasols through the gardens, sang and danced (see figure 7.3), dressed in fancy costumes, played cards and other games and took afternoon rides in the Victoria.

"We are only ten miles from the sea," wrote Frances, "and the roads are perfect for bicycling."[25] The cyclists were Rudyard Kipling and

7.3 Journalist and author Poultney Bigelow drew this picture in the guest book at Maytham Hall, June 30, 1901. Courtesy of the personal collection of Penny Deupree.

Henry James; James rode a tricycle. Kipling lived nearby in Sussex. James, who had been a frequent visitor at Frances's London home, lived at Lamb House in Rye, ten miles from Maytham, on the English Channel. He liked the flat, coastal setting, calling it "somewhere I can, without disaster, bicycle."[26]

"We are neighbours and can borrow cabbages from each other,"[27] claimed Frances, who actually saw less of James in the country than she had in London. She sent him peaches and figs from her garden.

"Noblest of Neighbours and Most Heavenly of Women!"[28] he wrote in his letter of thanks, but still he resisted her invitations.

She pursued him steadily, once knocking on his door at Lamb House. The maid turned her away. James was desperately writing *The Awkward Age*, which was being serialized in *Harper's* before the story was even finished. Like Frances, he needed to write to pay his monthly bills. His books earned far less than hers did.

Frances's friend, the author Ella Hepworth Dixon, visited Maytham frequently. She told how Henry James invited their house party to lunch. As they ate, he rose abruptly from the table to go write.[29] Nothing he did seemed to offend, or discourage, Frances.

Frances traveled to America in 1899. She had planned to visit Vivian at his first job, as a reporter in Colorado, but the altitude there was ruled unsuitable for her weak heart. Instead, Vivian came to see her in Washington, D.C. In February 1900 Frances sailed for Genoa, where Stephen met her and where they were married.

The news made headlines in England and in America. Stories about older women marrying younger men sold newspapers in 1900, the same as now.

In *The Shuttle* Rosalie quickly learns that her marriage is "one of those nightmare things in which you suddenly find yourself married to someone you cannot bear and you don't know how it happened, because you yourself have had nothing to do with the matter. She felt that presently she must waken with a start and find herself breathing fast, and panting out, half laughing, half crying, 'Oh, I am so glad it's not true! I am so glad it's not true!'"[30]

This passage echoes a letter Frances wrote to a friend just months after her own wedding: "It is all so grotesquely hideous—it is like some wild nightmare which I surely *must* waken from."[31]

During this same time Frances wrote to her sister Edith that Stephen "scarcely seems sane half the time. . . . He is like some spiteful hysterical woman. He will work up scenes. He will not let things alone."[32]

"You will do as I order you," Sir Nigel tells Rosalie in *The Shuttle*, "and learn to behave yourself as a decent married woman should. You will learn to obey your husband and respect his wishes and control your devilish American temper."[33]

Frances wrote to Edith,

> He talks about my "duties as a wife" as if I had married him of my own accord—as if I had not been forced and blackguarded and blackmailed into it. It is my duty to end my acquaintance with all such people as he suspects of not admiring him. . . . It is my duty to make my property over to him . . . he is to be provided with money enough to keep his chambers and spend as much time there as he likes. It is my duty to work very hard and above all to love him very much and insist on his writing plays with me. If I had married him because I loved him and believed he loved me what hades I should have passed through.[34]

In *The Shuttle* Frances describes a husband's blackmail. Sir Nigel knows that women are "trained to give in to anything rather than be bullied in public, to accede in the end to any demand rather than endure the shame of a certain kind of scene made before servants, and a certain kind of insolence used to relatives and guests."[35] Sir Nigel torments his wife for years over an innocent letter she wrote to the vicar, threatening to ruin both of them by exposing what he considers to be proof of an affair.

Stephen used the same techniques. "If a man is sufficiently indecent & unscrupulous—" Frances wrote to a friend, "if he will rave before your butler & makes scenes before your maid & if you are a woman who has horror of publicity such a man can gradually attain almost anything he has in view."[36] Steven tormented Frances with her past (she had almost certainly had other lovers before him). Even the accusations, made public, would have been sufficient to destroy her career. Sometimes Stephen threatened to enlist her first husband's assistance in bringing her to ruin.

All the classic signs of abuse, which were not so well-known in Frances's lifetime, are catalogued in *The Shuttle*. Sir Nigel isolates Rosalie from her family and friends, refusing to let her parents see her when they travel to England. Stephen tried this with Frances, too.

"I told him I would not let him cut people off from me—" she wrote to Edith, "I said I would call on a few of my men friends— . . . Kenneth [Campbell], Henry James etc. to talk the situation over with him—that the matter must be decided. He was mad with fury but I think he saw I meant what I said. . . . He threatened that he would drive me from Maytham."[37]

Henry James would seem an unlikely rescuer, but Frances's threat calmed Stephen. Their lives cycled from upset to calm and back again, but she knew that she could never trust him. "When a man shows himself a blackguard, a liar and a bullying coward, one does not forget,"[38] she wrote to Edith.

In *The Shuttle* Sir Nigel is also "a liar and a bully and a coward."[39] His bride Rosalie "was almost more afraid of [Sir Nigel's] patronizing, affectionate moments than she was of his temper."[40] Rosalie knows that his rages will return and she soon learns that they can end in violence. He hits her when she is pregnant and later beats their seven-year-old son.

In *The Shuttle*, after twelve terrible years, Rosalie's younger sister Betty comes from America to England to rescue her. It must have satisfied Frances to show the courageous Betty standing up to her villainous brother-in-law. "All your life," she tells him, "you have counted upon getting your own way because you saw that people—especially women—have a horror of public scenes, and will submit to almost anything to avoid them. . . . That is true very often, but not always. . . . I, for instance, would let you make a scene with me anywhere you chose—in Bond Street—in Piccadilly—on the steps of Buckingham Palace . . . and you would gain nothing you wanted by it—*nothing*."[41]

"Damn her!" Sir Nigel cries out about Betty later. "If I had hung her up and cut her into strips she would have died staring at me with her big eyes—without uttering a sound."[42] In the book's climax, Betty hides in a hedge as he hunts her, to rape her or kill her or both. Frances lets the reader imagine his exact plan.

Frances was so unhappy with Stephen that she longed to die. "Oh, God, if I have ever done a good deed in my life, kill me before the day is over,"[43] she wrote.

She rented a house in London for the winter of 1900. There, in just two weeks, she wrote *The Making of a Marchioness*, a light-hearted

Cinderella story. It, too, draws on Maytham as its poor but genteel heroine is invited to help at a house party in the country. But even in the sequel to this sunny book (*The Methods of Lady Walderhurst*), the villain beats his wife. Sadly Gretchen Holbrook Gerzina concludes that this domestic abuse was "likely to have been drawn from [Frances's] personal experience."[44]

Frances's sister Edith rejoined the London household, where Stephen was on good behavior. He published a novel, *A Thoroughbred Mongrel*, about an author, Mrs. Flufton Bennet, who has a country house. The story, told from her dog's point of view, received excellent reviews.

"Why can't you love me? Why can't you trust me?"[45] he demanded, but Frances could not.

"Dearest," wrote Vivian, "don't ever think for a moment that in the troubles you are having my heart has ever left you."[46] He offered to come at her call, but he did not visit. "Because [Stephen] is the head of your house," he wrote, "and because he has shown himself my enemy more than once, it would be both a task and a risk for me to sleep under the same roof with him and you."[47]

Frances, Edith, and Stephen returned to Maytham in March 1901. Now she implemented a plan to "keep visitors in the house,"[48] as they offered protection.

In July Frances planned a large house party with croquet, tennis, a cricket match, a band, and "tea on the field."[49] Apparently Vivian, who was touring Europe, visited Maytham around this time; accounts vary but Vivian himself reported that he had had a "brief taste of Maytham life,"[50] without saying whether Stephen was present, and his signature appears in the guest book.

In December 1902, Frances, Edith, and Vivian sailed for America. "At no period of her life," wrote Vivian, "had Mrs. Burnett been in so nervous a condition. The task of keeping the surface of things at Maytham smooth while struggling with the temperament of Stephen had brought her to the last frayed edge of her endurance."[51]

Frances checked herself into a sanitorium in Fishkill-on-Hudson in New York. Stephen soon followed, but in this refuge Frances finally found the courage to tell him that the marriage was over. Gretchen Holbrook Gerzina says that she paid him off.[52]

Frances did not return to Maytham until the summer of 1904. With Stephen gone, she devoted herself happily to writing and entertaining. Elegantly attired in white gowns and hats, she spent summers in the rose garden. "It was my habit," she said, "to sit and write there under an aged writhen tree, gray with lichen and festooned with roses. The soft silence of it—the remote aloofness—were the most perfect ever dreamed of."[53] A Japanese tent umbrella sheltered her from the sun.

The only disturbance came from a robin. Frances, holding perfectly still, imitated his call. Later she wrote about the bird in a sappy little book called *My Robin*: "Each morning when I came into the rose-garden he came to call on me and discover things he wanted to know concerning robins of my size and unusual physical conformation."[54] He perched on her hat, she said, and took crumbs from her hand. She named him Tweetie.

Neighbors came to call, but not the Vicar's wife, who sent a friendly note, regretting that "circumstances have kept the Hall and Vicarage apart."[55] That is, the Vicarage could no longer call on the Hall now that Frances was separated from a second husband.

Ellen Terry, the actress, had no such reservations, having suffered her own share of problems with two husbands and a lover. She lived in a sixteenth-century timbered house called Small Hythe, just two miles from Maytham. On a visit to Frances she liked the look of a grassy slope between the terrace and the lawn. "What a lovely place to roll down!"[56] she said and did just that.

Ellla Hepworth Dixon brought publisher William Heinemann down in a motor car, and he joined Maytham's circle of friends. Later he would publish the British edition of *The Secret Garden*.

Frances spent happy summers at Maytham and winters in New York or, one year, in Montreux. In her beloved rose garden, she wrote *A Little Princess*, incorporating material she had used in the play version of *Sara Crewe*, and fairy tales as told by Queen Crosspatch, including some set in the garden. Another book from this time is *The Dawn of a To-morrow*. *The Shuttle* proved hard to finish—the writing of this novel, so closely aligned to her life, lasted longer than her marriage to Stephen: "It simply holds on to each obstacle it is dragged past," she wrote about the book, "and screams and kicks up its heels and tries to dig its toes into the ground."[57] She finally finished it for serialization in *The Century* in November 1906.

Frances had to leave Maytham in 1908 after the owner sold the house. It was too expensive for her to buy but she soon built a home of her own, at Plandome, on Long Island. *The Shuttle*, that painful and most difficult novel, paid for the whole place.[58]

From 1909 to 1910, Maytham was rebuilt and enlarged by the famous architect Sir Edwin Lutyens to the way it looks now. Lutyens restored the exterior to a red brick, Georgian formality, adding a high, hipped roof with dormer windows. In front of the house he placed a clock house over the entrance, which was through the stables, and added a new drive. In the back, where Ellen Terry had rolled down the hill, he built a terrace and a series of steps leading down to the lawn. Now the house became known as Great Maytham Hall.

During World War II it was used by the National Institute for the Blind and the army. After the war it fell into disrepair as it passed from one owner to another. In 1955 the well-known landscape architect A. Du Gard Pasley happened on Maytham when he pulled into the driveway to turn his car around. Recognizing it as a Lutyens masterpiece, he convinced the Kent County Council to hold an enquiry on the building's future.

As a result, the house was preserved. It became part of the Mutual Households Association, later the Country Houses Association. This group was set up to save historic houses threatened with demolition. From 1961 to 1965 Maytham was renovated, and made into apartments. The new residents, like Frances before them, cleared the walled gardens of debris and took over some of the flower gardens. Later they became tour guides on days when the gardens were opened to the public.[59]

My mother, Jean Shirley, and I began writing our biography *Frances Hodgson Burnett: Beyond the Secret Garden* in 1988, before there was widespread access to the Internet. With no travel budget, we relied on the mail, writing to libraries, museums, historical societies, and tourist agencies where Frances had lived or visited.

One response came from Dr. B. G. Burgess, the Hon. Curator of the Tenterden Museum, which is near Maytham. Dr. Burgess sent the Maytham phone number and urged me to visit, adding

> The present Great Maytham Hall bears little resemblance to the building in F. H. Burnett's time. But the modern building (now prestigious flats for the elderly) is still in a very rural situation, surrounded by woodland, about a half a mile from the main village of Rolvenden. . . . My wife and I frequently take a walk on a public footpath from Rolvenden Church across a meadow through the woods adjacent to the Maytham Estate. It is still a very peaceful place, where you may

see and hear wild birds (including the robin) and perhaps catch a glimpse of a wild fox. I am personally interested in your enquiry: my great-great-uncle, Nelson Burgess, was the licensee of the only pub in Rolvenden Layne around the turn of the century, so I am sure he must have known about the gentry at Great Maytham Hall![60]

On a hot, sunny afternoon in May 1992, two years after the book had been published, my husband, daughter (then a university student), and I visited Great Maytham Hall where our tour guide was Bill Brewin, a resident and a retired court stenographer. Seeing Maytham, especially the garden, for the first time, was an overwhelming experience for me. It was a thrill to see the place I had written about, based purely on the descriptions of others. And, of course, *The Secret Garden* had been one of my favorite childhood books. I laughed; I cried; I took hundreds of photographs; and Richard, Carey, and Bill gave me all the time and space I needed.

The biggest surprise of the rose garden is how very large it is, 210 feet by 150 feet. This garden is not a secret by any means. To reach it, we went through the house and down the back terrace steps to the kitchen garden. Here were raised planters, filled with blooming irises. These brick boxes are Georgian; they were probably used for herbs in earlier times.

The door from the kitchen garden into the walled garden looked familiar: rounded on top and overgrown with ivy. Frances's walled garden was landscaped simply when we visited, for minimal maintenance. Most of the interior was grass, with borders of mixed flowers. A wisteria arbor divided the lawn. A small brick house with a peaked roof stood in the southeast corner. Bill said that Frances wrote there on cold days, but I could find no record that she did. On a later visit, someone suggested that this house was a Lutyens addition; this idea seemed more believable.

Standing in that walled garden felt like magic to me. It was practical magic: I heard sheep bleating and crows cawing, unfortunately, too late to put these sounds into our book! Mother insisted on having all five senses in every chapter, if possible.

"Where are the Laurette Messimy roses?" I asked, but alas, there were none. For years I visited gardens and nurseries, looking for these flowers, and never found any. But when my husband and I returned in 1998, Bill proudly escorted us to a garden by the little house. There were several Laurette Messimy bushes, a bit scraggly in their first year, blooming with fragrant pink roses.

Beyond the walled garden is a wood of tall oak trees. From the back, Maytham looks south over a vista of "rise and hollow, between the sheep-dotted greenness of fields and the scented hedges"⁶¹ toward the English Channel.

Walking around the house on our first visit we found an enormous chestnut tree (the British say horse chestnut) in full bloom and, by a lucky chance, the bluebells at their very best, a sea of purple under tall trees. Frances bragged about the bluebells at Maytham, and she was right: of all the bluebells in Kent that week, none were so lush as those. They carpeted the grounds from the front of the house to the edge of the property, to the public footpath, the one that leads to Rolvenden Church.

For years Bill Brewin's letters kept us informed about goings-on at Maytham. "Some of the people who come," he wrote, "know nothing about the house, Frances Hodgson Burnett or Edwin Lutyens and have to be told all about it, but others, like yourselves, know more than we do and can put us right when we are going through our spiel. On one occasion one of our guides was asked 'Are you allowed out?' as if it was some kind of reformatory!"⁶²

In June 1998 he described, "The daffodils made a brave show all over the grass areas at front and back of the house, followed by swathes of bluebells . . . and succeeded by common spotted orchid, the most frequent wild orchid in England. . . . The gardens proper are looking very good, tended by our indefatigable two lady gardeners."⁶³

Paddy Ferrier, who, with her husband, lived at Maytham at the same time as Bill, wrote,

> The guiding takes up a lot of our time from May to September, but it helps to bring in extra revenue to the House. The Secret Garden of course is a great attraction for our visitors—and we send them off round the garden to find the five-trunked tree to put a merry-leaf in their pocket!
> . . . Last summer we had a young man and his wife visit from Newcastle-under-Lyme. He was tracing his family history and said that his great-grandfather had been the gardener at Maytham when F. H. B. was in residence and that he had apparently been a curmudgeonly old man just like the gardener in the book.⁶⁴

In 2004 the Country Houses Association, citing rising maintenance costs, sold Great Maytham Hall. The residents, who had thought that they had a home for life, were given six months to find new accommodations. Then the buyer, a company called Heritage Living, began converting Maytham to pricey condominiums for people over the age of fifty-five. When I last visited, in May 2005, the bluebells were in full bloom and the construction was nearly done. The gardens were closed then, private gardens being a selling point for prospective customers. But Roger Watts, the new resident manager, said that there was "an enormous budget to fix up the garden." He thought that a time would come when the gardens would be opened again, perhaps as part of a national scheme of garden opening days. "Sooner or later," he said, "the new residents will want to show them off."[65] In the meantime he was seeking approval from his board to apply for a blue plaque to post outside. This plaque, like the one on Frances's London townhouse in Portland Place, would indicate that a great person had lived on the premises.

Near the end of Frances's life, when she was living on Long Island, her friend Rosamund Campbell wrote to tell her that she was still loved in Kent.

"It goes to my heart," Frances replied, "to be told that Rolvenden remembers me kindly. I loved the place so. Maytham was *home* to me."[66]

In *The Shuttle*, Frances describes the first wave of American tourism to England:

> The journey being likely to be made once in a lifetime, the traveller's intention was to see as much as possible, to visit as many cities, cathedrals, ruins, galleries, as his time and purse would allow. People who could speak with any degree of familiarity of Hyde Park, the Champs Elysées, the Pincio, had gained a certain dignity. The ability to touch with an intimate bearing upon such localities was a raison de plus for being asked out to tea or dinner. To possess photographs and relics was to be of great interest, to have seen European celebrities even at a distance, to have wandered about the outside of poets' gardens and philosophers' houses, was to be entitled to respect.[67]

Today wandering about the outside of Great Maytham Hall entitles the visitor to beauty and, as the landscape is so unchanged since Frances lived there, a feeling of time travel. Frances wrote that the Shuttle, "weaving new threads into its web each year, has woven warp and woof until they bind far shore to shore."[68] Now her words are woven tightly into the hearts of readers, wherever English is spoken, and in other languages, where her books have been translated. People have visited Maytham from many countries around the world.

Great Maytham Hall and its rose garden pleased her, consoled her, entertained her, fulfilled her, and inspired her. Vivian said, "The particular fragrance and outdoor beauty of her later books begins here at her contact with the English gardens at Maytham."[69]

How those gardens will affect Maytham's future residents is for them to tell, but the influence on recent visitors is powerful and evident. It can be seen in the 2003 Frances Hodgson Burnett conference, in Gretchen Holbrook Gerzina's new biography of Burnett, and in this book you are reading.

NOTES

1. Frances Hodgson Burnett to Vivian Burnett, February 28, 1898. Vivian Burnett, *The Romantick Lady (Frances Hodgson Burnett): The Life Story of an Imagination* (New York: Charles Scribner's Sons, 1927), 286.

2. Henry James to Mrs. Hugh Bell, January 7, 1892. *Henry James: Letters, Volume III, 1883–1895*, ed. Leon Edel (London: Macmillan London Limited, 1980), 369.

3. Frances Hodgson Burnett to Vivian Burnett, 1891. V. Burnett, *The Romantick Lady*, 221.

4. Henry James to Mrs. Hugh Bell, January 7, 1892. *Henry James: Letters, Volume III, 1883–1895*, 370.

5. Frances Hodgson Burnett, *The Shuttle* (New York: Frederick A. Stokes, 1907), 32–33.

6. Frances Hodgson Burnett to Vivian Burnett, February 28, 1898. V. Burnett, *The Romantick Lady*, 286.

7. Frances Hodgson Burnett, *My Robin* (New York: Frederick A. Stokes, 1912), 3–4.

8. F. H. Burnett, *The Shuttle*, 128.

9. Frances worked in her own garden but her contemporary, Elizabeth von Arnim, author of *Elizabeth and Her German Garden*, who also loved Laurette Messimy roses, wrote, "I wish with all my heart I were a man, for of course the first thing I should do would be to buy a spade and go and garden, and then I should have the delight of doing everything for my flowers with my own hands and need not waste time explaining what I want done, to someone else." Elizabeth von Arnim [Kathleen Mansfield Beauchamp], *Eliz-*

abeth and Her German Garden (New York: J. S. Ogilvie, n.d. [the book was first published in 1898]), 94.

10. Frances Hodgson Burnett, Introduction to Frances Browne's *Granny's Wonderful Chair* (New York: McClure, Phillips & Co., 1904), xxxv.

11. Frances Hodgson Burnett to Vivian Burnett, 1898. Ann Thwaite, *Waiting for the Party: The Life of Frances Hodgson Burnett, 1849–1924* (London: Faber and Faber, 1994), 182.

12. Frances Hodgson Burnett, *The Secret Garden* (Boston: David R. Godine, 1987), 62.

13. Frances Hodgson Burnett to Rosamund Campbell, 1898. V. Burnett, *The Romantick Lady*, 293.

14. V. Burnett, *The Romantick Lady*, 295.

15. F. H. Burnett, *The Shuttle*, 5.

16. F. H. Burnett, *The Shuttle*, 19.

17. F. H. Burnett, *The Shuttle*, 28.

18. F. H. Burnett, *The Shuttle*, 5.

19. F. H. Burnett, *The Shuttle*, 33.

20. F. H. Burnett, *The Shuttle*, 41.

21. V. Burnett, *The Romantick Lady*, 287.

22. Frances Hodgson Burnett to Vivian Burnett, July 28, 1898. Penny Deupree private collection (seen in Gretchen Holbrook Gerzina, *Frances Hodgson Burnett: The Unexpected Life of the Author of* The Secret Garden [New Brunswick, NJ: Rutgers University Press, 2005], 205).

23. F. H. Burnett, *The Shuttle*, 38.

24. Frances Hodgson Burnett, *The Making of a Marchioness* (London: Persephone Books, 2001), 61–62.

25. Thwaite, *Waiting for the Party*, 179.

26. Thwaite, *Waiting for the Party*, 179.

27. Frances Hodgson Burnett to Henry James. Thwaite, *Waiting for the Party*, 179.

28. Henry James to Frances Hodgson Burnett. Thwaite, *Waiting for the Party*, 184.

29. Ella Hepworth Dixon, *"As I Knew Them": Sketches of People I Have Met on the Way* (London: Hutchinson, 1930), 98.

30. F. H. Burnett, *The Shuttle*, 28.

31. Frances Hodgson Burnett to Katherine Thomas, May 24, 1900. Special Collections, University of Virginia Library, MSS 6817-d (seen in Gerzina, *Frances Hodgson Burnett*, 217–18).

32. Frances Hodgson Burnett to Edith Jordan, May 30, 1900. Penny Deupree private collection.

33. F. H. Burnett, *The Shuttle*, 49.

34. Frances Hodgson Burnett to Edith Jordan, May 30. 1900. Penny Deupree private collection (seen in Thwaite, *Waiting for the Party*, 191–92).
35. F. H. Burnett, *The Shuttle*, 21.
36. Frances Hodgson Burnett to Katherine Thomas, May 24, 1900. Special Collections, University of Virginia Library, MSS 6317-d (seen in Gerzina, *Frances Hodgson Burnett*, 217–18).
37. Thwaite, *Waiting for the Party*, 195.
38. Thwaite, *Waiting for the Party*, 193.
39. F. H. Burnett, *The Shuttle*, 116.
40. F. H. Burnett, *The Shuttle*, 38.
41. F. H. Burnett, *The Shuttle*, 411.
42. F. H. Burnett, *The Shuttle*, 435.
43. Thwaite, *Waiting for the Party*, 193.
44. Gretchen Holbrook Gerzina, Afterword to Frances Hodgson Burnett's *The Making of a Marchioness* (London: Persephone Books, 2001), 303.
45. Thwaite, *Waiting for the Party*, 199.
46. Thwaite, *Waiting for the Party*, 195.
47. Thwaite, *Waiting for the Party*, 196.
48. Thwaite, *Waiting for the Party*, 201.
49. Thwaite, *Waiting for the Party*, 203.
50. V. Burnett, *The Romantick Lady*, 302.
51. V. Burnett, *The Romantick Lady*, 302.
52. Gerzina, Afterword, 303.
53. F. H. Burnett, *My Robin*, 4.
54. F. H. Burnett, *My Robin*, 14.
55. Thwaite, *Waiting for the Party*, 210.
56. Dixon, "*As I Knew Them*," 82.
57. Frances Hodgson Burnett to Kitty Hall Brownell. Thwaite, *Waiting for the Party*, 206.
58. Thwaite, *Waiting for the Party*, 217.
59. *Great Maytham Hall: A Brief History* (Banbury, England: Country Houses Association, n.d.).
60. Dr. B. G. Burgess, letter to Angelica Carpenter, March 5, 1989.
61. F. H. Burnett, *The Shuttle*, 102.
62. Bill Brewin, letter to Angelica Carpenter, July 15, 1992.
63. Bill Brewin, letter to Angelica Carpenter, June 2, 1998.
64. Paddy Ferrier, letter to Angelica Carpenter, December 4, 2001.
65. Roger Watts, interview by Angelica Carpenter, May 9, 2005.
66. V. Burnett, *The Romantick Lady*, 405.
67. F. H. Burnett, *The Shuttle*, 2.
68. F. H. Burnett, *The Shuttle*, 2.
69. V. Burnett, *The Romantick Lady*, 287.

• 8 •

"A Delicate Invisible Hand": Frances Hodgson Burnett's Contributions to Theatre for Youth

Barbara Jo Maier

Shortly after her death in 1924, Frances Hodgson Burnett's friends proposed the construction of a Secret Garden in New York City's Central Park. It was to be "tucked away within reach of the great Fifth Avenue, yet so hidden by rock and shrubbery that one needs must seek for it in earnest in its nook."[1] Today the Secret Garden in memory of Burnett is listed in New York City guidebooks, yet visitors must diligently look for the boy playing a pipe and the girl holding a shell in her hands. The small memorial gets lost in the larger landscape, much like the accomplishments of Frances Hodgson Burnett in the history of theatre for youth. Burnett is acknowledged in this area of study primarily because two of her plays for children were produced on Broadway near the turn of the century: *The Real Little Lord Fauntleroy* in 1888 and *A Little Princess* in 1903. Rarely mentioned is a third Burnett play, *Racketty-Packetty House*, selected in 1912 as the show to open "the first playhouse in the world devoted to children" located on the roof of the Century Theatre overlooking Central Park.[2]

At the dedication of the memorial fountain, Frances's lifetime friend Kitty Hall Brownlee predicted that the writings of Burnett "will have a delicate invisible hand in future."[3] Frances Hodgson Burnett's plays for children deserve to be visible and recognized as the beginnings of a new genre of theatre focused on youth.

Several sources offer insights into the origins of Frances's literary creations for child audiences. Her autobiographical sketches, published first as a series of stories in *Scribner's Magazine*, were compiled in 1893 into a book titled *The One I Knew the Best of All: A Memory of the Mind of a Child*. Frances divides the autobiographical sketches into chapters parallel to stages of the development of her imagination. She writes in third person for a child audience and refers to herself as the Small Person. She explains in the preface dated 1892 that her motivation to write sketches of her life was based on her fascination with children: "I have so often wished that I could see the minds of young things with a sight stronger than that of very interested eyes, which can only see from the *outside*. There must be so many thoughts for which child courage and child language have not the exact words. So, remembering that there was one child of whom I could write from the inside point of view, and with certain knowledge, I began to make a little sketch of the one I knew the best of all."[4] The sketches must be accepted as fictionalized versions of her memories, yet are important because Frances admits the circumstances of her life led to her career as a writer. The 1894 *American Writers of To-Day* biography collection reveals her inspiration: "In that charming autobiography of hers which so delightfully entertained the readers of *Scribner's Magazine*, under the title of *The One I Knew Best of All*, she tells us that from her earliest recollection she lived in an ideal world, and was an unconscious playwright and romancer even in the nursery. She could not see anybody who impressed her at all without making him or her a character in these dramas and romances, and inventing all sorts of deliciously impossible adventures for them."[5]

In the 1927 biography of his mother, Vivian Burnett details the childlike lens through which Frances viewed her life. *The Romantick Lady: The Life Story of an Imagination* begins with a warning: "To those who knew Mrs. Burnett with any intimacy it was plain that in all her thinking and doing was something not quite to be measured or weighed according to the usual mortal methods. Approached in the right spirit, the whole matter was easy of explanation. One had merely to admit that she was partly fairy. That such a thing might be, she herself was quite willing—even eager—to admit."[6] Vivian claims, "Realism was the smallest part of Frances Hodgson as she lived and wrote."[7] The part-fairy woman not only had the gift of a fantastic imagination, but also a gift for storytelling.

Dramatizing came naturally to Frances. Her minimal education took place at the Select Seminary for Young Ladies and Gentlemen where lessons were taught by the Hadfield sisters in the rooms of their luxurious house located in Islington Square, Manchester, England. Frances loved to read and entertain her schoolmates with stories she made up. Frances's sister Edith describes her storytelling sister: "She was just like her own Sara Crewe. These stories were very romantic. Someone in them would be forlorn, sickly or miserable—pitiful in one way or another. And there would be someone else, who was brave and strong and helpful. The strong one would have to go through all sorts of trials and tribulations. But in the end things would come out right for everybody in a fairy tale sort of way."[8]

Things didn't necessarily go right for Frances's family. When her father died, they struggled to survive financially. In 1865, when Frances was fifteen, her family moved to the United States, just as the Civil War ended. Mrs. Hodgson's brother in Knoxville offered employment to Frances's brother. The rest of the family moved into a deserted log cabin in the village of New Market, twenty-five miles from Knoxville.

To assist her mother in the support of the family, that winter Frances practiced storytelling as the teacher of her own Select Seminary in New Market. Her eight students paid tuition with vegetables and eggs.[9] The following spring the Hodgson family moved to Knoxville, but there were not enough children in the new neighborhood to open another school.

Frances enjoyed reading *Godey's Lady's Book*, a women's publication her mother brought home. Magazines were beginning to prosper in America with the expansion of steam-powered presses. There were no international copyright laws. Publishers could print any foreign writer without paying royalties. Frances had the opportunity to read Scott, Thackeray, Dickens, and Shakespeare, which were mixed in with articles encouraging women to participate in community affairs and with serialized romantic stories.[10] The magazine stories inspired Frances to submit a story of her own. In 1868, at the age of eighteen, Frances was the paid author of two published stories. Thwaite cites the titles as "Hearts and Diamonds" and "Miss Carruther's Engagement."[11] Vivian reports the story titles as "Aces or Clubs" and "Miss Desborough's Difficulties."[12] The titles are not significant. What is significant is that Frances's career as a writer was launched with a payment of $35 for two stories.

Only two years later Frances became the primary breadwinner of the family when her mother died in 1870. With the acceptance of her first stories, Frances began to write five or six stories a month that were published in "every magazine in America except *Harper's*, *Scribner's*, and the *Atlantic*.

'I was not sufficiently certain of my powers,' she wrote years later, 'to send anything to them. It would have seemed to me a kind of presumption to aspire to entering the world of actual literature.'"[13] It was not until 1871 that she decided to send a story to the prestigious *Scribner's Monthly* magazine. Turned down because sixteen pages was too long for a short story, Frances submitted another that was warmly received by R. W. Gilder, assistant editor. Gilder remained her primary literary and publication advisor until he died in 1909. After 1871 Frances's stories appeared monthly in *Scribner's*, *Harper's*, *Peterson's*, *Leslie's*, and *Godey's Lady's Book*.

Spurred by the continuous acceptance of her stories and the encouragement of editor Gilder, Frances started work on her first major novel. On the strength of the first few chapters, *Scribner's Monthly* began to serialize her *That Lass o' Lowrie's* in 1876. In April of 1877 Scribner published *That Lass o' Lowrie's* in book form and it was highly praised by American critics. The *New York Herald* had "no hesitation in saying that there is no living writer (man or woman) who has Mrs. Burnett's dramatic power in telling a story. . . . The publication of *That Lass o' Lowrie's* is a red letter day in the world of literature."[14] A book published in 1894 that offers overviews of important American writers of the time suggests the level of fame Frances achieved with *That Lass*:

> In 1877 appeared "That Lass o' Lowrie's," having first had an honorable career as a serial in "Scribner's Monthly." This gave the author her first real taste of fame, and the book was so great a success that more substantial reward was hers at once. From that time on the world has gone well with her, if a large bank account and the praise of men can make a woman happy. As each of her books has appeared, it has been greeted with a chorus of approbation, and even when the critics have doubted, as critics sometimes will, the public has stood by its favorite and bought without a qualm of a doubt.[15]

Excellent reviews of the novel in England helped thirty thousand copies sell quickly in Frances's homeland.[16] Several British authors dramatized and staged Frances's story. A review of the London production in the *New York Times* dated September 3, 1877, describes how the American "authors were summoned to receive the congratulations of the audience" at the end of the opening night performance. The critic goes on to suggest his hope that "'Liz' will be quickly produced in America, where Mrs. Burnett has a novelist's right in her story."

The theft of Frances's story plus the need to support her family due to the struggling eye specialist practice of her husband Swan Burnett inspired her to write her first play. Not the kind of woman to let others take an opportunity away from her, Frances wrote to Charles Reade, one of the British dramatists: "I wrote *Lass* here [the United States], copyrighted it here, reserved stage-rights here (which *can* be done be in the United States), wrote my play here, copyrighted that here, and it will be played here."[17] Frances's first play opened on Broadway in November of 1878, but her debut as a playwright was not as successful as her debut as a novelist. A *New York Times* critic spoke at length about the faults of the script, claiming it lacked "the true dramatic sprit. . . . . Mrs. Burnett and Mr. Magnus [Julian Magnus, a writer for the stage] have not written a drama; they have taken several scenes from 'That Lass o' Lowrie's,' attached these in the best manner possible, and presented the result as a play. . . . Throughout these scenes there is no action that can be called dramatic, and no situations that can be called effective."[18]

Even though Frances's Broadway debut as a playwright was not a success, the fact that a woman writer had a play produced on Broadway is significant. How did Burnett's play find its way onto Broadway at the time?

Prior to 1870 New York theatre producers staged long-running melodramas with stars who could draw audiences. A Broadway manager either owned or leased a theatre and hired a company of performers, preferably with one or more stars. Often the managers like Lester Wallack, Laura Keene, Dion Boucicault, William Mitchell, or Edwin Booth, were the stars.[19] A company became identified with a certain theatre and performed in the same space for as many seasons as possible. Stock companies performing a small repertory of plays for loyal patrons satisfied the theatre-going crowds.

In the decades following the Civil War, New York was becoming not only the major U.S. port, but also a leading manufacturing center and the headquarters of major banks, insurance, and publishing companies. Retail shops, restaurants, hotels, and theatres blossomed along Broadway from Fourteenth Street to Twenty-third Street, making it a mecca for city dwellers, commuters, and visitors. With the completion of the transcontinental railroad in 1869, and the expansion of telephone communications, New York became the center of theatrical activity and an exporter of entertainment. Theatre became not just an art form, but a means of making money. In 1870 the population in New York was close to a million.[20] The annual income per capita rose from $779 to $1,164 while the work day decreased from twelve hours to ten hours a day, and for many, Saturday afternoons were holidays. Minstrel shows, vaudeville, and burlesque shows attracted many New Yorkers. Middle-class citizens had the time and money for entertainment.[21] (See figure 8.1.)

As potential audiences increased, so did the demand for new venues and plays. By 1870 there were fourteen theatres on Broadway.[22] In 1869 Edwin Booth invested over a million dollars to build his dream of a theatre at the corner of Twenty-third Street and Sixth Avenue, away from Broadway. Theatre companies discovered that if they specialized in a certain form of theatre they had a better chance of survival. Booth's Theatre became noted for foreign and domestic stars. Only five years after it opened, Booth was forced to declare bankruptcy. Thus Booth's Theatre was available to independent producers in 1878 when Frances's play was produced.

The *New York Times* reviewer reports his theory that a large crowd came to see *That Lass* "attracted thither, not simply by the announcement that a new play was to be produced, but chiefly by the fact that one of the most popular novels of the day was to be witnessed in dramatized form."[24] Frances's love story had thousands of readers. Many Americans wanted to forget the psychological and physical brutality of the war and so sought escape in romantic fiction. Frances's name was known in public circles because of her numerous and popular magazine stories. Producing a play based on a popular novel by a known author made good business sense, especially because a version of the novel had already succeeded on stage in London. In the next four years, Frances had three other novels published and her second play for adults, *Esmeralda*, opened on Broadway at the Madison Square Theatre on the first of October 1881.

Frances collaborated on her second script with William Gillette. Daniel Frohman produced *Esmeralda* at the Madison Square Theatre, which was managed by Steel MacKaye. In 1877, MacKaye took what had been the Fifth Avenue Theatre and redesigned the interior, adding innovations such as a crude form of air conditioning in which air was blown over huge blocks of ice before it entered the house. MacKaye addressed the problem of delays caused by set changes by adding space for a separate scene to be lowered into position, shortening "stage waits"

IN ONE OF THE BOXES.

8.1 Illustrator Reginald Birch portrayed a theatrical setting in Giovanni and the Other: Children Who Have Made Stories *(New York: Charles Scribner's Sons, 1893), 51.*

that sometimes took up to two minutes. With the installation of gas lighting, MacKaye embraced and experimented with new concepts in the use of lights to enhance the text or mood of a play.[25] Frances's second Broadway production was staged at a theatre with a prestigious reputation. The reviewer of *Esmeralda* frames his remarks with his opinion that Frances "is one of our essentially dramatic writers. She is not known, it is true, as a play-maker; her dramas are her novels. . . . But the play as a whole—with its subdued realism, bright characterization, agreeable features of humor, and thorough genuineness in its sentiment—is inherently a good work, and a very charming and interesting one. Its chief and somewhat amusing weakness is . . . an excess of optimism."[26] Less than enthusiastic reviews did not prevent the show from running for 350 nights and earning a fair-sized profit. Two years later the show opened in London as *Young Folks' Way*. Henry James reviewed the London production and suggested the play would be better as a moral tale for the young. He actually predicted the next phase of Frances's focus as a writer.

In her thirties, for the next few years Frances did not publish anything, but she was working on a story featuring her own son Vivian. In November of 1885, *Little Lord Fauntleroy* began as a serial in *St. Nicholas*, a magazine aimed toward a child audience. Editor Mary Mapes Dodge, who had started the publication, encouraged Frances to write wholesome and entertaining stories to offset the didactic element so commonly found in literature for the young.[27] *Little Lord Fauntleroy* was published as a book in 1886; over a million copies sold in English and it was translated into more than a dozen languages. Thwaite explains, "Frances had produced a book which fit perfectly the taste of the time."[28]

Around the turn of the century two distinct literary genres were developing for children: 1) the domestic novel focused on moral character development and written primarily by women and 2) adventure novels focused on action-filled plots rather than character development; these were written mostly by men. Both genres shared the didactic tradition often associated with children's fiction. Characters in novels and stories for children reflected characteristics of the emerging middle class: high moral standards, perseverance, practicality, and independence.[29] Frances's stories fit right into the popular domestic fiction of the times, and she was writing in a period when books for children became profitable. Improvements in book printing and binding, improved transportation, and cheaper household lighting made books more available and affordable to a larger population. Literacy rates were improving as more children attended school and public libraries were expanding. Both in Britain and America, the growing middle class valued family time, which included reading aloud to children.[30] *Little Lord Fauntleroy* was a product the public wanted. Vedder cites *Little Lord Fauntleroy* as "the most successful book for children ever written by a American. It extended the author's fame more than another sort of book could have spread it, for in capturing the hearts of the little ones she won those of fathers and mothers the whole country over; and thousands who would never have heard of the author of *That Lass o' Lowrie's* feel themselves on terms of familiar acquaintance with the author of *Little Lord Fauntleroy*."[31] Vedder stated that *Little Lord* is best considered more an "article of commerce than a work of art," which he justifies because "the hero of the tale is too faultily faultless. . . . [Fauntleroy] is always irreproachably dressed, exquisitely polite, and his conduct is without a flaw . . . far too much of a mama's darling; he just comes short of being a prig."[32] The less-than-masculine little boy did not hinder the story's popularity, which began with installments in *St. Nicolas* and increased with the publication of the complete story in novel form. The popularity of the serialized story and then the novel might explain how another of Frances's stories became a hit on the stage.

In 1887, while living in Florence, Italy, with her sons, Frances received a letter from British citizen E. V. Seebohm informing her that he had dramatized *Little Lord Fauntleroy*. When Frances vehemently objected, he offered her half the profits if she would collaborate with him. She refused. She immediately began writing her own script and instigated a lawsuit filed with the British High Court of Justice. In a letter to a friend, Frances explained, "A thief has quietly dramatized Fauntleroy and I am engaged in fierce battle with him. . . . The brigand, whose name is Seebohm, *knew* he was doing a miserable, dishonest thing, and knew I thought myself protected by the 'All rights reserved' on the title page. . . . But I will not sanction for any profits if my dear little boy is spoiled."[33] Seebohm's play opened at the Prince of Wales Theatre in London on February 23, 1888. On May 10, 1888, Frances won a favorable verdict in her court case, which clarified that no play could be licensed unless a copy was filed with the Lord Chamberlain, protecting authors' rights to dramatize their own novels. Four days after the victory in court, Frances's stage version of her novel which she titled *The Real Little Lord Fauntleroy* opened at Terry's Theatre in London; Seebohm's version was closed.

A review of *Fauntleroy* written by William Archer in the London *World*, May 23, 1888, was found in the scrapbook of the child actress who played Cedric. The reviewer compares Frances's version to Seebohm's: "The pirate plot-grabbers have fled confounded before the little champion. Novelists need no longer fear to see their brain-children kidnapped, distorted, and sent forth to pick up pence for the kidnapper in the theatrical highways and byways. This great reform they owe to Little Lord Fauntleroy, 'a hero in a happy hour conceived.' The new Fauntleroy at Terry's Theatre is altogether superior to the pseudo-Fauntleroy at The Prince of Wales's."[34] Frances's play was hit, and broke a record by "going beyond its fiftieth "morning" performance, as the British say. After a run in London, the show toured the provinces for nearly two years.[35]

The woman with the courage, money, and time to fight and win an international copyright battle was honored in July 1888 by the Society of British Authors. A banquet was given in Frances's honor, where she was presented with a diamond ring and matching bracelet inscribed "To Frances Hodgson Burnett, with the gratitude of British Authors."[36] Arthur Pinero and Oscar Wilde along with eighty-two other British authors contributed to the gift for Frances.[37]

In America, R. M. Field of the Boston Museum made arrangements to produce the Fauntleroy play as a matinee with his Boston company of actors. The play opened on September 10, 1888. When it was discovered that the play appealed to adults as well, the show was given the usual evening hours and matinees. Oliver Wendell Holmes attended the play in Boston and later wrote to Frances: "The tears that will not flow for real grief will sometimes come unbidden at the call of the writer of fiction who knows the human heart, and has access to its hidden fountains. It is a long time since I have been to the theatre. . . . I have had much to sadden me, and overshadow my daily life of late years, and this rush of natural emotions with all its tears and heart beats was like an angel's visit."[38] The week the play opened in Boston, news of the play's success is the reason given for E. V. Seebohm's suicide in London. A paper reported his suicide with the reminder that

"Mr. Seebohm dramatized *Little Lord Fauntleroy* and was stopped by an injunction."[39]

T. H. French of Samuel French and Company was one of the producers who arranged for the production of the Fauntleroy play in New York at the Broadway Theatre at 41st Street, a new theatre that had opened in March 1888. When built, the theatre was considered a folly because it was so far uptown, but the location did not stop crowds from coming to see Frances's third Broadway production.[40] The review in the *New York Times* predicted "*Little Lord Fauntleroy* will run for many weeks at the Broadway Theatre and it may last all Winter. Every mother will like the pretty play, the children will be taken to see it, and few others will object to it. No one but a crusty old bachelor or a shallow selfish young one will withhold his praise from the stage version of Mrs. Burnett's charming story."[41]

Frances's successful Broadway play strengthened a fashion fad hated by many young boys. "Reluctant small boys were forced by their mothers into black velvet suits with lace collars and other outfits based on Cedric's clothes."[42] Other merchandise also became popular: Fauntleroy playing cards, writing paper, toys, chocolates, and even a perfume. The New York production reached its one hundredth performance with no decrease in audiences. After twenty-three weeks the play closed, reports Vivian, because "it carried into the hot season."[43] The show moved to Chicago where it played for six weeks and then continued on a national tour.

Right after writing *Little Lord Fauntleroy* Frances wrote the story that was to be her next Broadway production for children. It first appeared in 1887 as a serial in *St. Nicholas* magazine entitled *Sara Crewe, or, What Happened at Miss Minchin's*. "The story sends multiple messages to child readers: practice self-control, use imagination to triumph over adversity, work hard, be kind to others, take care of yourself."[44] In 1902 Frances rewrote the story into a play, adding characters and dialogue, condensing scenes to three—one for each of the acts—and changing the ending. In her original story, after regaining her fortune, Sara returns to a bakery to make arrangements for the orphan Anne. The stage version titled *The Little Princess* eliminated the final visit to the bun shop, although the scene was restored in the novel published in 1904 after the play's success on Broadway. The novel expanded the story to nineteen chapters, more than three times the original length.[45] The final scene when Sara visits the bun shop is changed again. Sara is not the rescuer of the orphan Anne, but an equal. Both understand the importance of helping others less fortunate.

The stage version opened in London in December 1902 with the title *A Little Unfairy Princess*. Frances changed the title to *The Little Princess* when the play opened in New York in January 1903. It was staged at the Criterion Theatre, a Broadway house built in 1895 between Forty-Forth and Forty-Fifth Streets as part of the emerging theatrical district at Long Acre [Times] Square. Broadway theatres and Frances's reputation as a playwright continued to expand. The *New York Times* review heaped praise upon the show:

> "Oh, but wasn't it the verily loveliest play! and oh, wasn't that Sara Crewe just the sweetest Princess! and oh, wasn't that Miss Minchin just the meanest old thing, and oh—" If the superlatives of the children may be relied upon—and there seems to be no real reason for dissenting from their opinion in this instance—Mrs. Frances Hodgson Burnett has written in "The Little Princess" a play not unlikely to duplicate the success of "Fauntleroy." . . . The "Little Princess" is a gem. . . . Little Sara's troubles go straight home to the heart of every man and woman in whom the springs of emotion are not absolutely and hopelessly dried up. Not that "The Little Princess" is a sad play. Mrs. Burnett knows her child life too well to heap on the misery, and about the time everybody is wondering why such a nice little girl should have so much trouble, along comes the good fairy and transforms her miserable attic into a veritable palace. . . . Mrs. Burnett knows child life, and her pictures suggest an intimate knowledge of the juvenile temperament. The dialogue, too, is capital. . . . It is hoped that "The Little Princess" will find permanent lodging in New York among the plays to be seen "at night," for jaded playgoers will find here a pure spring where they may refresh themselves with clean and wholesome entertainment.[46]

Several years later the "clean and wholesome entertainment" was perfect material for the Educational Alliance of New York, a settlement house dedicated to the acculturation of immigrants living on the East Side. Unlike other settlement houses that imported theatrical entertainments, the Educational Alliance of New York created speech and action classes taught by Miss A. Minnie Herts enabling neighborhood children to become successful actors in the amateur theatre productions. Described in a 1907 *Theatre Magazine* article, "The [NY Educational Alliance's] Children's Theatre has become a moral and social force second to none on the East Side of New York."[47] The Alliance staged plays for youth every Sunday afternoon between October and May. Scripts had to be suitable for child audiences; their themes were required to underscore "an ideal which is necessary to impress upon the neighborhood."[48] Following a performance of a Children's Theatre production of *The Tempest*, a little girl remarked, "I always remember *The Tempest* with great pleasure because all the people in the neighborhood know about it—that is, the educated ones do, and those that isn't educated, I tell them about it."[49] The Educational Alliance recognized "the missing link, as it were, between parents and the children. It meant that the ideas which were impressed upon the children through the plays could be transmitted to the parent, and that these ideals might permeate the whole family life."[50]

To reach a young audience (ages eight to fifteen), the Educational Alliance specifically selected *The Little Princess*, which ran for two seasons. "The children never seemed to tire of this story. . . . It spelled hope for them, and meant that the tenement house apartment in which each of them lived could after all be made to seem like a palace, just as the garret had been for the little princess."[51]

Helping others less fortunate was the theme of Frances's third play for children produced on Broadway in 1913, a special year for children's theatre. "There was a year in New York—1913, to be exact—when it seemed as though our parents were going to the theater to see nothing but children's plays."[52] The season included *Snow White* at the Little Theater, *Hansel and Gretel* at the opera, *Puss in Boots* in vaudeville, and Frances's *Racketty-Packetty House*, (see figures 8.2 and 8.3), chosen to open The Children's Theatre, built on the roof of the Century Theatre, formerly the New Theatre. It was cited as "the first playhouse in the world devoted exclusively to children."[53] The seats were lower than those in a regular playhouse and the proscenium arch was decorated with sculptures of characters and animals from fairy tales. Going to the theatre was described in the *Theatre Magazine*:

> You go up and up and up in an elevator until you arrive high in the sky somewhere in a room that looks as though it were made of gray clouds. At one end is a big curtain festooned with garlands and garlands of roses, and music that seems to come from all over everywhere, fills the air. You have just decided that this must be heaven, when Little Red Riding Hood comes up and asks you to show her your ticket—and then, of course, you know that it is fairyland. Sure

"The Little Girl Princess picked up Meg and Peg and Kilmanskeg and Gustibus and Peter Piper as if they had been really a Queen's Dolls."

8.2 Harrison Cady's illustration shows the dolls of St. Nicholas XXIV, no. 3 (January 1907): 201.

8.3 Child actors portrayed the dolls in the play version of Racketty-Packetty House. *Photographer not credited; photo is from Clara Platt Meadowcroft's "At the Children's Matinée" in* St. Nicholas *XLI, no. 4 (February 1914): 353.*

enough, there's Little Bo Peep and Miss Muffett (you're sort of glad she hasn't brought the spider) and Cinderella and the Queen of Hearts and, yes, that must be Jill, because she is carrying water.[54]

The Children's Theatre at the Century had been financed by William K. Vanderbilt and George Tyler as a gift to the children of New York, but little thought had been given to the "policies and problems involved" of maintaining a program of theatre dedicated to children.[55] The Children's Theatre closed at the end of the year.

Frances Hodgson Burnett's gifts to children, the stories and plays she wrote based on her bitter memories of being poor, continue to have a "delicate invisible hand" that shapes the content and style of scripts focused on young people today. Her imagination and storytelling skills helped establish theatre for youth as a genre in America. Mrs. Frances Hodgson Burnett, the woman who believed herself to be part fairy, deserves to be highly visible in the chronicles of children's theatre.

NOTES

1. Montrose J. Moses, *Another Treasury of Plays for Children* (Boston: Little and Brown, 1927), 183.
2. "The Children's Theatre," *Architectural Record* (January–June 1914): 271.
3. Gretchen Holbrook Gerzina, *Frances Hodgson Burnett: The Unexpected Life of the Author of* The Secret Garden (New Brunswick, NJ: Rutgers University Press, 2004), 305.
4. Frances Hodgson Burnett, *The One I Knew the Best of All* (New York: Scribner's, 1915), xi.
5. Henry C. Vedder, *American Writers of To-Day* (Freeport, NY: Books for Libraries, 1894), 159–60.
6. Vivian Burnett, *The Romantick Lady (Frances Hodgson Burnett): The Life Story of an Imagination* (New York: Charles Scribner's Sons, 1927), v.
7. V. Burnett, *The Romantick Lady*, vi.
8. Ann Thwaite, *Waiting for the Party: The Life of Frances Hodgson Burnett, 1849–1924* (New York: Charles Scribner's Sons, 1974), 19.
9. Thwaite, *Waiting for the Party*, 30.
10. Thwaite, *Waiting for the Party*, 32.
11. Thwaite, *Waiting for the Party*, 34.
12. V. Burnett, *The Romantick Lady*, 46.
13. Thwaite, *Waiting for the Party*, 37.
14. Thwaite, *Waiting for the Party*, 55–56.
15. Vedder, *American Writers of To-Day*, 11–12.
16. Thwaite, *Waiting for the Party*, 61.
17. Jacob Blanck, *Bibliography of American Literature: Volume One* (New Haven, CT: Yale University Press, 1955), 418.
18. "That Lass o' Lowrie's," Rev. *New York Times*, November 26, 1878, 5: 1.
19. Mary C. Henderson, *The City and the Theatre: New York Playhouses from Bowling Green to Times Square* (Clifton, NJ: James T. White, 1973), 135.
20. Henderson, *The City and the Theatre*, 126.
21. *This Fabulous Century: 1870-1900* (New York: Time-Life, 1970), 248.
22. Henderson, *The City and the Theatre*, 131–34.
23. Henderson, *The City and the Theatre*, 136.
24. "That Lass o' Lowrie's," *New York Times*, 1.
25. Henderson, *The City and the Theatre*, 151.
26. "*Esmeralda*: Mrs. Burnett's New Play." Rev. Madison Square Theatre: New York City. *New York Times*, October 30, 1881, 9: 1.
27. Thwaite, *Waiting for the Party*, 82.
28. Thwaite, *Waiting for the Party*, 94.

29. Gail Schmunk Murray, *American Children's Literature and the Construction of Childhood* (New York: Twayne Publishers, 1998), 52.
30. Murray, *American Children's Literature and the Construction of Childhood*, 53.
31. Vedder, *American Writers of To-Day*, 164–65.
32. Vedder, *American Writers of To-Day*, 165–66.
33. V. Burnett, *The Romantick Lady*, 162–63.
34. V. Burnett, *The Romantick Lady*, 168.
35. V. Burnett, *The Romantick Lady*, 170.
36. V. Burnett, *The Romantick Lady*, 170–71.
37. Thwaite, *Waiting for the Party*, 114.
38. V. Burnett, *The Romantick Lady*, 175.
39. Thwaite, *Waiting for the Party*, 115.
40. Henderson, *The City and the Theatre*, 216.
41. "Little Lord Fauntleroy." Rev. *New York Times*, December 4, 1888, 5: 2.
42. Thwaite, *Waiting for the Party*, 118.
43. V. Burnett, *The Romantick Lady*, 180.
44. Janice Kirkland, "Frances Hodgson Burnett's Sara Crewe Through 100 Years," *Children's Literature in Education* (December 1997): 191.
45. Kirkland, "Frances Hodgson Burnett's Sara Crewe," 195.
46. "The Little Princess: An Idyll of Childlife by Mrs. Burnett at the Criterion," Rev. *New York Times*, January 15, 1903, 9: 3.
47. "A Kindergarten for Future Playgoers," *Theatre Magazine* (June 1907): 155.
48. "A Kindergarten for Future Playgoers," 156.
49. "A Kindergarten for Future Playgoers," x.
50. "A Kindergarten for Future Playgoers," x.
51. "A Kindergarten for Future Playgoers," xii.
52. Moses, *Another Treasury of Plays for Children*, 181.
53. "The Children's Theatre," 271.
54. "Racketty-Packetty House," *Theatre Magazine* (February 1913): 16.
55 Nellie McCaslin, "A History of Children's Theatre in the United States" (dissertation, New York University, 1957), 65.

· 9 ·

The Film Adaptations of Frances Hodgson Burnett's Stories

Paul H. Frobose

Editor's note: The material in this article was originally presented at a conference organized by Angelica Carpenter, "Frances Hodgson Burnett: Beyond the Secret Garden," at California State University, Fresno, in 2003.

Frances Hodgson Burnett was a prolific writer of adult fiction, novels, and short stories. She also crafted children's stories and stage adaptations of some of her fiction. Today she is principally remembered for three children's classics: *Little Lord Fauntleroy*, *The Secret Garden*, and *A Little Princess*. In the early days of motion pictures, many of her stories were adapted to the silver screen. These same three children's stories have been made and remade, but screen adaptations of her adult novels ceased before the coming of talking pictures. Whether in film, on stage, or in books, her enduring legacies are these three timeless childhood tales. While her place in the pantheon of children's authors is well established, little historical attention has been given to screen adaptations of her adult novels.

Frances Hodgson Burnett is known primarily because of the film and television adaptations of her trio of children's classics. The 1936 motion picture version of *Little Lord Fauntleroy* is still viewed and enjoyed, thanks in part to cable television and video recordings. Likewise, the Shirley Temple version of *The Little Princess* (1939) remains popular and can be purchased from the supermarket video rack. *The Secret Garden* (1949) starring Margaret O'Brien and Dean Stockwell also continues to be enjoyed by new generations of film viewers. New adaptations of *A Little Princess* and *The Secret Garden* were produced during the 1990s, and their success underscores the timelessness of these Burnett stories.

Between 1913 and 1919, during Burnett's lifetime, motion picture companies filmed eleven different Burnett stories. Eight of these silent films derived from her adult fiction and three from her well-remembered children's stories. Her children's classics, *Little Lord Fauntleroy*, *The Secret Garden*, and *A [The] Little Princess*, have been filmed most often and are still being adapted to the screen today as both feature films and made-for-television movies. While film-makers continue to find inspiration in Burnett's juvenile stories, none of her adult stories has been adapted for the screen since 1924, when remakes of *The Dawn of a Tomorrow* and *A Lady of Quality* were released. Since most silent films have not been preserved, it is difficult to generalize about what these films may have been like.[1] This essay examines the screen adaptations of Frances Hodgson Burnett's stories, and addresses why some of her works continue to be made into movies while films derived from her adult fiction died with the silent film era. Early film adaptations of Burnett's stories will be examined in the context of the dynamic changes taking place during the early years of motion picture production.

Including made-for-television productions, there have been at least twenty-three film adaptations of the works of Frances Hodgson Burnett. Twelve of these twenty-three productions were remakes. Therefore, eleven different Burnett stories have been adapted for motion pictures. *The Secret Garden* has been made into films five times. Four screen adaptations each have been produced from Burnett's *A Little Princess* and *Little Lord Fauntleroy*.[2] Excluding the three children's classics, the remaining eight film titles are screen adaptations derived from Burnett's adult fiction.[3] All eight of these films were made during the silent film era.

At the beginning of the twentieth century, moving pictures were an entertainment novelty, coexistent as side-show attractions with other inexpensive acts. By the teens, however, motion pictures had risen to prominence as a major entertainment force. In the twenty years between Thomas Edison's experimental ten-second film strips in 1895 and the rapid emergence of the silent feature film in the early teens, the American motion picture industry grew into the most dominant form of mass entertainment yet devised. Bootstrap film companies gambled whatever money they could muster on hunches. Many struck a chord with audiences, causing some companies to become multimillion-dollar corporations. So much money changed hands as the result of this dynamic growth that, by 1916, the motion picture business was the fourth largest industry in the United States. Movie studios contributed $30 million that year to the greater Los Angeles economy.[4]

Along with this phenomenal growth, the industry underwent some profound changes. As certain actors became recognizable to film audiences, the studios began promoting them more, and the actors commanded higher salaries. The result was what came to be known as the star system, and it changed the way films were made and advertised. As films became the dominant force attracting Americans' discretionary dollars, movies became longer and more skillfully crafted. Studios grew into miniature cities, and their production methods became extremely sophisticated and mechanized. The area in southern California where many studios set up operations became known generically as Hollywood, and the motion picture industry became quite literally a dream factory, manufacturing films for a vast, worldwide audience.

Frances Hodgson Burnett was a keen observer of the motion picture phenomenon. By 1911, motion picture trade journals had begun reporting on experiments with longer films. Even then Burnett recognized the importance of selling screen rights to movie producers, for they would likely "represent definite income in the future."[5] She remained cautious, however, resisting all requests to film her stories. In a landmark 1912 case dealing with adapting motion pictures from dramatic and literary sources, the Supreme Court held that film companies could not use copyrighted literary or dramatic material without first obtaining the owner's consent.[6] This precedent opened the door to the selling of screen rights. Sometime during her trip to Europe during late 1913 and early 1914, Burnett had an epiphany about the new medium, realizing the "universality of the appeal of the moving picture."[7] These factors may have contributed to her decision to sell the screen rights of some of her stories to the Kinemacolor Film Company in 1913.[8] The company initially planned to film *The Dawn of a Tomorrow* and *Esmeralda*, but fell on hard times. The only film released by Kinemacolor was a production of *Little Lord Fauntleroy*, shot in England with a cast of British stage actors. It premiered in New York in June 1914.[9]

Despite the misfortunes of the Kinemacolor Company, Burnett's timing was fortuitous. Movie audiences flocked to see the new, feature-length films. Prior to 1912, commercial films were quite primitive. Cheap to produce and usually made in less than one week, early films had simple plots and exaggerated characters. The villain might typically have a long, bushy moustache, and the damsel in distress would be highly prone to fainting. Most motion picture producers geared their films to audiences who were mainly urban and lower class. These early movies were formulaic and short. The standard film story was contained on one reel of film, and lasted no longer than ten to fourteen minutes.[10]

During the second decade of the twentieth century, however, movies gradually became longer and more fully developed with complex plot lines and deeper characterizations. Many production executives, content with the successful format of one- or two-reel films, resisted the change. But the longer format proved a huge success at the box office and movies expanded to five, six, and seven or more reels. This change coincided with and in part derived from the rise of the motion picture "star." Longer films also benefited from improved production values, and their success led producers to open their pocketbooks and apply larger budgets to produce these new "feature" films. Leading this movement in the United States was a novice film producer named Adolph Zukor. Toward the end of 1914, Frances Hodgson Burnett sold him the screen rights to *The Dawn of a Tomorrow*.

Fifteen-year-old Adolph Zukor had immigrated to the United States in 1888, arriving in New York City with $40. The Hungarian-born Zukor soon got a job as a furrier's errand boy. By age eighteen, he had become a journeyman furrier. He went to Chicago and built up a successful business in the fur trade. Twelve years later he invested his savings in a modest chain of movie theaters.[11] Zukor immersed himself in learning all he could about his new avocation, the motion picture business. His chain proved successful, but he decided that he wanted to produce moving pictures. Zukor had an idea for a new kind of film, one that would broaden the appeal of motion pictures. He saw a tremendous future in multiple-reel, or feature-length films.[12] He envisioned feature films expanding the market to include the middle classes, and consequently, expanding the producer's profits. Zukor dreamed of producing films of stage actors recreating their roles in famous Broadway plays. If these films succeeded, Zukor believed that the prejudice against moving pictures as "low class entertainment" would begin to disappear.

On April 12, 1912, Zukor incorporated his new film producing company as the Famous Players in Famous Plays Company.[13] He bought the rights to exhibit a four-reel French film, *Queen Elizabeth*, starring the internationally famous stage actress Sarah Bernhardt. Zukor hired and received encouragement from former Edison director Edwin S. Porter, the man who filmed the first American narrative film, *The Great Train Robbery* (1903). He identified three things he needed to make his new company successful: stories, actors, and a "big name." Zukor needed someone who could add legitimacy to his new company, someone with connections to the theatrical world who could help him attract top stage actors. He approached Broadway impresario Daniel Frohman.

By the turn of the twentieth century, Charles and Daniel Frohman were, along with David Belasco, the leading theatrical producers in New York. In 1881, at the age of thirty, Daniel Frohman had produced Frances Hodgson Burnett's *Esmeralda* at the new Madison Square Theatre. In three decades, Daniel Frohman's name had become synonymous with high class theaters.[14] In 1912, Zukor invited Frohman to meet with him. He told Frohman of his belief that feature-length films were the future of the motion picture, and how he wanted to film stage plays using the original actors recreating their roles. Finally, Zukor explained how he needed Frohman's help "in securing the plays and the players."[15]

Although he had reservations about the ability of stage actors to adjust to the lack of dialogue in motion pictures, Frohman was impressed, particularly with Zukor's purchase of the European film *Queen Elizabeth*. He soon joined Famous Players as managing director, "much to the derision," Frohman later wrote, "of my fellow managers, especially my brother Charles." Frohman described Adolph Zukor as "a man of shrewd and far-seeing vision, [who] saw possibilities in the industry which up to that time had not been touched."[16] To inaugurate their new association, Frohman arranged for the American premiere of *Queen Elizabeth* to be screened at his Lyceum Theater in New York on July 12, 1912. As the opening night curtain went up, "Daniel Frohman Presents *Queen Elizabeth*" opened to a packed house. Zukor had been right. The feature film or "photoplay" would soon become the standard film fare.

Frohman brought instant credibility to the company. He also brought the stage actors: James O'Neill,[17] James K. Hackett, Minnie Maddern Fiske, John Barrymore, Lily Langtry, and many others.[18] Frohman became "a powerful advocate of the movies in the theatrical world."[19] While not all of the stage actors proved able to make the transition to film acting, Famous Players nonetheless began regularly producing feature films.

It is surprising that theatrical impresario Daniel Frohman agreed to join Zukor's fledgling film company. Up to this point, the theatrical world and the film industry had occupied different niches in the American entertainment scene. In the early twentieth century, entertainment preferences divided along class lines, especially in the major cities like New York. The stage, referred to as the "legitimate" theater, was the choice of the middle class. It was a dignified and respectable form of entertainment. Middle class patrons and stage actors alike looked down on the "flickers" and the audiences who attended them. Movies were the province of the urban masses, especially in ethnic enclaves and immigrant neighborhoods. Since the films were silent, a knowledge of English was not a prerequisite to following the plot. Movie producers understood their audiences and kept the stories uncomplicated. Most film producers believed that motion picture audiences were incapable of sustaining interest in a film longer than one or two reels.[20] The monopolistic Motion Picture Patents Company, a consortium headed by Thomas Edison composed of the largest film production companies, dominated motion picture production and distribution. The Patents Company arbitrarily limited most films to one reel in length. But by 1912 the Patents Company was losing its iron grip on the film industry.

Within a year there were several similar movie companies making feature films.[21] The most important of these was the Jesse L. Lasky Feature Play Company. Organized by vaudeville producer Jesse Lasky in 1913, the company also included among its founders former glove salesman Samuel Goldfish (later Goldwyn) and playwright-actor Cecil B. De Mille. Like his rival Adolph Zukor, Lasky hired New York stage actors such as John Barrymore, Laura Hope Crews, Robert Edeson, Dustin and William Farnum, Pauline Frederick, and H. B. Warner. The company began production in a converted Hollywood barn in early 1914, and quickly grew to be one of the top feature film companies. By the summer of 1916, these two successful companies merged forming the Famous Players/Lasky Corporation, with Zukor as president.

Perhaps Zukor's greatest coup was signing the number one box office film star to a contract with Famous Players. In 1914, stage-trained Mary Pickford was the most famous name in the motion picture business. She had honed her film acting skills with D. W. Griffith at Biograph. By the time she signed with Famous Players, she was the most recognizable face in films. Audiences knew her as "Little Mary" and

"America's Sweetheart." Aware that her value to film companies was increasing, Pickford met with Adolph Zukor. Both Pickford and Zukor were keen business minds. Pickford negotiated a contract with Zukor at the astounding salary of $500 a week. Within a year she was earning double that. Pickford stayed with Famous Players for five and a half years.[22]

Now Zukor had his "name," Daniel Frohman, and his stars, including top box office queen Mary Pickford, and he had screen rights to many important novels and plays. Zukor ultimately obtained the screen rights to eight Burnett stories, releasing the films as follows: *A Lady of Quality* (1914); *The Pretty Sister of José*, *The Dawn of a Tomorrow*, and *Esmeralda* (1915); *A Fair Barbarian* and *A Little Princess* (1917); and *Louisiana* and *The Secret Garden* (1919). Famous Players Film Company produced six of the eight films adapted from Burnett's adult fiction, as well as two of the first three versions of her children's classics.

The early film adaptations of Burnett's stories starred the biggest names in the motion picture industry. Besides Mary Pickford, leading actors appearing in Burnett films included Marguerite Clark, Mae Busch, Constance Talmadge, Noah Beery Sr., House Peters, Jack Pickford, and Harry Carey. Directing these productions were major talents such as James Kirkwood, Marshall Neilan, and Rollin Sturgeon, all tops in their field at the time. Legendary cinematographers James C. Van Trees and Charles Rosher, among others, filmed the movies. Famous Players/Lasky-Paramount and Universal were large operations, which meant that these early features were supported by the best technical staffs of the biggest studios with the largest budgets. Burnett made a good choice in signing with Famous Players.

To adapt novels and stories to the medium of film, motion picture companies needed specialized writers. A strong story was a critical element in the success of a silent film, where written dialogue was replaced by gesture, action, and pantomime. But novels and stories had to be adapted to the unique requirements of motion picture production. Film plots for silent movies were called scenarios, and later, after the introduction of sound, they were renamed screenplays.[23] For this crucial job, a new kind of artist emerged: the scenario writer, or scenarist. The motion picture business, which was dominated by men in the early years, expanded rapidly. As feature films came to prominence, many women rose to positions of power and importance. Nowhere was this more evident than in the writing of scenarios. Many of the important early scenarists were women: Anita Loos, Nell Shipman, Jeanie MacPhearson, Bess Meredyth, Lois Weber, June Mathis, Eve Unsell, Marion Fairfax, Lenore Coffee, Alice Eyton, and Frances Marion, to name a few. Scenario credits for Burnett films include Eve Unsell, Marion Fairfax, Marian Ainslee, Margaret Turnbull, Alice Eyton, Edith M. Kennedy, and the incomparable Frances Marion.[24] Marion, wrote scenarios for *The Dawn of a Tomorrow* (1915), *Esmeralda* (1915), and *A Little Princess* (1917), all three starring Mary Pickford. (See figure 9.1.)

By the time Famous Players Film Company began producing films from Burnett stories, feature film production had become highly sophisticated. Famous Players turned out feature after feature, and Zukor and Frohman constantly searched for new stories to bring to the screen. But as Zukor explained, "We could not produce fast enough to satisfy the market." The hiring of Mary Pickford significantly improved the fortunes of the company for, as Zukor put it, she was a "surefire money-maker."[25]

Burnett was not the only novelist who benefitted from the rapidly growing motion picture industry. Popular fiction from best-selling authors was a major source for plots in during the silent film era. One film historian has concluded that between the years 1896 and 1915 there were approximately three thousand film titles derived from books and plays.[26] Modern estimates of the literary sources of screenplays run as high as 50 percent.[27] Even in the early days of movie making, some film producers paid huge sums for the exclusive right to adapt a successful novel for the silver screen.[28] Frances Hodgson Burnett joined the ranks of other popular writers such as Gertrude Atherton, Rex Beach, James Oliver Curwood, Richard Harding Davis, Peter B. Kyne, and Jack London, who sold the screen rights to their stories. Burnett sold the screen rights to eleven different novels and stories to motion picture companies: eight to Famous Players, two to Universal, and one to Lewis Selznick's Select Pictures. Burnett's eleven are more than any other female author of the time except for Mary Roberts Rinehart. For the silent feature film period, Burnett's total tops that of Peter B. Kyne, Mark Twain, Charles Dickens, and Robert Louis Stevenson, and ties her with Jack London.[29]

After Burnett sold the screen rights to *A Lady of Quality* to Famous Players in 1913, contracts for scenarios from other Burnett works fol-

9.1 Mary Pickford as Sara Crewe in the 1917 film A Little Princess. *Courtesy of the Academy of Motion Picture Arts and Sciences.*

lowed. Famous Players would have been an easy choice for Burnett. She had known Daniel Frohman for more than thirty years, and if she were going to trust the film adaptations of her stories to anyone, it surely would be Frohman. Burnett most likely would have been aware of how important the signing of Mary Pickford was to Famous Players.

For its second Burnett screen adaptation, Famous Players tapped Mary Pickford's younger brother Jack to star in *The Pretty Sister of José*. The supporting cast included Marguerite Clark[30] as Pepita, Edythe Chapman as the mother, and future film director Rupert Julian as the famous bullfighter Sebastiano. This film debuted on May 31, 1915.

One week later, Famous Players released *The Dawn of a Tomorrow*. Mary Pickford was the obvious choice for the role of Glad. With a strong scenario from Eve Unsell, and skillful direction from James Kirkwood, one of Mary's favorites, the film was one of the biggest hits of the year.[31] Pickford had been earning the unheard-of salary of $2,000 a week since November of 1914.[32] In September 1915, Famous Players released *Esmeralda*.[33] Mary Pickford was again cast in the leading role, and her director once more was James Kirkwood.[34]

Universal Pictures produced the next motion picture adaptation of a Francs Hodgson Burnett story. Like Famous Players, Universal had grown rapidly in the first few years of feature filmmaking. A Universal subsidiary, Bluebird Photoplays, released *Secret Love* in January 1916. The film was adapted from *That Lass o' Lowrie's*. Under director Robert Leonard's guidance, Burnett's social drama of the plight of coal miners was turned into a straightforward melodrama starring the reliable Harry Carey as Fergus Derrick, Helen Ware as Joan Lowrie, and other veterans of the Universal stock company.

The newly formed Famous Players/Lasky Company released *A Fair Barbarian* in December 1917, although Lasky had completed the production prior to the merger. Of note in this production was the cinematography of James C. Van Trees and the performance of Mae Busch, a tremendous actress adept at comedy or drama whose credits included *The Birth of a Nation*. Mary Pickford produced, starred in, and released *A Little Princess* in late 1917. For this film, Mary retained Marshall Neilan, one of the silent era's best directors, and her friend Frances Marion as the scenario writer.[35] She also picked some outstanding character actors such as Norman Kerry, Theodore Roberts, and Katherine Griffith in the major roles. Pickford gave the part of Minchin's slave girl to an unknown actress by the name of Zasu Pitts, a future star whose comedic gifts sustained her through nearly fifty years in movies and television.[36]

Select Pictures Corporation, an independent studio operated by Louis J. Selznick, released *The Shuttle* in early 1918. The star was Constance Talmadge, who became one of the silent screen's best comedic actresses in the 1920s. The film was directed by Rollin Sturgeon and photographed by James C. Van Trees. Margaret Turnbull and Harvey Thew wrote the scenario. Famous Players/Lasky brought out *The Secret Garden* and *Louisiana* in 1919. *The Secret Garden* starred eighteen-year-old vaudeville veteran Lila Lee and stage-trained Spottiswoode Aitken. The scenarist for this production was Marion Fairfax. *Louisiana*, which opened on July 20, 1919, had a scenario by Alice Eyton and starred Vivian Martin, Robert Ellis, and Noah Beery Sr.

The next Frances Hodgson Burnett story to be adapted for the silent screen is one of the all-time greats of the silent era. *Little Lord Fauntleroy* was directed by Alfred E. Green and Jack Pickford, and released in November 1921. By this time Mary Pickford had cofounded United Artists and was exercising more creative control than ever. Mary produced and starred in this well-received version of Burnett's story in which she played a dual role as the young Cedric and as his mother, "Dearest." The film contains some of the most outstanding cinematography of the silent era, including one double exposed scene in which Cedric kisses Dearest. Even modern filmmakers marvel at the technical sophistication of Charles Rosher's camera work. Loved by critics and the public as well, this was one of the most popular films of 1921.[37]

The year 1924 saw two Burnett adaptations released, both remakes of earlier films. *The Dawn of a Tomorrow* was a Zukor/Lasky production. Jacqueline Logan starred as Glad. Logan was no Mary Pickford, and only David Torrence's capable acting kept this film from being a total clunker, according to a *New York Times* review.[38] Universal also tried to capitalize on past success by releasing *A Lady of Quality*. With a scenario by Marion Fairfax, Arthur Ripley, and Marian Ainslee, this version was well received. A solid cast, including popular leading men Earle Foxe and Milton Sills, helped elevate this production above a mere costume drama.

Since the advent of sound in motion pictures, several notable productions of Burnett stories have appeared on the screen. In 1936 David

O. Selznick inaugurated his new production company by giving the full Hollywood treatment to *Little Lord Fauntleroy*. Starring Freddie Bartholomew, C. Aubrey Smith, Dolores Costello Barrymore, and Mickey Rooney, the film created an atmosphere described by critic Frank S. Nugent as "warm, sentimental and gently humorous."[39] MGM's 1949 release of *The Secret Garden* has been seen by generations of Burnett fans and remains a classic. With Margaret O'Brien, Herbert Marshall, and Dean Stockwell leading the cast, this production reflects the golden age of motion picture production. BBC Television's 1984 remake of *The Secret Garden* includes location photography that adds to the mood and atmosphere of this well-acted production. Recently, however, a new version has captivated film audiences. In 1993, Francis Ford Coppola's American Zeotrope Studios produced a beautifully filmed version of *The Secret Garden*. Directed by Agnieszka Holland and with a screenplay by Caroline Thompson, this lavish production retains the essential magic of the Burnett story. The film is notable for its fine performances from Kate Maberly as Mary Lennox, Maggie Smith as Mrs. Medlock, and Hayden Prowse, whose restrained and subtle Colin helps this film set a new standard for this Burnett classic. Alfonso Cuarón's beautifully filmed *A Little Princess* (1995) is a stunning achievement. Unlike the 1939 version, which was a vehicle for box-office champ Shirley Temple, Cuarón's film evokes the magic and mysticism of the original story while realistically portraying the harshness of Miss Minchin's treatment of Sara Crewe.

It was partly good fortune and partly good business sense that led Burnett to sign with Famous Players. Her business acumen is attested to by the number of contracts for screen rights she signed between 1913 and 1924. Ironically, because of the huge impact of the motion picture industry, even in its infancy, it is probable that more people knew of Burnett from the movies than from her books. That she lived to see so many of her stories made into motion pictures must have been a satisfying experience for the author. That her juvenile stories are still being adapted for the modern screen is a posthumous tribute to their timelessness. Only a handful of stories have continued to be remade for successive generations of film audiences. Mark Twain's *Huckleberry Finn* and *Tom Sawyer* have both been remade several times. Louisa May Alcott's *Little Women*, James Fenimore Cooper's *Last of the Mohicans*, Charles Dicken's *A Christmas Carol*, and Jack London's *White*

Fang stand out as examples of timeless stories that continue to serve as material for new generations of filmmakers. Frances Hodgson Burnett's three children's classics have all been remade at least once in the past twenty years. Eighty years after her death, her trio of classic children's stories still inspires motion picture producers. Thanks to the enduring nature of her juvenile classics, generations to come will continue to derive pleasure from television and film adaptations of classic Burnett stories.

NOTES

1. Many silent films were victims of an indifferent attitude on the part of early studios; little effort was given to the preservation of silent films.
2. It has recently come to my attention that the BBC has produced a television drama based on *Little Lord Fauntleroy* called *Guilty Hearts*. I have not examined whether any foreign language motion pictures have used Burnett stories.
3. The definitive source for motion picture production information is *The American Film Institute Catalogue of Motion Pictures Produced in the United States* edited by Patricia King Hanson. (Berkeley: University of California Press, 1988), xi.
4. *Moving Picture World* 29, no. 8 (August 19, 1916): 1230.
5. Ann Thwaite, *Waiting for the Party: The Life of Frances Hodgson Burnett, 1849–1924* (London: Secker & Warburg, 1974), 231.
6. The loser of the case was the Kalem Company, Inc., which produced motion pictures from 1907 to 1916. The case revolved around Kalem's production of *Ben Hur* in 1907, and the company was sued by the publisher, the estate of author Lew Wallace, and the producers of the stage version of the story.
7. *Vanity Fair*, June 1914 (seen in Thwaite, *Waiting for the Party*, 232).
8. Kinemacolor was the earliest commercially successful motion picture color process. It was developed in England by Edward R. Turner, with financial support from F. Marshall Lee, and later Charles Urban. Turner died and his research was continued by G. Albert Smith. The first public demonstration of their two-color process was on May 1, 1908. In 1909 Urban and Smith founded the Kinemacolor Film Company, and the American branch was founded in 1910. Despite considerable financial backing, the company had difficulty turning a profit. For a time it had studios in London, New York, and California, but the Hollywood studio folded in June 1913. World War I effectively ended the European activities of the company, and the company's color process lost its

patent protection on a legal technicality. Terry Ramsaye, *A Million and One Nights: A History of the Motion Picture Through 1925* (New York: Touchstone Books, 1986), 562–71.

9. *New York Times*, June 23, 1914, 11. Several members of the cast appeared in other British films. Gerald Royston, who played Errol, appeared in only four more films, the last in 1915. Scott Palmer, *British Film Actor Credits, 1895–1987* (Jefferson, NC, and London: McFarland & Company, 1988), 903.

10. One reel of film was approximately one thousand feet long. Due to the lack of uniformity in sprocket holes, and the variable speed of projectors, there was no precise length of time to view "one reel." Eileen Bowser, *The Transformation of Cinema, 1907–1915*. Vol. 2 of the *History of the American Cinema*, ed. Charles Harpole (Berkeley: University of California Press, 1994), 191.

11. Will Irwin, *The House That Shadows Built* (New York: Doubleday, Doran, & Company, Inc., 1928); Adolph Zukor and Dale Kramer, *The Public Is Never Wrong: My Fifty Years in the Motion Picture Industry* (New York: G. P. Putnam's Sons, 1953).

12. In June 1911, the motion picture trade journal *Moving Picture World* prophesied that the multiple reel film "is bound to come and in two or three years will be the rule rather than the exception."

13. *Motion Picture News* 11, no. 15 (April 17, 1915): 43.

14. Among his many other stage productions were Burnett's *The First Gentleman of Europe* in 1897 and *The Pretty Sister of José* in 1903. Charles had produced *A Little Princess* at the Criterion Theater in 1903.

15. Zukor and Kramer, *The Public Is Never Wrong*, 66.

16. Daniel Frohman, *Daniel Frohman Presents: An Autobiography* (New York: Lee Furman, Inc., 1937), 275.

17. James O'Neill was the father of American playwright Eugene O'Neill.

18. Other prominent stage actors who worked for the Famous Players Company included Hazel Dawn, William Farnum, Cecelia Loftus, Carlyle Blackwell, H. B. Warner, Marguerite Clark, Tyrone Power, John Emerson, Edward Abeles, Marie Doro, William H. Crane, Cyril Scott, and Malcolm Williams.

19. Zukor and Kramer, *The Public Is Never Wrong*, 67.

20. Robert Sklar's *Movie-Made America: A Social History of American Movies* contains a good discussion of the early motion picture industry. For a more detailed look at early film production, the Motion Picture Patents Company, and the rise of the feature film, see Eileen Bowser's *The Transformation of the Cinema, 1907–1915*.

21. By 1915, more than sixty film studios were in operation in the Los Angeles area. *Moving Picture World* 26, no. 8 (November 13, 1915): 1288.

22. Mary Pickford, *Sunshine and Shadow: The Autobiography of Mary Pickford* (New York: Random House, Inc.), 97–98.

23. Louis Jacobs, *The Rise of American Film: A Critical History* (New York: Harcourt, Brace and Company, 1939), 130–32.

24. Frances Marion's career is detailed in Cari Beauchamp's *Without Lying Down: Frances Marion and the Powerful Women of Early Hollywood* (New York: A Lisa Drew Book/Scribner, 1997). Marion's delightful autobiography *Off with Their Heads!: A Serio-Comic Tale of Hollywood* (New York: Macmillan & Co., 1972) gives further insight into her immense talent.

25. Zukor and Kramer, *The Public Is Never Wrong*, 121.

26. Denis Gifford, *Books and Plays in Films, 1896–1915: Literary, Theatrical, and Artistic Sources of the First Twenty Years of Motion Pictures* (London: Mansell Publishing Limited, 1991)

27. Robert B. Ray, "The Field of 'Literature and Film,'" in *Film Adaptation*, ed. James Naremore, 42 (New Brunswick, NJ: Rutgers University Press: 2000).

28. Among the many sources that have been used for motion picture plots are biographies, poems, operas, songs, science fiction, mythologies, historical events, cartoons, and comic strips.

29. Only a few authors have more total screen adaptations to their credit. London, Curwood, Beach, Richard Harding Davis, Bret Harte, Zane Grey, and O. Henry each had eleven or more screen adaptations from their works.

30. Marguerite Clark was second in audience popularity only to Mary Pickford among Famous Players' actors.

31. This film proved so popular that Paramount rereleased it in January 1919.

32. Mary Pickford's income skyrocketed during the teens. At Biograph Studios in 1912 she was earning $175 a week. When she moved to Famous Players in 1913, her weekly salary jumped to $500. One year later it doubled to $1,000 a week, and a few months later it doubled again to $2,000. In 1915, she was earning $4,000 per week.. In 1916 Famous Player's founder Adolph Zukor re-signed Mary at the staggering sum of $10,000 a week plus one-half the profits of her films with a $300,000 signing bonus, making her the highest paid actor in the movies. She also got her own production company, Mary Pickford Film Corporation; a new distribution company (Artcraft) set up only to distribute Mary's films; and 50 percent of the profits of all her films. Robert Windeler, *Sweetheart: The Story of Mary Pickford* (New York: Preagar Publishers, 1974), 71–95.

33. *Esmeralda* captivated the *New York Dramatic Mirror* critic Vachel Lindsay, who ranked it one of Pickford's three best films to date. *New York Dramatic Mirror* 74, no. 1917 (September 15, 1915): 32–33.

34. Kirkwood directed Mary Pickford in some of her best-loved films of the teens, including *Mistress Nell*, *Cinderella*, *Little Pal*, and *Rags*.

35. Howard Hawkes was an uncredited assistant director of the film, filling in when Marshall Neilan's drinking interfered with his work.

36. Mary Pickford, producer as well as star of the 1917 version of *A Little Princess*, chose Zasu Pitts to appear in the first screen version of Burnett's story. *A Little Princess* was directed by Marshall Neilan and had a Frances Marion scenario. Some scenes were directed by a newcomer Howard Hawks (uncredited).

37. A "public domain" version of this film is available for purchase on VHS.

38. *New York Times*, March 26, 1924, 19.

39. Frank S. Nugent, review of *Little Lord Fauntleroy*, *New York Times*, April 3, 1936, 27.

• *10* •

Snugness:
The Robin in Its Nest

Jerry Griswold

Editor's note: The material in this article was originally presented at a conference organized by Angelica Carpenter, "Frances Hodgson Burnett: Beyond the Secret Garden," at California State University, Fresno, in 2003.

I am engaged in a book-length study of pleasures particular to childhood. To explain what I mean, I often point, as an example, to the joy children get from playing under tables or behind couches or in tents made of chairs and blankets. I know few adults who enjoy playing under tables.

That particular example has led me to explore, among others, the topic or poetics of snugness in children's literature. I should also add that my studies began shortly after September 11, 2001, when I was haunted by stories my daughter, a schoolteacher, told about her first graders' drawings after 9/11; what those pictures seem to indicate was a deep concern with vulnerability. So, in an essay ("Reading Differently after September 11") for an Irish journal, I explored "vulnerability" as an opposite of snugness or coziness.[1]

While I mean to examine here a very small passage in *The Secret Garden* in relation to all this, and by way of preamble, let me give you a rather quick summary of some of the various ways this issue of snugness appears in children's literature.

One of the real great examples of snugness occurs in *The Wind in the Willows* when Mole, after having been lost and snowbound in the Wild

Woods, finally finds his way to Badger's cozy, underground abode. The vision Kenneth Grahame gives us of Badger's welcoming kitchen, the merry fire that greets the shivering Mole, that simple but welcoming place with its baskets of eggs and smiling plates—all these suggest the very picture of the snug abode and how snugness is a kind of friendly patina laid down on top of brute objects, how snugness is a spiritualization of feelings added to a place.

Felicitous space is often enclosed and protected; sounding very much like Robinson Crusoe talking about his stockade, Badger says of his underground home, "Nothing can happen to you, and nothing can get at you. You're entirely your own master."[2] You might also think, in this regard, of the familiar childhood drawing of the "happy house": a squat home very much rooted in the world, with eye-like windows, a welcoming door, and a chimney with smoke pouring out to indicate it is inhabited; and, of course, the sun happily shining on all of this.

There are, of course, certain times of year and day that are more conducive to evocations of snugness. Winter, especially after snow has fallen, and Christmastime are special in this regard; consider, for example, the tableau of the family in Louisa May Alcott's *Little Women*, all gathered together around the fire when father returns at Christmas; or Clement Moore's poem "The Night Before Christmas" when "The children were nestled all snug in their beds, / While visions of sugarplums danced in their heads."[3] And as for time of day, the moment for nesting is when sleep comes; here the great tableau may be in Johanna Spyri's *Heidi* when grandfather, both when Heidi first arrives and when she returns from Frankfurt, steals up the ladder to look at the slumbering child in the nest she has made for herself from hay in the attic. To be brief: a snug place is a place where one can sleep peacefully.

Of course, as I have suggested, the opposite of snugness is vulnerability: they are a pair. So, Peter Rabbit's return to his mother at the base of the fir tree is all the more welcome because of the precariousness of his time with Mr. McGregor; and Mole especially prizes Badger's underground retreat, or his own Dulce Domum, after his anxiety in the Wild Woods. But perhaps the sense of vulnerability in the immensity of space is most acute in *Little House on the Prairie* where Laura Ingalls feels ill at ease: "All around them there was nothing but grassy prairie spreading to the edge of the sky," she writes. "The land and sky seemed too large, and Laura felt small." Laura feels that way at least until the house is built.[4]

All this by way of preamble, then. We turn now to the question of how anxiety might be allayed. How can confidence and security, well-being and trust, be created and enclosed?

In this regard, I think we can view snugness as a retreat, but as an active retreat—a withdrawal associated with a sense of renewal rather than with torpor or defeat. In the safe anchorage of the snug place, calmness and confidence are restored and well-being enclosed. And from this safe center—like the swallow that builds its nest, as it were, from the inside out, from mud and its own saliva—these feelings of well-being can expand out into the universe. You might think, in this regard, of Erik Erikson's notion of Basic (or existential) Trust.

In the Sufi tradition, as passed along by Idries Shah, there is a story of a student who wishes for enlightenment and approaches a teacher who is resting in a courtyard. When the student asks to be instructed, the teacher tells this seeker that he will not give him any instructions until that time when the student can enter a courtyard and not cause the birds to fly away, as they just did. For twenty years, the story goes, the student did whatever was necessary to change so that when he entered a courtyard the birds didn't fly away. At the end of the twenty years, Shah notes, the student no longer had any need for a teacher.

This presents an interesting question. What would a person need to change or do so that when one enters a place, the birds don't fly away? Frances Hodgson Burnett's *The Secret Garden* tells such a story, about such a transformation, and about creating the conditions where others feel comfortable and snug in *their* places.

In the beginning of the book, Mary and Colin are irritable, contrary, colicky children. But under the tutelage and example of Dickon, a rural boy with whom all the animals of the Yorkshire moors feel at ease, Mary and Colin change and their instability is replaced with a calmness that allows others to feel secure. This is most evident in a scene where Burnett tells how the three children share the space of the Secret Garden with a nesting robin and his mate (see figure 10.1):

> In the robin's nest there were Eggs and the robin's mate sat upon them keeping them warm with her feathery little breast and careful wings. At first she was very nervous and the robin himself was indignantly

watchful. Even Dickon did not go near the close-grown corner in those days, but waited until by the quiet working of some mysterious spell he seemed to have conveyed to the soul of the little pair that in the garden there was nothing which was not quite like themselves— nothing which did not understand the wonderfulness of what was happening to them—the immense, tender, terrible, heart-breaking beauty and solemnity of Eggs. If there had been one person in that garden who had not known through all his or her innermost being that if an Egg were taken away or hurt the whole world would whirl round and crash through space and come to an end—if there had been even one who did not feel it and act accordingly there could have been no happiness even in that golden springtime air. But they all knew it and felt it and the robin and his mate knew they knew it.

At first the robin watched Mary and Colin with sharp anxiety. For some mysterious reason he knew he need not watch Dickon. The first moment he set his dew-bright black eye on Dickon he knew he was not a stranger but a sort of robin without beak or feathers. He could speak robin. . . . His movements also were robin. They never startled one by being sudden enough to seem dangerous or threatening. Any robin could understand Dickon, so his presence was not even disturbing.[5]

The robin feels less trusting, however, about the other children, about Mary and Colin, especially since the latter comes to the garden in his wheelchair and moves awkwardly until he learns to walk. But that discomfort eventually disappears as well:

At the outset it seemed necessary to be on guard against the other two. In the first place the boy creature did not come into the garden on his legs. He was pushed in on a thing with wheels. . . . That in itself was doubtful. Then when he began to stand up and move about, he did it in a queer unaccustomed way and the others seemed to have to help him. The robin used to secrete himself in a bush and watch this anxiously, his head tilted first on one side and then on the other. He thought that the slow movements might mean that he was preparing to pounce, as cats do. . . . When the boy began to walk by himself and even to move more quickly it was an immense relief . . . [and] the nest in the corner was brooded over by a great peace and content.[6]

Since we have been discussing snugness in children's literature by means of a kind of photo album of images, this image of the robin snug

"IN HIS MOST THRILLING TONE AND WITH AN AFFECTED MANNER."

10.1 Frances Hodgson Burnett (in the background) and the robin in her walled garden in Kent. Illustration by Alfred Brennan for My Robin (New York: Frederick A. Stokes, 1912), frontispiece.

in its nest may be the best one with which to end. Instead of a world where Burnett's robin fears the cat is about to pounce, it is a trustworthy universe of "great peace and contentment." Instead of a garden where Peter Rabbit trembles because of Mr. McGregor, or a snowbound wood where Mole crouches in fear, or a vast prairie where Laura feels dwarfed and vulnerable, it is a cozy hole where Peter is snug in his own bed, and Badger's underground abode where Mole can finally relax, and grandfather's attic where Heidi slumbers. The image in *The Secret Garden* of the robin in its nest—absent of fear and full of trust—presents a strong picture of the conditions of snugness. Moreover, as with the Sufi story of the teacher and the student and the courtyard full of birds, it also suggests what must be done to give rise to such ease in others.

NOTES

1. Jerry Griswold, "Reading Differently after September 11" *Inis* (Autumn 2002): 6–7, 15.
2. Kenneth Grahame, *The Wind in the Willows* (New York: Charles Scribner's Sons, 1953), 75.
3. Clement C. Moore, *The Night Before Christmas* (New York: Weathervane Books, 1976), 2.
4. Laura Ingalls Wilder, *The Little House on the Prairie* (New York: Harper & Row, 1971), 54.
5. Frances Hodgson Burnett, *The Secret Garden* (New York: Grosset and Dunlap, 1938), 328–29.
6. Burnett, *The Secret Garden*, 329–32.

• 11 •

Cultural Work: The Critical and Commercial Reception of *The Secret Garden*, 1911–2004

Anne Lundin

Editor's note: The material in this article was originally presented at a conference organized by Angelica Carpenter, "Frances Hodgson Burnett: Beyond the Secret Garden," at California State University, Fresno, in 2003. A slightly different version of this article was first published in The Secret Garden, A Norton Critical Edition, *edited by Gretchen Holbrook Gerzina. Reprinted by permission of Norton.*

"A book of the new century,"[1] wrote Ann Thwaite in her early biography of Frances Hodgson Burnett, *Waiting for the Party*. A book of "the New Thought" from an apostle of "beautiful thoughts," asserted Gretchen Holbrook Gerzina in her 2004 biography, *Frances Hodgson Burnett: The Unexpected Life of the Author of* The Secret Garden.[2] Indeed *The Secret Garden* is, to many critics and converts, the most significant children's book of the twentieth century, with mythic roots connecting the generations, celebrating creativity and healing, for young and old. Although both England and America claim the book as their own, it is known the world over, translated into dozens of languages. An exploration of the critical and commercial reception of the book in its multiple adaptations attests to the power of the text as cultural work. If, as Jane Tompkins suggests in *Sensational Designs: The Cultural Work of American Fiction, 1790–1860*, certain popular novels resonate with the contemporary cultural discourse, "providing society with a means of thinking about itself, defining certain aspects of a social reality which the authors and their readers shared,"[3] Burnett's best-known novel shows how a literary text can serve as a means of ordering the world for its readers in a way where effects are represented in myriad visions and revisions.

The Secret Garden's agency in achieving these ends is demonstrated in the ways in which people received and revived the text over the century since its first publication. It was well received when it appeared, but fell into a long period of not only neglect but derision as critics re-evaluated which children's books would become classics and which deserved oblivion. The literary critic Barbara Hernstein Smith speaks of the "dynamics of endurance" by which literary stature is created through social acts of publishers, critics, librarians, and teachers.[4] Despite the critics, *The Secret Garden*'s slow rise to classic status demonstrates how popular works not only fit the culture but may change the culture. To Jane Tompkins, readers see different texts and look at texts from different angles. "Looking," says Thompkins, "is not an activity that is performed outside of political struggles and institutional structures, but arises from them." The value of literary works lies in their ability to provide the culture "with a means of thinking about itself," thus "doing work, expressing and changing the social context that produced them."[5] Reception theory is a continuum in which a contemporary "read" of a text relates to its larger life and textual adventures in the world, a world changed by its existence. The interpretations given a literary work by its contemporary context make meaning, rather than merely finding it. This construction makes these early reviews, mostly unsigned, so critical to the cultural work of *The Secret Garden* over the last century.

The Secret Garden's reception was shaped by its format. It first appeared as a serial in a 1910 literary magazine for adults. That the book appeared first as a serial was not uncommon at the time; periodicals were often the first format for literary works, and their serial structure influenced how the story emerged. Burnett's first best seller, the hugely popular *Little Lord Fauntleroy*, first appeared in *St. Nicholas*, an esteemed children's magazine, before its publication as a novel in 1886. However, *The Secret Garden*'s publication in the *American Magazine* in 1910, the year before book publication, meant that although Burnett believed it to be the first children's novel to be published first in an adult magazine, the public perceived the text as adult fiction. Advance notice of the book itself appeared in *Publishers' Weekly*, August 12, 1911, announcing in a full page illustrated advertisement the book's arrival on August 25th and featuring a picture cover by Maria L. Kirk (see figure 11.1), a popular illustrator. Citing three of Burnett's previous works, only one of them for children, the ad proclaimed that the new book "has the tenderness and charm of *Little Lord Fauntleroy*, the imagination and power of *The Dawn of a Tomorrow*, and the dramatic suspense of *The Shuttle*. All the qualities which have made Mrs. Burnett the most beloved American storyteller are here, intensified and enriched."[6] Success seemed assured.

The book was initially marketed as an adult book, with some overlap in the juvenile market. As with all of Burnett's books, the first edition sold readily; *Publishers' Weekly* featured an ad less than a month later announcing "2nd Large Edition—25,000 Copies" and quoted the *Minneapolis Journal*'s praise of Burnett as "a writer of optimistic fiction."[7] An October *Publishers' Weekly* advertisement predicted that the book would be the most popular of the season because "it appeals to both young and old. It combines the qualities of her best works. It is full of optimism, health and joy."[8] While this prediction may have been overly optimistic, the rationale was convincing as to the book's resonant reception: ageless appeal, connection to previous work, and hopeful, healthy theme.

The press awarded the book attention worthy of a new book by a famous author and literary celebrity. The reception may have been somewhat tame, tempered by the text's overshadowing predecessor, *Little Lord Fauntleroy*. The presence of this 1886 blockbuster dwarfed other works by the author, who was endlessly blessed and cursed by her *Fauntleroy* fame. *The Secret Garden* struggled to assert its own identity as a different kind of story that spoke to both the romanticism and modernism of a new century. Burnett inscribed in the text some of the popular philosophy of the age—the power of positive thinking, the therapeutic message of health and healing—in language and forms that spoke to adults in particular. These ideas found expression in a favorite and familiar subject for Burnett: gardening. While gardening at her new Long Island estate, she recalled the makeover of an neglected orchard in Kent into a rose garden and an earlier childhood visit to an abandoned garden in Manchester, which her mind's eye had transformed from squalor to splendor. Her first childhood book was *The Little Flower Book*, in which each letter of the alphabet was illustrated with flowers that grew into a garden before her eyes. She also may have been

11.1 Cover by Maria L. Kirk for The Secret Garden (New York: Frederick A. Stokes, 1911).

familiar with an earlier garden restoration story published a decade before: *Elizabeth and Her German Garden*, a popular book whose central figure and author was Elizabeth von Arnim, an Australian-born writer who had been raised in England and who had married a German count. In this book, the character Elizabeth discovers a large neglected garden on her husband's country estate and begins its restoration. Burnett, transplanted to America, also recalled her own childhood reverie with green places magically transformed.

While the critics did not connect intertextually with von Arnim, they did instinctively connect to Burnett's other writings for adults and children. Her success in both realms and in several genres made her a true crossover author, long before that term circulated. Impressively, the critics did not seem to have Burnett categorized as one type of author with a certain audience in mind. Reviews also suggest that adult readers found pleasure in books on childhood experience, which is not assumed today. The earliest American review of *The Secret Garden*, in the *Literary Digest* of September 2, 1911, announced its arrival with a sense of eager anticipation. Relating the book to Burnett's earlier novel *The Dawn of a To-morrow*, the critic lauded its similar "allurement of mystery, the fascination of child-life, and the joyous and sane philosophy of life." Susan Sowerby, Dickon, and Ben Weatherstaff and even the robin are mentioned glowingly.[9] The *New York Times*, which wrote a lengthy review a day later entitled "What Was Hid in a Garden," appreciated the book's dual appeal and the author's rare talent in attracting young people and "their elders who love young things, for whom literary craftsmanship is a source of enjoyment and a quiet, beautiful tale."[10]

That same year the *Independent* characterized the author as someone able to speak to children, as she had in *Fauntleroy* and *Sara Crewe*. While *The Secret Garden* was a worthy successor to those books, the review said, it might not appeal as much to sophisticated readers, who might notice similar themes in her recent play *The Dawn of a Tomorrow*. The book's charm seemed to lie in its "fresh-air gospel" and garden imagery, which might inspire a similar project of one's own, though "the transformation it may work will be less startling."[11]

On September 16, 1911, *Outlook* wrote a lengthy summary of the plot and mentioned in particular the "agency of the garden" and the "innocent conspiracy" as factors leading to "an exposition of nature-cure and mental healing." Despite the "unnecessary mysticism" at the end of the story and the "little holding forth by the ex-hysteric," the reviewer found the book simple, natural, nondidactic in its "out-of-door spirit" and poetic tone.[12]

The *Nation* mentioned characters' names, the three children and Mrs. Sowerby, and approved of the charming story, with its absence of two objectionable qualities: "the children's faults are not such as to invite imitation; and the young are not reformers of the old."[13]

R. A. Whay in the New York *Bookman* found the book difficult to review because it was hard to tell who was the leading character and whose story it really was: the various possible heroes or heroines, or the moor itself? After characterizing the story as romance, the reviewer decided that "*The Secret Garden* is more than a mere story for children; underlying it there is a deep vein of symbolism."[14]

The *American Monthly Magazine*, the novel's first publisher, not surprisingly, found the book to be a worthy if not superior successor to *Little Lord Fauntleroy* in its lack of sentimentality and piety and its appeal to "those grown-up people who love children and out-of-door pleasures, the open moor, and flowers, and sweet scented mystic 'secret gardens.'"[15]

The *Dial* mentioned the book in an article appraising the best of the season's juvenile offerings as one among the many "to be accounted permanent."[16] *The Secret Garden* seemed comfortably on its way to becoming a popular book, if not necessarily a classic.

At the end of 1911 the book was selected as one of the best of the season in American holiday reviews. The *New York Times* published "One Hundred Christmas Books," which included *The Secret Garden*, stating that the book "is so very near to the common lot of humanity that its readers cannot be defined by age, class, or literary taste."[17] Picking it as one of the fifty best books of the season, the *Literary Digest* applauded its broad appeal—"I like to believe that every one will get hold of this tale"—and mentions by name the character modern readers identify as the hero, Dickon.[18] The book sold briskly that season, according to monthly reports in *Bookman*, where it was seen in the top six best-selling category for fiction, and occasionally for juveniles in

Boston, Minneapolis, Baltimore, Cleveland, Albany, Washington, D.C., and Providence.

The British reviews were more sparing in coverage but quite ardent. The book was published in England in October 1911 by Heinemann with illustrations by the distinguished Charles Robinson, aesthetic illustrator of classics. The edition included a prefatory advertisement for Burnett's most recent adult novel, *The Shuttle*, a vehement denouncement of marriages between American heiresses and greedy and impoverished English noblemen, with effusive blurbs from six British newspapers. Recalling *The Secret Garden*'s earlier serial appearance, the critic Katherine Tynan in the *Bookman* (London) raved, "It is a *hortus inclusus* of a book— a very fragrant book, sweet with the sweets of the Hidden Garden, and with certain other flowers that grow in the soil of the human heart." She commended Burnett for applying her talents to writing stories for children, and the illustrator, Charles Robinson, for his imaging of Mary at her various stages of growth. Noting its touch "of the grown-up heart and experience," Tynan decided that the book belonged "as much to general literature as to the literature of the schoolroom . . . [to please people aged] from seven to seventy-seven."[19]

The *Athenaeum* reviewed it as a new adult novel with "graceful descriptive writing," a distinctive Yorkshire dialect, and eight illustrations by Charles Robinson.[20] Across the Atlantic, the *Canadian Magazine*'s review focused on the crippled boy finding healing "through the most tender and faithful of teachers," presumably either Mary or Mother Nature herself. Appreciating the author's sensitivity for youth, the critic found there to be little plot or narrative but, instead, a lesson of gentle suggestion.[21]

The only negative review seems to have appeared in *Booklist*, the reviewing journal of the American Library Association. Writing in the [adult] "Fiction" section, the reviewer declared that "the hours spent in rescuing the 'secret garden' from a state of wildness are the means of redeeming the lives of two lonely, selfish English children. A 'new-thought' story, over-sentimental and dealing almost wholly with abnormal people. The moral is obvious but sensible, and both it and the character of the story will appeal to many women and young girls."[22] While idiosyncratic, this review is apparently unique among those that appeared shortly after the book's first publication. Yet after a promising start, *The Secret Garden* languished in obscurity.

Burnett's obituaries in 1924 reveal that *The Secret Garden* was indeed dormant. Commentators fondly aligned Burnett with the enormously popular *Little Lord Fauntleroy*. The London *Times* dismissed *The Secret Garden* by saying that "in her other books and plays Mrs. Burnett was less successfully Dickensian, sentimental, naive."[23] The *New York Times* published three pieces about Burnett when she died. The first was a lengthy review that heralded *Fauntleroy* but omitted any mention of her other children's books, commenting instead on her novels for adults. The second was a letter to the editor from a friend who extolled her love of gardens, mentioning *The Secret Garden* as a corner of her rose garden at Maytham Hall, Kent, where Burnett had spent some of her happiest years and where she no doubt first conceived the idea for her story within her walled gardens, a tamed robin by her side. The third, entitled "Fauntleroy," placed that novel among "the gallery of immortal children" and mistakenly referred to "The Secret Orchard."[24] A long memorial tribute in *St. Nicholas* mentioned several of her juvenile works and other fiction, without referring at all to *The Secret Garden*.[25] In a tribute titled "A Portrayer of Lovable Children," *Outlook* mentioned the title as possessing "a singular outdoor charm mingled with much that was mystical."[26] With Burnett's death, the book now considered her masterpiece seemed to have passed on as well.

The Secret Garden's revival was a slow process. That new generations found the text is evident from references in the literature, despite the lack of interest by some important figures in the library field. The selection bible, *The Children's Catalog,* began listing *The Secret Garden* as a recommended title only in the third edition (1917), but did not list it as a starred selection until the ninth edition of 1956; *Little Lord Fauntleroy* remained Burnett's leading title in this work until 1951. *The Secret Garden* was entirely absent from the influential *Book Shelf for Boys and Girls*, edited by Clara Hunt from 1918–1931; this guide influenced Bertha Mahony who drew upon it to compile the collection for her children's bookstore and for the *Horn Book* magazine that followed. Mahony did mention the book in her massive tome, *Realms of Gold* (1929), under the category "Home and School Pleasures," with this brief annotation: "The story of how health and friendships came to a little sick boy in a 'secret' garden."[27] The book was not mentioned in Alice Jordan's esteemed "Children's Classics" recommended list, first published in 1947 in the *Horn Book* and reprinted in five editions, three revised by Helen Adams Masten (1952, 1960, 1967). Paul Heins's 1976 edition finally restored the garden to its rightful place.

What is surprising is that although the book remained popular with children and had been appreciated by adults as well, it continued to suffer the neglect of librarians and critics. Louise Seaman Bechtel, the pioneer children's book editor for Macmillan and a mover and shaker in the field of children's literature, dismissed the book in various speeches published in her work, *Books in Search of Children*, as "sub-literature," and grouped it with other landmarks "not necessarily a rightful inheritance, however popular."[28] Referring to the results of a 1926 "favorite books" survey in the popular family magazine *Youth's Companion*, in which *The Secret Garden* ranked twelfth, she bemoaned "the frank indifference to literary quality, the lack of fairy tales, and the conservative staying appeal of the misnamed 'children's classics.'"[29] In an essay on what constitutes a classic, the editor listed the book as one among others unnecessary today as "strange survivals."[30]

The most influential figure, Anne Carroll Moore, matriarchical maven of the children's book field as mainstay of the New York Public Library, gave modest mention of the book on one of her recommended lists of "Books for Middle-Aged Children," reprinted in her collection, *My Roads to Childhood*: "One of the first of a new order of mystery stories appealing to girls on the edge of the teens. Its setting is a very lovely garden in Yorkshire. Written many years later than the *Little Princess* [*sic*], its characters are less distinct. One remembers the garden better than the boy and girl characters. Mrs. Burnett was a lover of gardens."[31]

In the first critical work on American children's literature, Cornelia Meigs's *A Critical History of Children's Literature*, Elizabeth Nesbitt, another notable children's librarian and educator, included the book in a discussion of the years 1890–1920, a period she called "Romance and Actuality"; she found in the *Secret Garden* the "combination of the old and the new." Amid the highly romanticized setting, she wrote, is a real problem rarely discussed by writers for children: "the conversion into mental and physical health by two children ... accomplished by a combination of self-development, the healing qualities of the outdoors and the self-forgetting love of growing things and, of all things, the principles of mental healing." While calling the book "over simplified and idealized," she said that the book's thesis remained that "a happy and normal child must care for something and must be cared for."[32]

Frances Clarke Sayers, Anne Carroll Moore's successor at the New York Public Library, mentioned the book in her collection of essays and speeches, *Summoned by Books*. Recalling an inveterate young reader of nine or ten in a school library she had visited, Sayers was struck by this overheard conversation: "'Have you read *The Secret Garden?*' the girl asked a young friend, not waiting for a reply, and stroking the back of the book as if she were petting a kitten."[33] This anecdotal evidence illustrates the power of a book's being passed from one reader to another, without the benefit of either institutional acclaim or selective tradition.

While the book may have received faint praise from librarians, it has long garnered acclaim through tributes of writers recalling their childhood reading. Lois Lowry, Katherine Paterson, Philippa Pearce, Joan Bodger, Jean Little, and others listed it among their favorites. Literary historians and critics have also been instrumental in preserving the work's longevity. The first to take notice were the British, who tended to claim Burnett as their own, despite her later American naturalization. Before children's literature became an accepted subfield of literary criticism, a lone literary study appeared in 1950: Marghanita Laski's *Mrs. Ewing, Mrs. Molesworth, and Mrs. Hodgson Burnett*. This slender book by a British critic elevated *The Secret Garden* to preeminent status as Burnett's major contribution to children's literature. Laski astutely perceived the metaphorical significance of an introspective, unhappy child figure learning how to cope by cultivating a garden. She, like many other readers then and now, appreciated finding herself in such an empathetic, comforting work, for which she felt that Burnett deserved to be richly remembered: "This is a book for introspective town children. I was such a child myself, and it is therefore the most satisfying children's book I know."[34] That this opinion was somewhat heretical is suggested by a reviewer from the *Saturday Review* who dismissed Laski's literary judgment with this comment: "The test of worth for children's books—Alice and Huck pass such a test—is whether they can be reread by adults. None of the books by the three ladies can. As for Mrs. Hodgson Burnett—how many squirming, sweating boys in velvet pants and lace collars have cursed the creator of Little Fauntleroy!"[35]

Nothing as eloquent as Laski's work on Burnett appeared for more than a decade, yet following her lead, British readers and critics seemed more receptive to the novel. The London *Times* in 1960 organized an exhibition called "The One Hundred Best Books for Children," which included *The Secret Garden* as its last item, due to the overwhelming voice of readers.[36] While Marcus Crouch in *Treasure Seekers and Borrowers* dismissed the book as a period piece in his 1962 history,[37] Roger Lancelyn Green a few years later in *Tellers of Tales* and in *Only Connect* praised the book's "great individuality and astonishing staying power."[38] Perhaps the most influential champion was the historian John Rowe Townsend, who in his 1965 *Written for Children* praised the book's complexity and its power to quicken the imagination for things that grow and children's longing for real achievement: making something, a subversive notion to Victorian sensibilities.[39]

From there the list of articulate British champions of the book goes on, with the exception of Humphrey Carpenter who borrowed the title for his own study of the golden age of children's literature, but begrudged it space in the canon. Of particular note is the commentary by Fred Inglis in his study of the social values of children's literature, *The Promise of Happiness*, which wove *The Secret Garden* into his central theme of the radical innocence of youth and the novelist's vision for the future: "our faith that our children will *have* a future."[40] To Inglis, the book framed powerful feelings on childhood and England: the secret garden of childhood and of England, a metonymy that shapes cultural ways of thinking and feeling. Ann Thwaite's 1974 biography of Burnett, *Waiting for the Party*, published fifty years after Burnett's death, established Burnett as a major writer and *The Secret Garden* as her most loved book. Children enjoyed it, Thwaite said, "not as a 'classic' urged on them by their elders, but as a living story of as much concern to them as any written more recently."[41]

The American critical response to *The Secret Garden* grew along with the scholarly discipline of children's literature, a phenomenon of the last quarter century. The major scholarly journals in the field—the *Children's Literature Association Quarterly*, *Children's Literature*, the *Lion and the Unicorn*, *Children's Literature in Education*, and *Signal*—all contain weighty responses to the work, which resonated with the burgeoning feminist consciousness. In 1986, the year the book entered the public domain, Faith McNulty, children's book editor of the *New Yorker* wrote her own homage and exclaimed, "There is hardly a literate female alive who hasn't read and loved it."[42] The list of those who have written about the book's generative themes is stellar, but the key player in this country is surely Phyllis Bixler, whose literary studies of Burnett and numerous articles, beginning in 1978, have quickened interest in the breadth of Burnett's contributions. Bixler's 1984 critical appraisal of Burnett and her 1996 study of *The Secret Garden* for Twayne's Masterwork Series placed the book within the context of Burnett's body of work and its critical and commercial reception. Works like Ann Thwaite's biography, Phyllis Bixler's criticism, and numerous scholarly articles have elevated *The Secret Garden* to a firm place in the academic canon, and they have recognized as well its sentimental stature as a beloved text. Literary scholarship has christened *The Secret Garden* as a classic much as have the small hands that were handing the book along.

The Secret Garden's bonding to our culture is witnessed by its many editions and adaptations, bespeaking its commercial viability and adaptability. The 1949 Lippincott edition illustrated by Nora S. Unwin charmed a generation of readers, if not Anne Carroll Moore, who expressed displeasure with the color illustrations. In her column "The Three Owls' Notebook" in the *Horn Book*, Moore wrote that the book "remains deservedly popular, for Mrs. Burnett's story is still a good story and might well have been accompanied by fewer pictures reflecting more of its essential atmosphere."[43] The trend toward more, rather than less, illustration was effected through Tasha Tudor's 1962 illustrated edition for Harper & Row. When the book entered the public domain in 1986, new editions and adaptations began to emerge, some abridged or transformed into audio books or picture books, illustrated by Graham Rust, Michael Hague, and Thomas B. Allen; some adapted to the theater or film, once again. The book was released as a film in 1919 by Famous Players, remade in 1949 by Metro-Goldwyn-Mayer, in 1984 by

BBC-TV, in 1987 by Hallmark, and in 1993 by Warner Brothers. The book was adapted to the Broadway stage in 1990, with the production winning many top awards of the season. At the time of this writing, there are 281 different published editions in English, seventy sound recordings, and thirty-five visual materials (VHS and DVD versions). The text's openness to interpretation and invention speaks to its currency and commerce in the culture.

The Secret Garden was indeed a book for the new century, but which century? The book seems poised to play this inaugural role again. Despite the resistance of librarians toward popular reading or the shadow of *Fauntleroy*, *The Secret Garden* found its audience, passed from hand to hand, among readers of all ages. Readers led what academics later mapped on their own adopted critical landscape. It is a text rich enough to romance a reader still seeking what is on the other side of the wall, and the magic beneath the surface. The mythic imagery of a restored garden, of something submerged awaiting discovery, of the secrets we bear, of the mysteries about, all speak to the larger revelations that this text offers. The world "dwells in Possibility," as Emily Dickinson says, and as Frances Hodgson Burnett shows in this personal as well as public myth of enduring appeal.

NOTES

1. Ann Thwaite, *Waiting for the Party: The Life of Frances Hodgson Burnett, 1849–1924* (Boston: David R. Godine, 1991), 221.
2. Gretchen Holbrook Gerzina, *Frances Hodgson Burnett: The Unexpected Life of the Author of The Secret Garden* (New Brunswick, NJ: Rutgers University Press, 2004), 263–64.
3. Jane Tompkins, *Sensational Designs: The Cultural Work of American Fiction, 1790–1860* (New York: Oxford University Press), xi.
4. Barbara Hernstein Smith, *Contingencies of Value: Alternate Perspectives for Critical Theory* (Cambridge, MA: Harvard University Press, 1988), 21.
5. Tompkins, *Sensational Designs*, 200.
6. *Publishers' Weekly*, August 12, 1911, 768.
7. *Publishers' Weekly*, September 16, 1911, 1040.
8. *Publishers' Weekly*, October 14, 1911, 1446.

9. *Literary Digest*, September 2, 1911, 361.
10. *New York Times*, September 3, 1911, 526.
11. *Independent*, September 7, 1911, 547–48.
12. *Outlook*, September 16, 1911, 136.
13. *Nation*, September 28, 1911, 290.
14. R. A. Whay, *Bookman* (New York), October 1911, 183–84.
15. *American Monthly Magazine*, December 1911, 342.
16. *Dial*, December 1, 1911, 457.
17. *New York Times*, December 3, 1911, 793.
18. *Literary Digest*, December 2, 1911, 1041.
19. Katherine Tynan, *Bookman* (London), December 1911, 102–3.
20. *Athenaeum*, November 18, 1911, 621.
21. *Canadian Magazine*, February 1912, 398–99.
22. *Booklist*, October 1911, 76.
23. *Times* (London), October 30, 1911, 16.
24. *New York Times*, October 30, 1924, October 31, 1924, November 16, 1924.
25. *St. Nicholas*, January 25, 1925, 306–10.
26. *Outlook*, November 12, 1924, 397.
27. Bertha E. Mahony and Elinor Whiteny, *Realms of Gold in Children's Books* (Garden City, NY: Doubleday, Doran, 1929).
28. Louise Bechtel, *Books in Search of Children* (London: Macmillan, 1969), 28.
29. Bechtel, *Books in Search of Children*, 145–47.
30. Bechtel, *Books in Search of Children*, 174.
31. Anne Carroll Moore, *My Roads to Childhood: Views and Reviews of Children's Books* (Boston: The Horn Book, 1961), 238.
32. Elizabeth Nesbitt, "A Rightful Heritage, 1890–1920," in *A Critical History of Children's Literature*, ed. Cornelia Meigs, Anne Eaton, Elizabeth Nesbitt, and Ruth Hill Viguers, 264, 377 (New York: Macmillan, 1953).
33. Frances Clarke Sayers, *Summoned by Books* (New York: Viking, 1965), 152–53.
34. Marghanita Laski, *Mrs. Ewing, Mrs. Molesworth, and Mrs. Hodgson Burnett* (New York: Oxford University Press, 1951), 88.
35. *Saturday Review*, March 29, 1952, 33.
36. Brian Alderson, ed., *Children's Books in England: Five Centuries of Social Life*, 2nd ed. (Cambridge: Cambridge University Press), 329.
37. Marcus Crouch, *Treasure Seekers and Borrowers* (London: The Library Association, 1962), 14.

38. Roger Lancelyn Green, "The Golden Age of Children's Books," in *Only Connect: Readings on Children's Literature*, ed. Sheila Egoff, G. T. Stubbs, and L. F. Ashley, 11 (Toronto: Oxford University Press, 1969).

39. John Rowe Townsend, *Written for Children* (London: Penguin, 1983), 88–89.

40. Fred Inglis, *The Promise of Happiness: Value and Meaning in Children's Fiction* (Cambridge: Cambridge University Press, 1981), 111.

41. Thwaite, *Waiting for the Party*, 220.

42. Faith McNulty, "Children's Books for Christmas," *New Yorker*, December 1, 1986, 115.

43. Anne Carroll Moore, "The Three Owls' Notebook," *Horn Book*, November/December 1949, 521–22.

• *12* •

Painting the Garden: Noel Streatfeild, the Garden as Restorative, and Pre-1950 Dramatizations of *The Secret Garden*

Sally Sims Stokes

In the sitting room of Noel Streatfeild's Belgravia flat, Eric Phillips, of *The Writer*, settled in to interview the popular author of dozens of books for young people. Phillips's account of the visit would appear in the magazine's January 1962 number. With "that touch of dignity and repose which you find in royalty and some great actresses," Streatfeild, a seasoned Shakespearean and erstwhile playwright, responded smoothly to a series of general questions about plot and vocabulary. She stressed the importance of solid research, and of knowing her characters intimately.[1] Two-thirds of the way into the session, Phillips inquired, "'Have you been influenced by other writers?' Streatfeild's guard was now up. 'By nobody,' was her brisk reply. 'To be a writer you must be an individualist. In writing for children you must be yourself telling the story. But,' she allowed, 'there are a number of writers of children's books whom I greatly admire—Mary Norton, Rosemary Sutcliffe, Elizabeth Enright and Arthur Ransome.'"[2]

If Phillips reported the interview accurately, then Streatfeild's rejoinder showed some economy with the truth, for in fact she had drawn upon the work of other writers for decades. Her conversation with Phillips transpired more than thirty years after she had begun writing for adults, and a full quarter-century after Streatfeild's first children's novel, *Ballet Shoes*, had swept her into the realm of eminent writers for the nine-to-fourteen set. Shakespeare, Lewis Carroll, and Frances Hodgson Burnett are present and palpable in *Ballet Shoes*: one of the child protagonists performs in a play of *A Midsummer Night's Dream*, another in a film of *Alice*, and all three little girls are read to from *The Secret Garden*. It could be argued that the uses of these works are simply

169

tools, and not evidence that the architects of Puck, the Red Queen, or Mary Lennox affected Streatfeild's style, philosophy, or perspective; but why did she not mention the authors in her interview?[3]

A dozen years before meeting with Phillips, Streatfeild had published *The Painted Garden*, a children's novel about an English family's postwar sojourn in Southern California. Everyone who knows her is surprised when the petulant middle child, Jane Winter, garners the role of Mary Lennox in a major studio's production of *The Secret Garden*.[4] It comes as shocking news to Jane that starring in a movie at Bee Bee Films, Inc., will require her to say lines from a screenplay that she considers phony and fallacious.

In *The Painted Garden*, Noel Streatfeild not only recounts Jane's usually less-than-valiant attempts to come off convincingly as Mary, but also ingeniously disperses the beloved chronicle of Mary, Colin, and Dickon into the fabric of her story. She does this by integrating facets of Burnett's book into her own, and by causing the lead characters in *The Painted Garden* to represent principal players from *The Secret Garden*.

Streatfeild wove together the two narratives in a manner snug, shrewd, and well secured. Whether she hoped that someone would eventually crack the code of her literary scheme remains a mystery to this day. One wonders why Phillips's question seemed to put her on the alert. Had he read *The Painted Garden*? Was he pressing her to admit to having fused her novel with Burnett's? In a separate article, I have offered my own explication of how Streatfeild mingled the two stories. The reader may wish to seek out a copy of that other commentary as a companion piece to the essay at hand.[5]

Some critics have charged that in *The Painted Garden* Streatfeild added a slick coating of Hollywood glamour to an otherwise amusing and inoffensive yarn;[6] but her intent in creating the fictional Bee Bee Films, Inc., was not to romanticize the movie industry. Rather, she meant to demonstrate to her young readers that working in films can be dull and hard; that not all children are suited for it; and that when filmmakers craft a movie from a cherished favorite such as *The Secret Garden*, the original story—as Jane Winter quickly discovers—will be altered, distorted, or lost.[7] In order to consider how Streatfeild might have come to choose *The Secret Garden* as the film in which Jane performs, it is useful first to review the pastoral themes in her earlier works.

NATURE AS RESTORATIVE IN EARLY STREATFEILD NOVELS

Born in 1895, Streatfeild was in her teens when *The Secret Garden* was published. Burnett's novel was popular, but not a runaway hit. Streatfeild could have been in her thirties before she ever turned its pages. She first mentions it in *Ballet Shoes* (1936), when she drops Burnett's story into a scene in which Pauline, Petrova, and Posy Fossil are having a cozy evening at home with their guardian, Sylvia. Streatfeild states simply, "They were reading a book called *The Secret Garden*."[8] Her use of the modifier "a book called" is revealing. It is a gesture of introduction, implying that her readers might not be familiar with Burnett's work, even though it had been released twenty-five years earlier. Had she instead written, "They were reading *The Secret Garden*," her phrasing would have suggested that the story was well-known to the English children of 1936 at whom *Ballet Shoes* was aimed. Streatfeild also intimates that *The Secret Garden* does not fully engage at least two of the Fossils: while Sylvia reads aloud, Petrova assembles a model airplane, and Pauline busies herself with her needlework.[9]

Traces of *The Secret Garden* had been drifting through her adult fiction for at least five years before *Ballet Shoes* drew Streatfeild into the ranks of best-loved children's authors. Streatfeild evokes the pastoral in her first novel, *The Whicharts* (1931), wherein three London half-sisters experience the rejuvenating powers of the countryside during a retreat to the Sussex downs. She expresses the impact of their time in rural Sussex by having the girls coin the catchwords "Sussex" and "Sussexly" to describe something in superlative terms: "Such 'Sussexly' chocolates. I do think my new frock's Sussex."[10] During Streatfeild's own growing-up years, explains her biographer Angela Bull, the "particular charm of the Sussex countryside imprinted itself lastingly on her spirit."[11]

Streatfeild presses full bore into the garden-as-curative theme in *Tops and Bottoms* (1933), another adult novel in which aspects of *The Secret Garden* are stunningly apparent. Seven-year-old Beaty, deprived, misunderstood, and regularly thrashed by her alcoholic stepfather, goes along on a school outing to the country with her Cockney classmates. Her mother has died that morning. Beaty wanders away from the group and into the garden of Miss Felicity Fortescue. She is overcome by the glory of Miss Fortescue's roses: "Beaty . . . stood spellbound with admiration. . . . She had seen a few, well out of reach, in a vase at school, and in small tight bundles sold on a cart, but never had she been near enough to one to touch it or smell it. Felicity's roses were at their best . . . , each iridescent with drops of dew."[12]

Soon after, Felicity adopts Beaty: "Permanent kindness brought confidence, . . . fresh air, good food, and plain but charming clothes, worked such marvels for her appearance that she felt, astounding though it was, that people thought her pretty."[13] This passage evokes the gratifying moment when Mrs. Sowerby sees Mary Lennox in the garden, and suggests to Mary that she is getting prettier.[14] As with Mary's transformation, "it was months before the real Beaty began to emerge from the repressed child" she once was.[15] Nancy Huse, in her 1994 survey of Streatfeild's work, notes that in *Tops and Bottoms* the pastoral is "subordinated . . . to urban survival"; Beaty does not develop strength of mind, but instead becomes "a victim of others' desires."[16]

Huse turns to *The Secret Garden* as a clear archetype for Streatfeild's 1940 adult novel *The Winter Is Past*, "the important differences being," in Huse's view, "that the child kept alive and strengthened through the pastoral setting is a Cockney boy billeted" at a manor during World War II, "and that the parent healed and regenerated . . . is a childless woman, not a grieving father."[17] *The Winter Is Past* is even richer in *Secret Garden* allusions than Huse indicates, and demonstrates that Streatfeild was, by 1940, well along in molding and buffing Burnett's story into new fictional forms. The seven-year-old boy Tommy's plea to the gardener for a little plot to till, and some bulbs to plant, is redolent of Mary Lennox's desire for "a bit of earth."[18] Streatfeild's book takes its title from the *Song of Solomon* 2:10-13: "My beloved spoke, and said to me: 'Rise up, my love, my fair one, And come away. For lo, the winter is past, The rain is over and gone. The flowers appear on the earth." A primary theme of *The Winter Is Past* is the tension between a young wife and husband at the start of World War II. Sara wants to get away in order to work out her feelings toward Bill; but it is Bill who leaves for a time, and comes back to a Sara who is now willing to try to revive their dying marriage. The demise of Lilias Craven had taken place ten years before *The Secret Garden* opens; Streatfeild, through the characters Sara and Bill, collapses into a matter of months Lilias's death and Archibald's time spent at Lake Como a decade later. Sara's miscarriage, her subsequent depression, and her coldness toward Bill signify death in body and spirit. Bill's war service (and a spate of dalliances) offers him time to ponder Sara's anguish, and in the end, as expressed in the title, there is promise of a new season of reconciliation.

AMERICAN DRAMATIZATIONS OF *THE SECRET GARDEN*, 1919–1949

While Streatfeild was actively drawing on themes from *The Secret Garden* for her adult novels, a synergy within the pre-1950 American cinema and theatre was whirring in the background. In order accurately to render the film studio in *The Painted Garden*, and to give Jane a script to act from and react to, Streatfeild needed to place herself in the role of screenwriter. More than a few sources may have informed her portrayal of Misselthwaite Manor and its inhabitants in the ersatz screenplay of *The Secret Garden* that she devised for *The Painted Garden*.

The Secret Garden on the Silver Screen

1919: Famous Players/Lasky
Augusta Appel, of Union Hill, New Jersey; Gustav von Seyffertitz of Bavaria: These are names that only film historians and silent movie buffs are likely to recognize today. Appel was the sometime ingénue Lila Lee, and von Seyffertitz, a.k.a. G. Butler Clonblough, was a Hollywood actor and director who flourished during the inter-war period. At Famous Players/Lasky Studios (soon to become Paramount Pictures), Clonblough directed Lila Lee, then eighteen years old, in the role of Mary Lennox in the 1919 Marion Fairfax silent screen adaptation of *The Secret Garden*. The movie had been conceived as a vehicle for Mary Pickford, who had played both Cedric and Dearest in *Little Lord Fauntleroy*. Pickford was not available, having just started her own film company, and the role went to Lee instead.[20]

Fairfax's best-known screenplay was the 1925 sci-fi thriller *The Lost World*. She also wrote *The Lying Truth* (1922), which involves a corpse found in a swamp. In true Fairfax style, her script of *The Secret Garden* is a model of creepy details and shifty, underhanded dealings.[21]

These include Mary's two forays into a bog, and Dr. Craven's plot to poison Colin so that the doctor can inherit the manor. The movie is designed to keep filmgoers in a state of pop-eyed anxiety, but it also gratifies the softhearted by interposing an especially doting Mrs. Sowerby, and by marrying off Colin and Mary, who in this version are not cousins. Fairfax's Mrs. Medlock is a punishing crone who forces Mary to hem towels as a penalty for having helped Colin remove a brace prescribed by the sadistic Dr. Craven. At the end of the picture, the garden is "full of bloom, and happiness reigns";[22] but an important function of this mysterious walled quadrangle on the grounds of Misselthwaite is to serve as a place of retribution in which the children bury Colin's brace, to even the score with the malevolent medic.[23]

Streatfeild probably did not see this motion picture when it was first issued. It does not appear to have been immediately distributed in England, where Streatfeild was still living in 1919.[24] Famous Players/Lasky was involved in a dispute with owners of British movie houses that year, and cinema managers refused to screen the company's films.[25] Lila Lee evidently enjoyed some celebrity in England, but the *Times of London* does not list any showings of the movie.[26]

1936: Paramount Pictures

The *New York Times* commented in July 1936 that "threats of a saccharine cycle continue to emanate from the coast": Paramount was planning a remake of *The Secret Garden*, with the role of Mary intended for Virginia Weidler, aged ten.[27] At Paramount, Weidler had appeared as Europena in *Mrs. Wiggs of the Cabbage Patch* (1934), and had the lead in *Girl of the Ozarks* (1936). *The Secret Garden* never came about, and Weidler moved over to Metro Goldwyn Mayer (MGM) in 1938. After a series of middling-to-good parts alongside Katharine Hepburn, Mickey Rooney, and Judy Garland, she retired from films in 1945.[28]

1949: Metro-Goldwyn-Mayer

The fall of 1948 found Angela Maxine O'Brien in front of the MGM cameras as Mary Lennox in Robert Ardrey's screenplay of *The Secret Garden*. For Angela, who had changed her name to Margaret a few years earlier, this would be the last film for MGM.[29] Already blossoming into adolescence during the autumn 1948 shooting, the nearly twelve-year-old O'Brien just barely carried off the role of ten-year-old Mary.

Noel Streatfeild traveled to the United States twice during the 1930s.[30] In 1938 she "met and studied most of the child film stars,"[31] but she set aside plans for a book about American cinema children until after the war. She returned to California in 1946,[32] and apparently rounded out her research during the fall of 1947 and the early part of 1948.[33] Before it was published as a book in 1949, *The Painted Garden* began a six-month serial run in *Collins Magazine for Boys and Girls* in July 1948. Casting for the MGM picture was still under way in September 1948, shooting did not start until October, and the film had its world premiere in May 1949.[34] Streatfeild unmistakably based her Bee Bee facilities on MGM's Culver City studios, but contrary to assumptions posited in other studies of her work, neither she nor anyone else could have observed the filming of MGM's *The Secret Garden* in 1947, simply because it was shot in 1948—too late for Streatfeild to have incorporated an "I was on the set" authenticity into the magazine installments of *The Painted Garden*.[35] Unless she returned to the United States *after* her serial commenced, she could not have experienced the film's Gothic chill, or witnessed a Hollywood-trained raven substituting for Ben Weatherstaff's robin, or heard the dissonant mix of British and American accents, until the film arrived in Britain in 1949. It is unlikely that Streatfeild saw Margaret O'Brien and Dean Stockwell on screen as the too-robust Mary and Colin, or Elsa Lanchester as a barmy bumpkin of a Martha, or Gladys Cooper as a near-villainess of a Mrs. Medlock until well after her serial concluded in December 1948.[36]

The Secret Garden on the Stage

Slotted into this period of Hollywood's exploitation of *The Secret Garden* were stage productions of the story from two notable American dramatists for children. A bellwether of children's theatre in the 1930s and 1940s was Clare Tree Major, founder of the Children's Theater of New York. In the early years of her enterprise, Major dispatched road companies to selected venues in the Northeast. Later, she sent casts and crews out as far as the Pacific coast, and into Canada. Each of her little convoys consisted of a carload of actors and production staff, and a truck packed with props, sets, and costumes. Across the country, Major's all-adult traveling troupes set up in school and college auditoriums and local halls, and brought such favorites as *Little Women, Mrs. Wiggs, Aladdin,* and *The Secret Garden* (as well as another Burnett favorite, *Sara Crewe*) to audiences from Boston to the Bay Area.

Major's company toured *The Secret Garden* in the 1931–1932, 1935–1936, and 1940–1941 seasons.[37] Scripts of Major's plays are elusive: Clare Tree Major collections at Arizona State University and the New York Public Library lack copies of Major's adaptation of *The Secret Garden*. But Michael Gamble's analysis of her playwriting techniques indicates that Major adapted stories in a "responsible" way, and that she tended to stick conservatively to the story line, sometimes to the point of rigidity.[38] On the other hand, she fancied slapstick ingredients such as pillow fights, and it is conceivable that she staged Mary and Colin's shout-downs as semi-comic scenes.[39]

In 1938, more than half of Major's local organizational sponsors were parent-teacher organizations;[40] but another font from which American children's theatre flowed was the Association of Junior Leagues of America. The first Junior League was founded in 1901 in New York, to provide a means for comfortably off women to aid the less fortunate. Hundreds of Leagues had formed in the United States, Canada, and Mexico by the 1930s. Over the next two decades, the Junior Leagues developed an exceptional record of establishing children's theatre in communities of every size. The Leagues gave benefit shows to support charitable causes, and they brought live theatre into settlement houses and hospitals. Junior Leagues throughout North America sponsored Major's visiting players, and some groups, including members of the Junior Leagues of New York and Boston, used Major's script to perform *The Secret Garden* themselves.[41] A 1937 New York Junior League Players flyer, advertising tryouts for *The Secret Garden*, featured a whimsical cartoon of a woman driving a truck full of props and sets, en route to the city's hospitals.[42] In anticipation of their 1942 performance, a representative of the Boston Junior League Players told the press that there was "a great need of bringing to children the wholesome influence of such plays to counteract wartime tensions."[43]

Another pioneer in the twentieth-century children's theatre movement was Winifred Ward, who in 1927 established the Children's Theatre of Evanston, Illinois, a partnership between the Evanston elementary schools and Northwestern University. By popular vote of children's audiences during the spring of 1937, Ward produced *The Secret Garden* that autumn.[44] The play opened with Mary Lennox and Misselthwaite's housekeeper, Mrs. Medlock, traveling in a gently swaying railway carriage, an effect that "excited the wonder of the large audiences," according to the *Evanston Review*. The newspaper praised set designer William McCreary for the "surprising illusion of reality in the train movement and sounds, as well as in the rain which appears to beat against the window." Area seventh-graders acted the juvenile roles, and "adults from the university [i.e. Northwestern]" took the grownups' parts.[45] Ward's papers at Northwestern University contain nineteen playscripts, but there is none on file for *The Secret Garden*. Ward did present other playwrights' works, and it is possible that she used Major's adaptation of Burnett's story. A rare playbill from a 1932 performance of Clare Tree Major's *Secret Garden*, sponsored by the Boston University Women's Council, reveals that Major's version of the play, like the one performed at Evanston in 1937, opens with Mary and Mrs. Medlock in a railway carriage.[46]

As a playwright, author, and theatre lover; as one who developed contacts efficiently to further her research and promote her books in America; and as a former child welfare and social service volunteer in the London slum district of Deptford,[47] Streatfeild would likely have been interested in Ward's work, in Major's traveling theatre program, and in the Junior League's efforts to bring uplifting stories like *The Secret Garden* to children at all levels of society. Ward had published a book on children's theatre in 1930, and had written two more by 1947. Major's road companies had reached countless American communities before Streatfeild's first U.S. visit. Streatfeild might have caught a Junior League–sponsored matinée in any region of the United States during the 1930s or 1940s. When assessing the possible influences that aided Streatfeild to devise her simulated cinematic dramatization of *The Secret Garden* for the Bee Bee studios, one must take into consideration the renown of Ward and Major, and the undeniable popularity of *The Secret Garden* in a performance mode.

CULTIVATING *THE PAINTED GARDEN*

In *The Painted Garden*, Streatfeild offers a realistic portrait of a film studio, and not just any film studio, but one that is unquestionably in the midst of producing *The Secret Garden*. She describes costumes and sets, and even makes certain that the Bee Bee studio's movie will transmute from black and white to Technicolor for the garden scenes—a climactic attribute of the MGM adaptation. Streatfeild insinuates in her foreword that she had carte blanche at MGM during her late-1940s visits to the Culver City studio.[48] Even though she had apparently returned to England months before Margaret O'Brien stepped before the camera as Mary, various resources were available to Streatfeild as a VIP guest on the MGM lot. The most compelling of these were access to some of the child stars and to the working drafts of Robert Ardrey's screenplay. The earliest draft of record is dated September 17, 1946. As it happens, this was one day after Streatfeild arrived in the States with the intent to collect, as she recorded in her memoir, "all the technical detail" for "a children's book with a Hollywood background"—a book that she would build around the filming of *The Secret Garden*.[49]

A fact gone missing from the annals of Streatfeild's oeuvre is that in May 1946, more than two years before the movie was shot, MGM had announced it would make *The Secret Garden* as an instrument for Claude Jarman Jr.[50] The winsome lad had just won a miniature Oscar for his role as Jody in *The Yearling*. MGM must have tagged little Claude as the perfect American Dickon—an unaffected Tennessee tow-head whose shy grin and gentle way with animals predicted box office bliss for Metro-Goldwyn-Mayer. Dean Stockwell and Margaret O'Brien were tentatively lined up as Colin and Mary. Movie columnists expressed periodic curiosity about the studio's plans, but 1947 came and went with little news trickling out of MGM's press office. As late as May 1948, Bob Thomas reported in the *Washington Post* that MGM intended to make *The Secret Garden* in England, with the core cast of children who had been on hold since 1946. The international strain over the export of American films to Great Britain may have interfered with any arrangements to film on location in the United Kingdom. Amidst the postwar fiscal crisis that gripped England, the British government had set strict limits on nonessential foreign goods: Import restrictions included heavy taxes on American films, to the tune of 75 percent of the ticket sales.[51] American movie companies desiring to shoot in Britain thus faced a hostile political and economic climate.[52] Meanwhile, even as MGM was backing and forthing on where and when to set up filming, Claude Jarman Jr. was rapidly overtaking his young costars in height. Hollywood gossip maven Hedda Hopper reported on August 14, 1948, that

Claude had achieved a lanky five feet, ten inches.[53] He was no longer an even remotely suitable Dickon Sowerby.[54]

By the summer of 1948, Margaret O'Brien and Dean Stockwell were also on the brink of outgrowing the parts of Mary and Colin. MGM aborted plans for filming in England, and quickly lined up the rest of the cast during August and September for the October shoot in Culver City.[55] In a flash of good sense, the studio turned the loss of Claude Jarman Jr. into a chance to reconsider the ideal Dickon. Hedda Hopper proclaimed on October 4 that, after a widely publicized casting call, MGM had selected British actor Brian Roper to act alongside Margaret and Dean.[56] Brian's open expression, his placid bearing, and the rich timbre of his native Yorkshire idiom made him an entirely credible Dickon. But during her visits between late 1946 and early 1948, the would-be Dickon whom Noel Streatfeild would have seen around and about the MGM lot was Claude Jarman Jr.; and it is Claude whom Streatfeild makes over into the fictional David Doe, the young actor who plays Dickon in the Bee Bee film. In the 1930s, her publisher had warned her about basing her characters on real people.[57] Careful not to go too far, Streatfeild ensures that David, although he comes from the mid-south and has just starred in an animal-themed film, does not look like Claude: David's red hair and green eyes are evocative of Dickon's features in the Kirk plates for the 1911 Stokes edition of *The Secret Garden*. But Streatfeild warrants that David, a Missouri native, is studying Yorkshire vernacular for his role, just as the real-life Tennessean Claude would have had to do in order to be believable in the role of Dickon. David's mother, mirroring Susan Sowerby, offers Jane nourishment (a strawberry milkshake and some strawberry shortcake instead of Yorkshire milk and bread); as well as nurture, in the form of kind welcome and wise counsel.[58]

The extent to which Streatfeild actually interacted with the Jarman family is not clear, but Streatfeild makes it plain in her foreword that she had met Margaret; the book is essentially dedicated to her.[59] Ursula Gidden, the Margaret figure in Streatfeild's story, is a phantasm: The reason there is an opening for Jane to audition as Mary Lennox is that Ursula has just been taken ill, and will not return to work for six months. Ursula never actually appears in the book, but her charm and talent are dead weight to Jane, who can scarcely breathe without being unfavorably compared to Ursula. Streatfeild had great respect for Margaret,[60] but she needed to set her aside and give Jane a go as Mary to make the point that not every aspiring actor, especially Jane, is destined to be a star.

Before Jane's screen test, the director asks her whether she has read *The Secret Garden*. Fractious little Jane brags that she has read it "lots of times."[61] Jane's answer, though flippant, is an indicator that by the 1940s Noel Streatfeild had come to identify Burnett's story not merely as "a book called *The Secret Garden*," but as approaching the status of a classic. Jane is appalled by Bee Bee's too-generous characterization of Colin, and by the portrayal of Dr. Craven as a cruel sort (he does get nicer), and she bristles when she learns that Mary will see Lilias Craven's ghost in the garden.[62] The Bee Bee version also contains a flashback to happier days at Misselthwaite, not a feature of Burnett's book. Streatfeild implies that tampering with the much-loved story is high effrontery, but she makes it plain that Jane had better button her lip if she wants to keep the part of Mary. (See figure 12.1.)

The screenplay that Streatfeild devised, and that Jane finds so unfaithful, is one of the cleverest bits of tinkering ever to be poured out of the Noel Streatfeild Bag of Literary Tricks. In order to maintain her VIP status with MGM, Streatfeild could not risk appearing to scoff at the upcoming 1949 film. Still, she needed to craft a script that would seem like a plausible Hollywood product—a script that would be recognizable as a Burnett derivative while at the same time deviating markedly from the original Burnett book. To give Jane the chance to show how well she knows *The Secret Garden*, Streatfeild allows some aspects of the Bee Bee screenplay to rise to Jane's standard, but assures that Jane will bridle at the more felonious alterations. Elements that occur in the two extant versions of the 1919 Marion Fairfax scenario, and in early MGM drafts by Robert Ardrey, provided Streatfeild with little slivers that she could glide dexterously into her Bee Bee script.

That Streatfeild must have had the opportunity to read the Fairfax and Ardrey texts (or, in the case of the Fairfax adaptation, to run up to Paramount Pictures and view the 1919 film in a studio screening room) is entirely evident. She was hardly shy about asking for such privileges, and energetically plied her network of contacts to help her gain entrée in Hollywood.[63] Fairfax's flashback to a romantic scene before Lilias's fatal accident, as well as a toned-down modification of Marion Fairfax's fiendish take on Dr. Craven, become components of

Monday's shooting started with Colin in bed and Mary sitting by his bed looking at him in a very interested way

12.1 Ley Kenyon provided illustrations for Noel Streatfeild's *The Painted Garden: The Story of a Holiday in Hollywood* (London: Collins, 1949), 227.

the Bee Bee screenplay. Neither Fairfax nor Ardrey indicates that Mary will see Mrs. Craven's ghost, but in two 1946 renderings of the screenplay, Ardrey describes the garden as "hauntingly beautiful" when Mary enters it for the first time.[64] Also in these early drafts, Ardrey makes two references to ghosts that directly suggest the spirit of Mrs. Craven: Ben Weatherstaff senses "the presence of a dead friend" when he picks a rose in the secret garden;[65] and Archibald Craven tells Colin that memories "rise like ghosts to haunt our lives."[66] These references began to be edited out by August 1948; all are absent from the 1949 continuity. If Streatfeild did browse Ardrey's various scripts, the spectral allusions surely acted as stimuli for her to introduce Lilias's ghost into the Bee Bee adaptation as a deliberately objectionable element.

Streatfeild's self-described "blotting paper memory" was at work all through her writing career, soaking up ideas for plots, characters, settings, and dialogue.[67] If only we could probe that memory today, to find out when she first read *The Secret Garden*, and how many times she returned to it over the years. In her 1971 memoir, she wrote of "the dear old *Secret Garden*," pointing out its timeless appeal to children, and implying how natural it was for them to want to read it again and again.[68] Indeed, when the lead character in her 1968 novel *Gemma* relaxes in the garden with a book, the child is rereading *The Secret Garden*.[69] By the 1960s, Streatfeild clearly expected that any literate girl would want to indulge in this pleasure of a summer afternoon.

If we could visit Noel Streatfeild, we might inquire whether she had ever joined a youthful audience at a Clare Tree Major production, or read Winifred Ward's treatises on children's theatre, or requested a private screening of the Lila Lee silent picture, or seen a prospectus for the abandoned 1936 Paramount film. We could ask if she rushed eagerly to Hollywood in 1946, hoping to watch Margaret and Claude in *The Secret Garden*, only to return twice within two years to face the increasingly bleak prospect of ever seeing the story filmed; and whether, in the end, she resorted to scouring Fairfax or Ardrey's screenplays, feverishly seeking out just the right pieces to fold into her own faux variation for the Bee Bee Studios, while trying to meet her publisher's deadline. If we could interview her, would she be, as Eric Phillips found her, sitting "upright in her chair," considering our queries "thoughtfully whilst smoking a cigarette through a ring-holder"?[70] Would she dispose of each question coolly, one by one, as she did with Phillips? How enchanting it would be if Noel Streatfeild were to succumb to a bit of cajolery, and to our fervent desire to know, and would at last reveal to us her own true thoughts about the influence upon her work of the dear old *Secret Garden*.[71]

NOTES

1. "Noel Streatfeild Talks to Eric Phillips," *Writer,* January 1962, 4–5.
2. "Noel Streatfeild Talks to Eric Phillips," 5.
3. The Streatfeild/Phillips conversation took place just three years after Streatfeild's *Magic and the Magician*, an analysis of the life and work of E. Nesbit, appeared; yet during her chat with Phillips, Streatfeild offered not so much as a nod to the creator of the Bastables in her log of esteemed children's writers. Marcus Crouch, in his 1972 *The Nesbit Tradition*, observes about E. Nesbit, "No writer for children today is free of debt to this remarkable woman"; and

Crouch specifically includes Streatfeild in the category of those beholden to Nesbit. Surely Streatfeild could have helped increase sales of *Magic* by indicating Nesbit on her roster of worthies; Marcus Crouch, *The Nesbit Tradition: The Children's Novel in England, 1945–1970* (Totowa: Rowman & Littlefield, 1972), 16, 19, 173, 79, 85, 224.

4. Random House published an abridged version in the United States under the title *Movie Shoes* in 1949.

5. Sally Sims Stokes, "Noel Streatfeild's Secret Gardens," *Children's Literature Association Quarterly* 29 (2004): 172–206.

6. Naomi Lewis, "The Swineherd and the Turtle," *New Statesman and Nation* 38 (December 3, 1949): 180; Angela Bull, *Noel Streatfeild: A Biography* (London: Collins, 1984), 195.

7. The title *The Painted Garden* suggests the artificiality of a movie set.

8. Noel Streatfeild, *Ballet Shoes* (London: Dent, 1936), 29.

9. Streatfeild, *Ballet Shoes*, 29.

10. Noel Streatfeild, *The Whicharts* (New York: Brentano's, 1932), 58; Bull, *Noel Streatfeild: A Biography*, 17.

11. Bull, *Noel Streatfeild: A Biography*, 16.

12. Noel Streatfeild, *Tops and Bottoms* (Garden City: Doubleday, 1933), 76.

13. Streatfeild, *Tops and Bottoms*, 101.

14. Streatfeild, *Tops and Bottoms*, 264.

15. Streatfeild, *Tops and Bottoms*, 101.

16. Nancy Huse, *Noel Streatfeild* (New York: Twayne, 1994), 34–35.

17. Huse, *Noel Streatfeild*, 60.

18. Noel Streatfield, *The Winter Is Past* (London: Collins, 1940), 203–4; Frances Hodgson Burnett, *The Secret Garden* (Philadelphia: Lippincott, 1949), 117.

19. I have found no evidence that any British films of *The Secret Garden* were made during this period. It is, of course, possible, and even likely, that schools and small drama societies staged the story in both England and America.

20. Hedda Hopper, "Looking at Hollywood," *Los Angeles Times*, November 29, 1946, A2.

21. The script for this film resides at the Margaret Herrick Library of the Academy of Motion Picture Arts and Sciences in Beverly Hills, California. A two-page synopsis, submitted as part of registration of copyright, is available from the Motion Picture, Broadcasting and Recorded Sound Division, Library of Congress, Washington, D.C.

22. *The Secret Garden*. By Frances Hodgson Burnett. Abstract of Screenplay. Adapt. Marion Fairfax. Famous Players/Lasky, 1919. Motion Picture, Television, and Recorded Sound Division, Library of Congress.

23. In the Fairfax script, when Archibald Craven leaves Misselthwaite, he goes to Egypt, not to Italy. The popular fascination with archaeologist Howard Carter's excavations of the tomb of Ramses VI probably contributed to this adjustment of Archibald's itinerary.

24. Bull, *Noel Streatfeild: A Biography*, 73.

25. "U. S. Film Enterprise in Britain: Proposed Trade Boycott," *Times*, June 25, 1919, 9.

26. "Ten Years of Motion Pictures," *Times*, February 21, 1922, iv.

27. "News of the Screen," *New York Times*, July 3, 1936, 23.

28. "Virginia Weidler," *Class Act: Those Golden Movie Musicals*, www.classicmoviemusicals.com/weidler2.htm (accessed September 28, 2005).

29. Allen R. Ellenberger, *Margaret O'Brien: A Career Chronicle and Biography* (Jefferson, NC: McFarland, 1999), 157.

30. Noel Streatfeild, *Beyond the Vicarage* (London: Collins, 1971), 96, 117.

31. Noel Streatfeild, "Myself and My Books," *Junior Bookshelf* 3 (May 1939): 123.

32. Streatfeild, *Beyond the Vicarage*, 96, 185.

33. Noel Streatfeild to Herman Ould. August 11, 1947, P. E. N. Archive, Department of Special Collections, McFarlin Library, University of Tulsa; "Noel Streatfeild's Books by Collins," (advertisement), *Collins Magazine for Boys and Girls*, November 1948, inside back cover.

34. Thomas F. Brady, "Paramount to Do Film on Jet Pilots," *New York Times*, September 28, 1948, 32; Edwin Schallert, "Ruth Warrick Changes Pace in Musical Opus . . . Elsa Lanchester in 'Secret Garden,'" *Los Angeles Times*, September 18, 1948, 9; "'Secret Garden' May 4," *Christian Science Monitor*, April 26, 1949, 5.

35. Noel Streatfeild, *The Painted Garden* (London: Collins, 2000), 5; Bull, *Noel Streatfeild: A Biography*, 189; Huse, *Noel Streatfeild*, 90.

36. For thorough critiques, see Gillispie and Wolf. Gillispie emphasizes that the MGM's film "takes on all the dimensions of a teasing thriller and embodies the multiple anxieties of the time." Wolf stresses that Ardrey "chose to use the novel's realism, very nearly removing its magic." Shirley Marchalonis, in "Filming the Nineteenth Century," covers three films of *The Secret Garden* made after 1984, but includes a note dismissing the 1949 MGM film as "not worth talking about"; Julaine Gillispie, "American Film Adaptations of *The Secret Garden*," *Lion and the Unicorn* 20 (1996): 132–52 (Project Muse); Virginia L. Wolf, "Psychology and Magic: Evocative Blend or a Melodramatic Patchwork [*The Secret Garden* (1911), Frances Hodgson Burnett]," in *Children's Novels and the Movies*, ed. Douglas Street, 126 (New York: Ungar, 1983); Shirley Marchalonis, "Filming the Nineteenth Century: *The Secret*

Garden and *Little Women*," *ATQ/The American Transcendental Quarterly* 10 (1996): 291.

37. Michael W. Gamble, "Clare Tree Major: Children's Theatre, 1923–1954" (dissertation, New York University, 1976) Ann Arbor: UMI, 2003. 276, 288, 300.
38. Gamble, "Clare Tree Major: Children's Theatre," 106.
39. Gamble, "Clare Tree Major: Children's Theatre," 108, 130.
40. Gamble, "Clare Tree Major: Children's Theatre," 193.
41. Major's sets typically were uncomplicated box affairs, but *The Secret Garden* was evidently a complex play to stage. Envoys from the national organization, assigned to review the effectiveness of various Leagues, sometimes included comments about the local group's theatre efforts. League representative Virginia Lee Comer visited the Boston Junior League in May 1943 to consider concerns "over the children's theatre program for the next year." Comer noted, "In talking with Miss Spencer last fall, I had urged that they not try *The Secret Garden*, which had been chosen, because it is such a heavy production. However, that was carried through, and, of course, proved a great headache. We discussed the fact that it would be very wise to give up the big production next year"; Virginia Lee Comer, Letter to Dorothy Rackemann and Patricia Spencer. Association of Junior Leagues of America Records. Box 10, Folder 97. Social Welfare History Archives, University of Minnesota; Gamble, "Clare Tree Major: Children's Theatre," 163.
42. "The Play's the Thing!," (flyer) 1937, New York Junior League Archives.
43. "Junior League Juvenile Play Is Next Week," *Christian Science Monitor*, December 24, 1942, 4.
44. "New U.S. Play, Ali Baba Ballet on Program of Children's Theater; Season Opens Oct. 30 with 'The Secret Garden,'" *Evanston Review*, October 14, 1937, 6.
45. "'Secret Garden' Saturday's Bill at Haven School," *Evanston Review*, November 11, 1937, 43.
46. *The Secret Garden*. By Frances Hodgson Burnett. Playbill. 1932. Adapt. Clare Tree Major. Boston University Women's Council Collection, Howard Gotlieb Research Center, Boston University; I describe the playbill as rare because Major discouraged the printing of programs, lest they be dispatched from the balcony in the form of paper airplanes, or, if printed on crisp paper, rustle during the performance; Gamble, "Clare Tree Major: Children's Theatre," 207.
47. Bull, *Noel Streatfeild: A Biography*, 125, 169.
48. Streatfeild, *The Painted Garden*, 5
49. Streatfeild, *Beyond the Vicarage*, 185.

50. "Screen News," *Christian Science Monitor*, 24 May 1946, 4; "Ayres to Appear in Warner Movie," *New York Times*, November 13, 1946, 41.

51. "Parliament," *The Times*, November 4, 1947, 2.

52. These problems in the 1940s ironically parallel the difficulties between Famous Players/Lasky and the British cinema managers in 1919. Each set of difficulties had an impact on an American film of *The Secret Garden*.

53. Hedda Hopper, "Alan Ladd Will Play New Sacrificial Role," *Los Angeles Times*, August 14, 1948, 8.

54. Hopper incorrectly states that Dean Stockwell would inherit Jarman's role.

55. Bob Thomas, "Young 'Jody' Prefers Grid to Screen," *Washington Post*, May 23, 1948, L1.

56. Hedda Hopper, "Brown Pacts British Lad for New Feature," *Los Angeles Times*, October 4, 1948, A6.

57. Streatfeild, *Beyond the Vicarage*, 84.

58. In contrast to Dickon in *The Secret Garden*, David Doe in *The Painted Garden* has a father. In Mr. Doe, Streatfeild offers a nearly unerring replication of Claude Jarman Sr.'s manner and speech. For the flavor of Mr. Jarman's style of expression, see Claude Jarman Sr., "My Boy and I," an "as told to" article he contributed to *Parents'* magazine about bringing up Claude Jr. in Culver City; Streatfeild, *The Painted Garden*, 169–71.

59. Streatfeild, *The Painted Garden*, 5.

60. Bull, *Noel Streatfeild: A Biography*, 190.

61. Streatfeild, *The Painted Garden*, 138.

62. Streatfeild, *The Painted Garden*, 153.

63. Streatfeild to Ould. August 11, 1947, P. E. N. Archive.

64. *The Secret Garden*. By Frances Hodgson Burnett. Screenplay. Adapt. Robert Ardrey. Metro-Goldwyn-Mayer, 1946; 1948, 1949. Margaret Herrick Library, Academy of Motion Picture Arts and Sciences. sc. 122.

65. *The Secret Garden*. By Frances Hodgson Burnett. sc. 177.

66. *The Secret Garden*. By Frances Hodgson Burnett. sc. 182.

67. Bull, *Noel Streatfeild: A Biography*, 38.

68. Streatfeild, *Beyond the Vicarage*, 197.

69. Noel Streatfeild, *Gemma* (New York: Dell Yearling, 1986), 135.

70. "Noel Streatfeild Talks to Eric Phillips," 3–5.

71. Not wishing to lead the reader to believe that *The Secret Garden* was the only Burnett story that Streatfeild incorporated into her books, I cheerfully direct him or her to Streatfeild's 1970 novel, *Thursday's Child*. Set in the late Victorian/early Edwardian period, *Thursday's Child* involves a traveling ensem-

ble of players whose presentation of *Little Lord Fauntleroy* has Cedric being played by a female (as was typical in early stage productions, and occurred in the Famous Players/Lasky film); and two little boys who discover that their grandfather is a lord. The story was later made into a BBC television play; no scripts survive in the BBC Written Archives Centre.

• *13* •

Dreams, Imaginations, and Shattered Illusions: Overlooked Realism in Carol Wiseman's Film Adaptation of Burnett's *A Little Princess*

Lance Weldy

Editor's note: *The material in this article was originally presented at a conference organized by Angelica Carpenter, "Dreams and Visions," the thirty-first annual conference of the Children's Literature Association, at California State University, Fresno, in 2004.*

It seems popular for young girls in children's literature who find themselves in complex and harrowing situations to exercise their healthy imaginations. Sara Crewe is such a popular heroine whose sense of fantasy and optimism provides calm relief through troubling circumstances. Sara, when she is a cold and hungry servant girl, finds a coin in the gutter and uses it to buy six hot buns. Then she gives five of them to a street girl who is hungrier than she. To compensate for her loss, Sara wonders about her remaining bun: "'Suppose it was a magic bun,' she said, 'and a bite was as much as a whole dinner. I should be overeating myself if I went on like this.'"[1] The chapter titled "The Magic" serves as the most poignant example of Sara's use of imagination as she provides a workshop of sorts for Becky on how to imagine an appropriate feast in the attic. Even with all of Sara's imagining, however, Sara remains in control of her reality, acknowledging to Becky that "we are going to *pretend* a party" (emphasis added).[2]

Connected to Sara's sense of imagination during adversity is the broader issue of trauma in children's literature. In Sara's case, her ability to dream helps her through the nightmare she lives. Hamida Bosmajian notes in "Nightmares of History—The Outer Limits of Children's Literature" that "children have often been singled out to suffer special brutalities."[3] Earlier in her article, Bosmajian lists "child abuse" as one element that scholars question having a part in children's literature, an element that I believe plays a major part in Burnett's *A Little Princess*. Not only does Miss Minchin starve Sara, but she also requires her to work grueling hours and sleep in substandard living quarters. It is perhaps because Sara endures so much in Burnett's story that two film adaptations, Walter Lang's (1938) and Alfonso Cuarón's (1995), decide to alleviate Sara's burden somewhat in the end. However, what surprises me is the lack of scholarly interest in Carol Wiseman's 1986 stellar representation of Burnett's same story. Manisha Mirchandani's article, "Colonial Discourse and 'Post'-Colonial Negotiations: *A Little Princess* and Its Adaptations," focuses only on the work of Lang and Cuarón. Mavis Reimer's "Making Princesses, Re-Making *A Little Princess*" and Mary Lou Emery's "Refiguring the Postcolonial Imagination: Tropes of Visuality in Writing by Rhys, Kincaid, and Cliff" look only at Cuarón's recent achievement. Though her article follows Burnett's story from a theater-historical perspective, Susan Applebaum's interesting essay manages to mention only three ensuing *Little Princess* film adaptations: Mary Pickford's 1917 performance, Lang's direction of Shirley Temple's 1939 rendition, and Cuarón's 1995 interpretation. Finally, a simple search on the MLA Database using the entry "Little Princess" reveals a handful of essays on Burnett's novel and adaptations, but nothing resembling or mentioning Wiseman's production. It seems that either people have not heard of this film or that they choose not to write about it.

What I believe sets Wiseman's adaptation apart from the other two is its engaging realism. Arguably, this realism reveals itself in no better fashion than by keeping Mr. Carrisford as Sara's benefactor rather than "resurrecting" Sara's father as the two more popular film adaptations do. Briefly, I want to focus on Burnett's classic novel and argue for Wiseman's superior production, not only because it follows the book closely, but also because it refrains from following the Hollywood template of the tidy, perfect ending, choosing instead to enhance its realism, most notably in "keeping" Mr. Crewe dead.

As Elizabeth Lennox Keyser notes, Burnett's writing style evolved in the period after *Little Lord Fauntleroy* (1885), moving from realism to romanticism: "It is as though Burnett, on reconsidering *Sara Crewe*, saw how the story could be made to justify her own romantic imagination and the turn that her career, a commercial but no longer a critical success, had taken. Yet the heightened romanticism of *A Little Princess* is accompanied by a subtle psychological realism, a realism also characteristic of *The Secret Garden*. This realistic strain, I would argue, betrays the very ambivalence toward romance that Burnett is attempting to conceal even from herself."[4] In essence, though Keyser notices a shift in writing style, arguably the two most popular of Burnett's stories cannot help but retain realistic elements. Sara Crewe's story is virtually a romantic Cinderella motif set in gritty, realistic London.

How to focus or prioritize realism in a book with an integral theme of imagination is quite difficult. On one hand, Sara Crewe relies on the magic of imagination to survive in utterly bleak times. On the other hand, Sara lives and remains in England, not in a far-away fairy world. As Mirchandani says, "Children's literature and films are usually comprised of magical, fantasy worlds within which the characters play out their stories. These worlds function as the playground for young imaginations and, often, they are elaborations of real historical and geographical counterparts."[5] We know that Burnett's historical representation of a seven-year-old girl living in a boarding school is realistic, and while Sara does engage in imagination with "fantasy worlds," she remains in the real world. Mirchandani's article provides a thorough account of both the 1938 Lang version as well as the 1995 Alfonso Cuarón version, and even though her focus is on postcolonial elements in both films, I appreciate how she acknowledges that both "film adaptations have liberally altered the narrative structure and the historical setting, making the final product quite different from the original novel."[6] It is evident that each film diverges from the Burnett text, but what makes Wiseman's adaptation more successful?

KEY PROBLEMS

Basically, I find two major faults with the Lang and Cuarón adaptations. First, the fact that the father is still alive at the end of the movie actually detracts from the story line. What does having Sara's father remain alive do to Burnett's original story? Does it reward Sara for being such a good girl and enduring great adversity? Possibly. Does it ease the story of war and give readers optimism that their loved ones too may return from war? Possibly. But what else does it do? It drastically transforms Sara's character from the character portrayed in the book. Keyser says about the book, "As the outcome of Sara's simple, unadorned, and realistic story, however, it can also be read as the triumph of her imagination—an imagination that no longer idealizes suffering so as to deny it but that can empathize with its victims."[7] In other words, Sara has suffered a great deal and been a victim of abuse. Nevertheless, if her father does return, the remaining level of believability in the story line is in jeopardy. It is probable that Sara's imagination could conjure a "father resurrection," but it is not as likely in the realm of natural law. Also, how changed would Sara be if her father returned and took her away from Miss Minchin's school? She would have born the scars of abuse for a time, but having both wealth and father reinstated could have easily wiped away the remembrance of her previous situation. To remain a plausible, empathetic victim, Sara needs to endure a conflict from which she cannot completely regain something of great importance, even with all of her amassed wealth: her father.

Second, both popular films give abysmal means by which the father returns. It is interesting that two movies produced fifty years apart chose the same ending—not only that the father returns, but that he does so suffering from amnesia so that he does not initially recognize Sara upon their reunion. I am no medical doctor, so I cannot honestly deny the possibility of the reunions portrayed in these films, especially reunions involving veterans. However, what is the purpose of the father's amnesia? Does it prove that he was in a war? Does it heighten the dramatic suspense at the end? Even if both producers were sincere at an intended effect, what really happens? Each father's "snapping out" of amnesia looks exceedingly cheesy, nothing more than sentimentality in action. Whether or not this flaw is the fault of the actor, the absurdity remains.

Though I highly recommend watching each film's scenes of Sara's notification of her father's death and the father's returning, I am limiting myself here to recount in words the representation of death or resurrection in the three films. In doing so, I will also draw upon what I consider one of the most useful Internet tools for educational or entertainment purposes: www.imdb.com. The Internet Movie Database is an invaluable tool that catalogs film and television productions, giving the researcher the ability to search by actor, title, producer, and so on. This website also offers members the chance to comment on particular movies or television shows. Often members sign their comments using only an e-mail address or a code name. This public, commercial website invites free memberships. Thus user comments may not always use academic (or logical) reasons to support their positive or negative responses. Nevertheless, I think it is beneficial to provide a sampling of what members have posted about all three of these films. Fortunately, the movies are so popular that they have drawn numerous comments. As examples, I quote six user comments, giving both a favorable and unfavorable review of each of the three movies, in appendixes A, B, and C. In these appendices, I have highlighted especially thought-provoking portions of each user's comment.

1939 SHIRLEY TEMPLE VERSION

Mirchandani says, "Released in 1938 during a moment of great anticolonial struggle in India, it is easy to deduce that the film motivates colonialist resolve while trying to suppress any element that might call attention to Britain's role in that particular political conflict."[8] In the reunion scene, Captain Crewe (Ian Hunter) is found by Sara (Shirley Temple) as she desperately searches the hospital for the slight chance that he may be there. She is actually running away from Miss Minchin and authorities and, in hiding from them, enters her father's room by accident. She shuts the door, remains in the room for a few seconds, then reopens the door and stands in the doorway, keeping one hand on the doorknob and peering into the hallway.

She seems to spend an unusually long time in this doorway, even when it is clear she has eluded the authorities, at least for the moment. Perhaps she is waiting for a cue from Hunter, who eventually moans her name. When she reenters the room and finds her father, she screams with delight. Unfortunately, he doesn't recognize her, though he repeats his daughter's name as though she were somewhere far away. Once she discovers he is not responding to her voice, she asks, "What's the matter, Daddy? Why don't you talk to me?" She calls for help and in a frenzy says, "Daddy, you've got to know me! Look at me! Look at me!" Still despondent, he says, "You mustn't cry. You mustn't cry. We must be good soldiers, you know." Sara responds, "But I have been a good soldier, Daddy, and you don't know me!" The captain continues a conversation with her, though he does not recognize her: "My little Sara never cries," to which Sara screams, "But I'm Sara! I'm Sara!" She sobs and shakes him a few more times. Conveniently, with just two hard blinks and a slight shake of the head, Captain Crewe manages to reverse the spell. This miracle leaves the viewer wondering two things: first, does it take just a few good shakes and a whole lot of crying to bring him back; and second, how does Sara's crying bring him back when the captain specifically says that his daughter doesn't cry?

I don't discount films just because they were made before the 1980s, nor am I inclined to agree with John Ulmer's comments that "Shirley Temple is as annoying and unlikable as ever" (see appendix A). While I appreciate the comments of Winslow Bunny that "Victorian England was captured well in this movie" (see appendix A), I cannot shake the tacky amnesia fix as the single most lasting impression of this film.

1995 ALFONSO CUARÓN VERSION

Again, in this scene, Sara (Liesel Matthews) is running away from Miss Minchin and the law. Miraculously she escapes to the adjoining house where her father (Liam Cunningham) resides temporarily. Believing that she is alone, she huddles on the floor to cry. A thunderstorm has shorted the electricity, making the room dark [this story is set during World War I]. A man is in the room, and the audience only sees a quarter of his face (theoretically Sara does too). In this film Sara does not recognize her father until long after he begins talking to her. More significantly, although they converse much longer than Ian Hunter did with Shirley Temple, the father still does not recognize his own daughter. Cunningham asks, "What is it? Why are you crying? Please tell me.

I won't hurt you. Won't you tell me your name?" She responds without looking up: "Sara." After Cunningham comments, "That's such a pretty name," the lights come back on. Sara immediately recognizes her father and lunges toward him, screaming, "Papa, it's me! It's Sara!" Resisting her embrace he asks, "Sara, do you know me?" In her crescendoed frustration, she screams, "Oh God, Papa, don't you remember me? Papa, please, you've got to know me. It's Sara, remember? Remember India, and Maya? Remember the Ramayana, and Emily, and the locket with Mama's picture in it?" Miss Minchin and the others soon find Sara screaming to her father to remember, and Miss Minchin, who has met Captain Crewe personally before, says, "This child has no father." As her father stands there, bewildered, Sara is taken away by authorities into the "dark and stormy night." Ram Dass walks straight into Crewe's face as the mystical Indian music starts, and suddenly, Crewe's eyes widen! With a melodramatic yell and a run outside into the rain, Crewe is reunited with Sara in a moving Hollywood resolution.

Unlike the father in the novel, the father in both films [Lang's and Cuarón's] survives. The father's subsequent survival can be read as another moment in the narrative when the true lovers who persevered against all odds are reunited.[9] Yes, the reunion is intended to be dramatic. Cuarón, famous for his magical realism, creates a visually stunning film here, as noted in the review by username corpusdza: "At the same time that the speech occurs [when Miss Minchin tells Sara of her father's death], a black balloon slowly displaces floating near, exploding at the very moment . . . when [Sara] says that she's completely alone in the world, symbolizing that her fantasies are dead and [that she] must face the crude reality" (see appendix B). However, instead of a fulfilling, dramatic reunion, Cuarón has essentially furthered a silly reunion— reminiscent of Lang's version—by creating more suspense at the climax and a more unlikely miracle to cure Captain Crewe's mind: the mere mysticism of Ram Dass. Username Rilchiam-1's comments resonate well here: "Because we lose [the father's death], we also lose the parallel, and heartbreaking, storyline about Carrisford searching for Sara everywhere except where she actually is. And Sara's hysterics when she meets her father again are inexcusable" (see appendix B).

1986 WISEMAN VERSION

Because her father remains dead in this film, I decided not to focus on the ending, but rather on the moment where Sara (Amelia Shankley) discovers that her father has died. As username oleander-3 notices, this particular film lacks the blockbuster Hollywood budget and special effects: "It doesn't rely on special effect interludes, like the '95 one, or cute little song and dance sessions like movie of '39. Here we just get the story as it is with all the characters presented in exactly the way the novel depicts them" (see appendix C). True, the special effects that were used in 1986 on the production's budget may seem laughable now, but this "minimalism" furthers the realism, giving this production an engaging story.

The blunt and terse Miss Minchin tells Sara on her birthday that her father is dead in the most insensitive way possible: "Now I want no crying, and no unpleasant scenes. I have some bad news." Sara asks, "Not, Papa?" Miss Minchin quickly replies without any emotion, "He's dead. And before he died, he lost every penny of his fortune. You are left a pauper on my hands." All Sara can say is "Dead?" Miss Minchin, meanwhile, begins taking down party decorations: "You are a beggar Sara, and it appears you have no other relatives to take care of you." Portions of her dialogue become muffled and indistinct to reflect Sara's mental confusion upon hearing the news. She continues, "Don't you understand what I'm saying to you? You are left quite alone in the world. There will be no more of your grand airs, no more of this princess nonsense." Sara cannot listen closely to her words thereafter but instead goes through a flashback of happier times with her father (one of the few uses of special effects in the whole film). The blowing out of birthday candles helps to bring Sara and the audience back to the present. Miss Minchin says, "If I choose to give you shelter, you must work for your living." With the reality of the pain already settling in, Sara responds, "Yes, if I can work, it won't hurt so much." The end of the scene demonstrates the beauty of this film's realism. Though Sara may dream and imagine, she is honest and real. Earlier she has denied being beautiful when Miss Minchin first met and complimented her. As she goes upstairs after this sad news to change clothes, Miss Minchin asks Sara, "Aren't you going to thank me?" Puzzled, Sara says, "Thank you?" Miss Minchin responds, "For my kindness in giving you a home." This final line from Sara superbly clinches the overall tone of the film. She says, "No, Miss Minchin. You are not kind, and this is not a home." As Sara walks out without properly excusing herself, the audience understands that she can be brave without being overly sentimental, but more important is the lack of the usual Hollywood soundtrack at places such as this, typically used to enhance emotions in an already overwrought audience. Here all the audience hears is silence.

SHATTERED ILLUSION

Mirchandani sees the shortcomings of Lang's and Cuarón's films when she argues that "the historical negotiations the films [Lang's and Cuarón's] try to make fail miserably for two reasons: firstly because the racial categories are highly over-determined; secondly, because the historical fact of colonialism and a corresponding imperial culture consciousness are so complexly interwoven within the narrative structure that they become indispensable to it."[10] Although my focus is not on elements of colonialism, I believe Mirchandani's point subtly reinforces my disappointment with the more popular representations of *A Little Princess*. Essentially, even though the audience accepts a significant amount of imagination in the plot, the audience also expects the imagination to be limited in terms of involvement in the resolution of the plot. Without a realistic ending, we as the viewers cannot be sure that Sara's well-being will survive in the real world. What is my shattered illusion? I am disappointed not only when films such as these two share the same name with a classic literary work yet depart in an all-too-familiar way from its spirit, but also when works that actually do convey the same spirit and name of a literary work—like Wiseman's— receive little or no attention, attention that they deserve.

APPENDIX A: IMDB USER COMMENTS FOR *A LITTLE PRINCESS*, THE (1939) SHIRLEY TEMPLE VERSION

Winslow Bunny, International Falls, MN. Date: May 7, 2004. Summary: Shirley Temple at her best!

"The Little Princess" is a reversal-of-fortune movie, so to speak. Sarah Crewe (Shirley Temple) is the daughter of a wealthy soldier sent off to the Boer War in 1899. Having no relatives, Sarah is placed in an exclusive girls school until her father returns. When her father is reported dead and their fortune is wiped out, the friendly headmistress becomes not-so-friendly toward Sarah, who is made to work off her father's debt to the school. Sarah is convinced that her father is alive, though, and searches the area hospital for him, eventually finding him.

    This movie serves as an excellent example of several things: movies like this just aren't made any more. Unfortunately, they can't be—people would say it was too corny. In the movie, Shirley portrays a child not only with unshakable hope but patience, manners, politeness, and kindness in the face of terrible adversity, with only a couple of cracks in her steadfastness. She meets Queen Victoria. Who would believe that a child under the duress that she suffers could be so gracious? Who would believe that, being a pauper, she could meet the Queen of England? Today's movie child star would have filled the air with sassiness and expletives under the same situation. But Shirley/Sarah doesn't, and that's a reason that I really like this movie—it shows someone who tries to make the best of a bad situation, and never gives up hope. *I also believe that the movie is an accurate portrayal of the life and times of the turn of the century, as it was made only 40 years after the Boer War. I think that Victorian England was captured well in this movie;* after all, we do a pretty good job of displaying the 1960s on film these days (emphasis added). Overall, though, it is Shirley Temple at her singing/dancing/acting best in this movie, and she does a wonderful job from start to finish.[11]

John Ulmer. Date: February 13, 2004. Summary: The remake is so much better!

Unarguably a family classic, although the compliments stop there. *Shirley Temple is as annoying and unlikable as ever as the "little princess" who is put in a crass orphanage after her father is believed to have been killed in the war* (emphasis added). The devilish headmistress, knowing she will no longer receive payment for the girl's keep, locks her in the attic where she remains cheerfully (and quite annoyingly, I might add) optimistic—despite everything that is going on. Remade some number of years later, with a much better lead actress (who was optimistic and yet also sad—making the character believable), this original version is one for the crap shoot. *Sorry, Ms. Temple—you're just a friggin' brat* (emphasis added).[12]

APPENDIX B: IMDB USER COMMENTS FOR *A LITTLE PRINCESS* (1995) ALFONSO CUARÓN

corpusdza. México, D.F., México. Date: April 21, 2004. Summary: A wonderful movie.

It's a fantasy film over the fantasy and the imagination, but showing realities of children mistreatment and cruelty that in the real world are truly worse than those exposed (maybe more outside of U.S.A. and certainly exists in the third world, including India). Alfonso Cuarón (`Y tu mamá también'), showed us in this film a masterful domain of the dramatic conduction combined with an excellent photography and a first-rate edition job. For example, a deserving scene is when Sara (Liesel Matthews) wakes up and starts getting up to find the transformation of the rickety attic in a marvelous environment just made with cloths, fruits, food and incense with Hindu reminiscent. It's a fast sequence of five different shots which emphasizes the magic moment for the girl. The astonishing surprise relaxes the magic to a real world that can be good, just with the appearance of the little monkey of the Hindu servant Ram Dass (Errol Sitahal), showing to us that he, in some way, transformed the attic in the meanwhile sleep of the two girls. Another exceptional, but very simple made scene, is when Miss Minchin (Eleanor Bron), in a crude way informs Sara that her father, an English captain of the British army, died in the war some weeks ago, and the British government confiscated all his properties, leaving her in misery. *At the same time that the speech occurs, a black balloon slowly displaces floating near, exploding at the very moment in when she says that she's completely alone in the world, symbolizing that her fantasies are dead and must face the crude reality* (emphasis added).[13]

Rilchiam–1. Date: December 25, 2003. Summary: So many things wrong with this!

I understand that having Captain Crewe serve in the Great War was probably considered more cinematic than diamond mines and "brain fever." But I despise any story where someone "dead" turns up again. That's a terrible thing for children to see, especially if they've already lost a loved one; they don't need that false hope. Furthermore, this change eliminates more dramatic tension than it creates. When someone goes off to war, you *know* there's a good chance they may die. I prefer the book's turning point: first, the too-good-to-be-true diamond mines; then Barrow's arrival to report that Crewe "died delirious . . . and didn't leave a penny." And because we lose this, we also lose the parallel, and heartbreaking, storyline about Carrisford searching for Sara everywhere except where she actually is. And Sara's hysterics when she meets her father again are inexcusable. Burnett's Sara would never have taken on so.

And *forget* the soot-down-the-chimney prank. Sara would have been beaten for that, not just made to wash dishes. As a servant, she was subjected to downright abuse. She didn't get regular meals, for instance. When Minchin told her she would get no meals the *next* day, that was after she'd had no dinner or supper *that* day. She also had to take a lot of guff from the cook, another character I'm sorry they left out.

And the last act is ridiculously overwrought. In the book, Minchin softened up again when Sara started getting "donations," because she assumed this mysterious benefactor could make trouble if they knew how she'd been treating Sara. Putting Sara in peril is a trite cop-out.

And I don't believe she could have pulled herself up onto that ledge anyway.

And Minchin being reduced to servitude is just stupid.[14]

APPENDIX C: IMDB USER COMMENTS FOR *A LITTLE PRINCESS* (1986) (TV) AMELIA SHANKLEY

oleander–3. London, Ontario, Canada. Date: August 30, 2000. Summary: Why is this the one that's overlooked?

If you read the comments for the 1995 version, many people seem to say (in more or less words) that *that* version has been sadly overlooked. But even sadder, here's a version (1986) that is far better, and few people know it exists. (Just read some professional reviews on the internet, and they'll only mention two—the 1939 and 1995.) Perhaps that's because quite a few haven't read the novel, or just because it's a classic, dismiss it as "boring" and "irrelevant" to today's society. But for those of us who have read the novel and loved it, this is by far the best movie of "The Little Princess" made. It doesn't rely on special effect interludes, like the 1995 one, or cute little song and dance sessions like movie of 1939. Here we just get the story as it is with all the characters presented in exactly the way the novel depicts them. Amelia Shankley did a wonderful job as Sara Crewe. She looked dark, thin and solemn, just as described in the novel, and acted quiet and wise as well. In fact, all the actors and actresses did a good job. Even if Lottie didn't look quite the way as described, she acted it out so well that it didn't matter at all. And that goes for everybody else who's in this. I watched this with my mother and she agreed that it was very well done, and that all the children were quite appealing. As well, the sets and costumes were not too bold, like in the 1995 version (can you tell I didn't like that one?). *Sara's surroundings are supposed to look drab and grey.* If you've never seen a version of "The Little Princess" or read the book—obviously read the novel first, then see this one. But if the thought of Frances Hodgson Burnett's lovely story doesn't appeal to you, then by all means, see the others. In general, I love BBC productions of novels, because of their faithfulness to the original stories, and because of their length. (My favourite BBC miniseries of a novel would have to be the 1978 "Wuthering Heights"—exactly like the novel, to the T. Make every possible effort to see that if you've read the book.[15])

tcurry. Houston, TX. Date: June 1, 2000. Summary: Way too long.

Let me first say that I like "The Little Princess." I adore both the 1939 and 1995 versions, but this one was just too long. They could have cut out much of it and still been faithful to the book. Nothing much seemed to happen, it was so long! Most, but not every actor was convincing (Nigel Havers and Amelia Shankley were excellent). Shirley Temple, Liesel Matthews and Amelia Shankley (this version) are all convincing as the kind-hearted but strong-willed Sara, which was exactly what Sara was. Forget the separate nuances, that Shirley Temple was too "cute" or snotty (she was never that). No movie has to be "completely" faithful to its book. But if you feel it has to be, you'll be disappointed more often than satisfied, and that's unnecessary. But too much length is bad for any movie. The film was well-executed, and the sets were realistic but mostly unattractive. I would have given it a much higher rating if it wasn't so long. 4/10.[16]

NOTES

1. Frances Hodgson Burnett, *A Little Princess, Being the Whole Story of Sara Crewe Now Told for the First Time* (London: Warne, n.d.), 158.

2. Burnett, *A Little Princess*, 180.

3. Hamida Bosmajian, "Nightmares of History—The Outer Limits of Children's Literature," *Children's Literature Association Quarterly* 8, no. 4 (Winter 1983): 20.

4. Elizabeth Lennox Keyser, "'The Whole of the Story': Frances Hodgson Burnett's *A Little Princess*," in *Triumphs of the Spirit in Children's Literature*, ed. Francelia Butler and Robert Rotert, 232 (Hamden, CT: Library Professional Publications, 1986).

5. Manisha Mirchandani, "Colonial Discourse and 'Post'-Colonial Negotiations: *A Little Princess* and Its Adaptations." *New Literature Review* 33 (1997): 11.

6. Mirchandani, "Colonial Discourse," 12.

7. Keyser, "'The Whole of the Story," 240–41.

8. Mirchandani, "Colonial Discourse," 21.

9. Mirchandani, "Colonial Discourse," 21.

10. Mirchandani, "Colonial Discourse," 16.

11. The Internet Movie Database. December 21, 2004. Accessed May 18, 2004 www.imdb.com/title/tt0031580/usercomments-15.

12. The Internet Movie Database. December 21, 2004. Accessed May 18, 2004 www.imdb.com/title/tt0031580/usercomments-14.

13. The Internet Movie Database. December 21, 2004. Accessed May 18, 2004 www.imdb.com/title/tt0113670/usercomments-62.

14. The Internet Movie Database. December 21, 2004. Accessed May 18, 2004 www.imdb.com/title/tt0113670/usercomments-58.

15. The Internet Movie Database. December 21, 2004. Accessed May 18, 2004 www.imdb.com/title/tt0090474/usercomments-6.
16. The Internet Movie Database. December 21, 2004. Accessed May 18, 2004 www.imdb.com/title/tt0090474/usercomments-4.

• *14* •

Discovering the Fiction of Frances Hodgson Burnett

Deborah Fox Bellew

Have you ever wondered what sort of romantic stories Sara Crewe may have shared with her enthralled audience in *A Little Princess*? Or what kind of books a Victorian lady like Colin's mother may have enjoyed in her *Secret Garden*? Some Frances Hodgson Burnett fans may not know that their favorite author wrote many stories in addition to her most famous works *The Secret Garden*, *A Little Princess*, and *Little Lord Fauntleroy*.

More than one hundred works are known, some meant for adults and some for children. While many were novella length or shorter, some were long enough to fill multiple volumes. Her twin specialties were romantic fiction and children's stories, but she wrote with skill and sophistication on many topics. Burnett was a great success in her own day as both a serious and as a popular author; though proud of her work, she considered many of her earliest efforts simply part of "her writing-for-remuneration past, which she wished to move beyond."[1] What all her writings have in common, aside from being mostly out-of-print today, is how extremely enjoyable they are to read. Burnett wrote best seller after best seller for a devoted mass audience for more than fifty years, and as she herself said, "With the best that was in me I have tried to write more happiness into the world."[2]

Fortunately, with a bit of research, Frances Hodgson Burnett's lesser-known stories are still accessible today. Here are some techniques for locating and acquiring these treasures based on my experience reading, collecting, and enjoying her fiction for fifteen years.

WHAT IS AVAILABLE?

Frances Hodgson Burnett published her fiction as books, magazine articles, and plays. An important first step to discovering her work is to learn what she actually wrote. There is no one definitive bibliography covering all forms of her fiction, which adds a treasure-hunt quality to the search for her publications.

Between 1877 and 1924, Burnett published approximately fifty-five books in America, most of which were published in England as well. Several good bibliographies of these books exist, both published and online. The most thorough book bibliography can be found in Ann Thwaite's *Waiting for the Party: The Life of Frances Hodgson Burnett*. Many books can also be found in the online Library of Congress catalog at www.loc.gov and in the Bodleian Library at Oxford at www.odl.ox.ac.uk.

During roughly the same time period (1868–1924), Burnett is also known to have published at least 121 magazine stories and articles, of which only 78 were later published in book or collection form. These magazines are now one of the few ways to access some of her more obscure titles. Academic research to date has focused almost exclusively on her books; no thorough published magazine bibliography exists. Some notable articles are listed in Gretchen Holbrook Gerzina's *Frances Hodgson Burnett: The Unexpected Life of the Author of The Secret Garden*. I have created a bibliography myself, available online at http://groups.yahoo.com/group/FrancesHodgsonBurnett/, which I update frequently as I discover new stories.

Burnett also published several plays, which are listed in the biographies by Gretchen Holbrook Gerzina and Ann Thwaite. However, not all her plays were actually sold to the public. Stand-alone copies of those that were published occasionally surface at used and rare bookstores.

For all of these forms, there are four major sources: free online versions, in-print books, out-of-print books, and out-of-print magazines.

Please note: other Burnett items that may potentially interest collectors include modern illustrated editions of her best-known stories, movies based on her works, dolls and collectibles based on her characters, personal and business letters, published poetry, photographs,

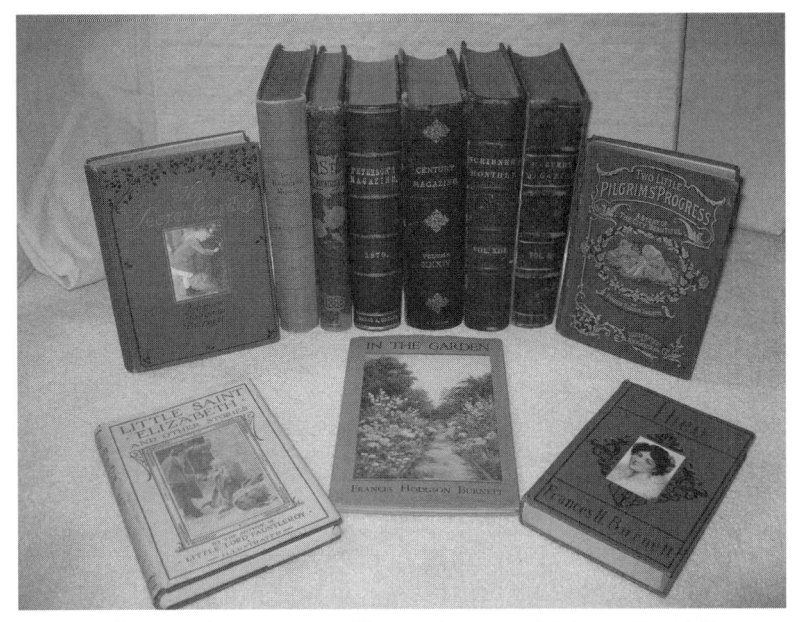

14.1 Collection of magazines and books. Courtesy of Deborah Fox Bellew.

foreign-language editions, reviews of her works, programs and posters from her plays, and so forth. In this essay I focus exclusively on her prose: fiction and articles.

Finding the Stories: Free Sources

Because most of Burnett's stories went out of print more than fifty years ago, her lesser-known titles are unlikely still to be on the shelf at your local library. University libraries may have some in their stacks (often you can search a library's collection online in advance to see if a trip is warranted) but unless you are affiliated with the institution you may not be able to check your finds out. Increasingly, the easiest and least expensive way to find Burnett stories is on the World Wide Web. There are a variety of websites devoted to preserving literature, notably Project Gutenberg at www.gutenberg.org. As of this writing, this site has twenty-one of her books available. The University of Virginia has a similar project (at http://etext.lib.virginia.edu), and the two sites are linked.

Other online sources can be found by entering "Frances Hodgson Burnett online books" into a search engine. Individual titles may be searched for in the same manner.

The advantage of online books, of course, is that these stories are easily accessible: no rummaging through used books, no driving to a bookstore or library, and no waiting for a book to be delivered. The service is free and the books can be read on-screen or printed to be perused at leisure. These works are in the public domain and can thus be freely distributed; you can send a link to a friend if you want to share a story. Some online sites such as University of Virginia even include the original illustrations.

On the other hand, simply reading the words on a screen or a printout cannot capture the full flavor of the era as compared to holding a Victorian or Edwardian book in your hands—the same book, perhaps, that one of Burnett's contemporaries held and enjoyed. With a tangible book, you can see the slightly faded cover art and perhaps a former owner's signature in old-fashioned writing, or an inscription from a loving parent or friend. They can be a very fast read as well: Burnett's novellas were often printed in somewhat large type with wide margins in order to fill a book, which means that it can be disconcerting to see how brief a story appears when viewed on a monitor or printed on ordinary paper.

Online fiction currently available as of December 2005 includes these books: *The Dawn of a To-morrow*, *Emily Fox-Seton* (*The Making of a Marchioness* and *The Methods of Lady Walderhurst*), *A Fair Barbarian*, *The Head of the House of Coombe*, *His Grace of Osmonde*, *In the Closed Room*, *A Lady of Quality*, *The Land of the Blue Flower*, *The Little Hunchback Zia*, *Little Lord Fauntleroy*, *A Little Princess*, *Little Saint Elizabeth and Other Stories*, *The Lost Prince*, *My Robin*, *Racketty-Packetty House*, *Sara Crewe*, *The Secret Garden*, *The Shuttle*, *T. Tembarom*, and *The White People* and these stories: "Esmeralda," "Lodusky," "Mère Giraud's Little Daughter," "Le Monsieur De La Petite Dame," "One Day at Arle," "The Plain Miss Burnie," "Smethurstses," "Surly Tim's Trouble," and "The Woman Who Saved Me." The play *The Little Princess* and the poem "What the Pug Knew" can also be found online.

Finding the Stories: In-Print Books

Little Lord Fauntleroy, *A Little Princess*, and *The Secret Garden* have never gone out of print. These can be found at all types of booksellers ranging from superstores to airport gift shops. Until recently, though, most other Burnett titles were not available. Fortunately, some of her other books are being brought back into print. While these may not be on the shelf at your local bookstore, they can be ordered for you by the bookseller or purchased from online book dealers.

Most online booksellers offer a search feature that permits you to find all their Burnett titles. Some are even available as downloadable "ebooks" or as audio books. However, do note that in the case of Burnett's stories, books in print are not necessarily cheaper than used copies. In particular, the rarer reprinted titles may even cost more than an ordinary new book due to the small print runs.

Some current publishers include Persephone Books, which recently published *The Making of a Marchioness*, and Books for Libraries Press, which offers *Jarl's Daughter and Other Stories*. The Kessinger Publishing Company has recently issued paperback versions of more than a dozen of the online titles listed above.

Finding the Stories: Out-of-Print Books

The most typical way to find Burnett's out-of-print books is to search secondhand book stores, either online or in person. An acquaintance once asked me, "Why buy an old book when you can get a new one?" I believe that owning a used book brings you closer to Burnett's world, with the decorative covers, quaint illustrations, antique advertisements in the back, and period typescript. Some collectors prefer books in pristine condition so they can feel as if they are the very first owner. I personally like to find a book that contains a previous owner's handwritten name and date, ideally a copy published during Burnett's lifetime, as it helps me imagine the era and bring home the sense of the book's age.

For me, shopping in person in used bookstores is the most satisfying way to add to my collection. There is the thrill of discovery while searching among the shelves, and, because of the sheer quantity of Burnett books that were printed, it is not too hard to find her most popular titles. *The Shuttle*, for example, was a best seller of 1907 and is still widely available. Furthermore, Burnett is famous enough that many booksellers will be able to direct you easily to the appropriate shelves if they have anything in stock. Depending on age, scarcity, and condition, used copies of her books frequently cost the same as or less than what you would pay for a new book. And it is satisfying to be able to hold the book in your own hands while you decide on it rather than relying on a written description in a catalog or website.

As you get further into collecting, you may no longer be able to find titles easily in stores. You may be tempted to overpay for a rickety book because you wonder if you will ever see that title again. In this case, online purchases are extremely convenient. The book that you have been hoping to find may be waiting for you in a shop nearby, across the country, or around the world—all you need to do is tell the seller and it can be mailed to your door. Comparing prices and overall condition is quicker online as well, even though you can't hold the book before buying it. I find it much easier to walk away from an overpriced book if I have invested only moments in finding it rather than years.

Wish lists or book-finding services can be a great convenience for those who do not frequently check their book sources: your favorite shop owner or online service simply contacts you when your book surfaces, and any associated fee or markup is worth the convenience. However, since I shop the same sources frequently myself, I omit this service for fear of accidentally introducing a middleman, and a price increase, into my transaction.

One other useful source for rare Burnett books is online auction sites. I have found these to have the most unusual items; most of the special treasures in my collection were found on these sites. The items offered change every day, more frequently than in other bookstores, so persistence is a must. The prices may surpass those at bookstores (sometimes in the last few moments of the auction) but occasionally there are bargains. I have found the built-in peer-review systems to be effective in determining if a seller will follow through on a sale. However, it is important to use caution, as those who are selling the books are very rarely experts (and if they are, they may price the book so similarly to online bookstores that you may as well buy it there). Treat with a grain of salt any claims of *"true* first edition," "very rare," "fine condition," and so forth. Also pay attention to what is unsaid: if someone rhapsodizes about the period advertisements in the back of the book without describing the text itself in detail, it may mean that the book is in such poor condition that only the ads are salvageable—or only the detached pages may be for sale rather than the whole book. Sellers also may not be experienced in interpreting versions: if someone says "first edition," this could mean the first printing, but it could also mean a much later reprint that happens to include the text of the first edition. Ask questions well ahead of the end of the auction and request a photo if one is not shown. For example, an occasional seller might not think to mention whether a book is actually an ex-library book, which decreases its resale value (if this is important to you). One person's "very good" condition may be another person's "poor" condition, so it is best to be as certain as possible before bidding.

With any collecting of old books, regardless of venue, buyers need to be aware of relative prices in order to recognize bargains and to avoid significant overpayments. The Internet is a great tool for research even for those who prefer to buy in person. Especially if you have a particular title in mind, it is worth taking a few minutes to visit a good online used book site to find out how many copies are offered and to assess the overall price range. Continuing with the example above, one online bookseller currently lists over one hundred copies of *The Shuttle* priced at $20 or less. Thus, I know that if I see a much more expensive copy I should ask if there is anything extraordinary about it—perhaps an inscription or a dust jacket. If an item is in fact mis-priced, the staff at the bookstore is often willing to negotiate because they do not want to keep the book on their shelves indefinitely. I myself am willing to pay somewhat more for a book I find in person because I don't need to pay shipping (and because I know I won't need to send it back); however, if I discover later that I paid two or three times the going rate, some of the book's luster seems to wear off.

A full discussion of used book pricing is beyond the scope of this essay, but briefly, expect to pay more for a book that includes any or all of the following characteristics: first edition, fine (just-off-the-press) condition, original dust jacket, author's autograph or inscription, and/or illustrations. A book with all of these characteristics can be extremely expensive relative to a "reading" (just passable) copy. Conversely, aspects that make a book more affordable though less "collectible" include anything that distances the book from its appearance when first sold: later edition, more battered condition, missing dust jacket (if one was originally present), marks in the book made by someone other than the author (such as library markings), and torn or missing pages or illustrations. There are exceptions but these are general guidelines. You may wish to buy an inexpensive copy at first and upgrade it later. Most important is that the text be intact and legible;

nothing is more frustrating than reading a good book only to discover that the final pages are missing.

Finding the Stories: Out-of-Print Magazines

My favorite way to read Burnett's stories is in their original magazine form. This is not a common way to read or collect her works but I find it extremely rewarding. Virtually all her stories were serialized first, so these periodicals can be thought of as "pre-first editions" that anticipate the books. The serialized versions sometimes differ slightly from the revised book text and can provide a careful reader with additional insight into the story. Even more significant to dedicated Burnett fans is the fact that some stories appear in magazine form only, so even if you have finished all her books, there are still more treats in store. To my knowledge, there is no complete list of her magazine articles and stories. Even Burnett herself may not have kept track of them, since she did not consider all of them her best work.[3] She was a very prolific author: so far I have counted 121 articles in nineteen magazines, 43 of which do not appear in any other published book or collection.

There are many advantages to reading her stories in magazine form. First, if you have access to a large library the magazines may already be there for you to consult—call ahead or check online to find out. Libraries frequently acquired bound volumes, so well-known journals like *Godey's Ladies Book*, *Scribner's*, *Harper's*, and *Peterson's* may still be available on the shelves or via interlibrary loan. If they are no longer in the stacks in book form they may be available on microfiche or microfilm. You can read them on the screen or even take the story home for the nominal cost of a printout or copy.

Another advantage of bound magazines is that, if you wish to own the stories, they are relatively cost-efficient. Though they often cost three to five times as much as a typical book from the period in comparable condition, they contain much more text. A single volume generally includes six or twelve months' worth of articles by a variety of authors, which, if published separately, would have made up dozens of books. For some of the more obscure titles, it is less expensive to buy the more common magazine version than to find the stand alone book. If you prefer to own individual issues of a magazine rather than a weighty tome, these are generally inexpensive and often have the advantage of including colorful cover art (generally not present in bound volumes), though, with paper covers only, they may be more fragile.

A magazine provides context, showing how the stories were originally experienced. The advertisements, the type styles and layout, and the surrounding non-Burnett stories evoke the target audience of Victorian and Edwardian readers. Such intriguing extras as fashion plates are included in *Peterson's* and *Godey's* along with dressmaking hints and patterns. The magazines may include illustrative drawings or engravings of Burnett's characters that were never included in the stories' later book form—and don't forget to check the magazine's frontispiece.

Other interesting Burnett-related pieces can also be found in magazines. After she became an established celebrity, reviews of her books and plays as well as profiles of her life begin to appear side by side with her fiction. She also wrote nonfiction pieces, accounts of interesting events in her past and tributes to other authors. Occasionally you can find pieces written by her first husband, Swan, or her son Vivian. In *St. Nicholas* children's magazine of 1888, there is even a piece called "The Dogs of Mrs. Frances Hodgson Burnett," in which she reminisces about her childhood pets.[4]

Finding Burnett stories in magazines is not always easy. The partial lists of published magazine articles are helpful but not complete, and further searching is time-consuming. Some bound magazines include a table of contents or an index, but others require laborious page-by-page checking to see if any of her stories are present. She was not always credited as "Frances Hodgson Burnett" either: in her first published story in *Godey's*, she used the pseudonym "The Second," in her second *Peterson's* story she was simply "The Author of the Modern Sir Launcelot," and prior to her marriage in 1874 she was credited as "Fannie Hodgson."

Acquiring the appropriate issues offers its own set of challenges. Not all magazines are readily available for sale at all times. When a candidate magazine is offered for sale, be mindful that other collectors may be interested for completely different reasons and this will be factored into the pricing. For example, two different issues of the *Children's Magazine* containing Burnett stories were simultaneously offered on an auction site. I was able to purchase one at a reasonable price, but the other sold for more than ten times that amount because it also contained an Oz story and thus attracted L. Frank Baum collectors. Another magazine was priced comparably to others even though it was in poor condition, since the seller was targeting collectors of antique advertisements and not collectors of the articles themselves. Magazines may be sold and dismantled by collectors of fashion plates, paper dolls, and cover art, all of which can be resold separately. Be aware of whether the magazine you are purchasing has had pages taken out. There is nothing wrong with buying a magazine from which the fashion plates have been removed but you should not be expected to pay the same price as if it were completely intact.

I locate candidate magazines by following biography references, researching the references at the library, and periodically checking online auctions. For example, in his biography *The Romantick Lady*, Vivian Burnett listed *Peterson's Magazine* as a place in which his mother frequently published, but he did not include many story titles. I went to the library and used their free resources to determine which particular months contained her stories. For those I chose to acquire, I used online bookstores (for bound volumes) and online auction sites (for either bound volumes or loose issues). I have been searching these sources for five years and though I am far from having a complete list of her writings, I always get a thrill of discovery when I find something new.

CONCLUSION

Whatever means you use to discover Frances Hodgson Burnett's extensive fiction, I hope you find it as enjoyable to discover and read as I have. There are benefits to all of the methods described above. Her little-known stories transport you to her world and time, and I trust that, having read some of them, you will have a richer sense of her writing when you do return to your long-time favorites.

NOTES

1. Gretchen Holbrook Gerzina, *Frances Hodgson Burnett: The Unexpected Life of the Author of* The Secret Garden (New Brunswick, NJ: Rutgers University Press, 2004), 71.

2. Vivian Burnett, *The Romantick Lady (Frances Hodgson Burnett): The Life Story of an Imagination* (New York: Charles Scribner's Sons, 1927), 409–10.
3. Gerzina, *Frances Hodgson Burnett*, 70–71.
4. Gertrude Van R. Wickham, "Dogs of Noted Americans," *St. Nicholas* (June 1888): 598–600.

• 15 •

The Frances Hodgson Burnett Online Discussion Group: A Modern History

Diana Birchall

The Frances Hodgson Burnett conference at California State University, Fresno, in April 2003 was so historic, so stimulating, such a heady gathering of scholars, authors, readers, and fans, that many participants felt that the excitement and sense of connection, the feeling of community in Frances Hodgson Burnett studies, should continue. It seemed time for the formation of a Frances Hodgson Burnett Society—but as conference attendees and Burnett lovers are so far-flung, and the era so electronic, it was decided to create an online literary group that would serve as a sort of worldwide Burnett bulletin board. As I had several years' experience participating in other online literary discussion groups, notably those devoted to Jane Austen, I volunteered to get the Frances Hodgson Burnett discussion group up and running.

This online group is one of thousands of Yahoo Groups sites, and can be found by going to http://groups.yahoo.com/group/FrancesHodgsonBurnett/. The archives are open to all members, containing all the messages members have sent to the list since the group's inception, in April, 2003. At the start, of course, there was an excited flurry of messages, with people introducing each other and discussing their favorite Burnett books. In time, the first burst of discussion died down, and the list subsided into less activity. Many such lists fade away into nonexistence, but this is not what happened with our Burnett list. Although not as incessantly busy as some lists, it remains reassuringly healthy, and very true to its purpose: it serves as a central place where people interested in Burnett can introduce themselves at any time, comment on having read a book or seen a filmed version of one of her stories, ask questions, make announcements of new books and conferences, and generally keep in touch. The group remains functional and active enough so that its membership has never dropped; there are over fifty members at present, and whenever anything new or interesting happens in the Burnett world, someone will always bring it to the attention of the list. If nothing else, it has proved to be a useful bulletin board tool for social and academic purposes; but it is more than that, for some fascinating and useful discussions have taken place on this list, as an examination of its archives and a review of its history will show.

After the first flurry of introductions and the posting of a bibliography of Burnett's works, we moved into an introductory discussion of which books were favorites, which ones we'd read, and which we wanted to read. There was a strong feeling that members, who were nearly all thoroughly familiar with *The Secret Garden* and *A Little Princess*, were extremely interested in reading some of Burnett's adult novels. The first one we discussed was *Robin*, which several people named as a favorite, but which many had never read before, and the connection between *Robin* and *The Head of the House of Coombe* was explained, as the two were originally serialized together. It was an important moment when Gretchen Hodgson Gerzina joined the list; she had been the keynote speaker at the conference, and at that point her epochal new biography of Burnett was still forthcoming and eagerly awaited. With her extensive knowledge of her subject, Gretchen has continued to be a most helpful and gracious explainer, elucidator, and reference point, throughout the list's existence.

The list took a detour from literary matters with a discussion of the Frances Hodgson Burnett/Secret Garden portion of Central Park, and the Frances Hodgson Burnett Memorial Fountain, a sculpture depicting characters from *The Secret Garden*. Penny Deupree, great-granddaughter of Frances, came on the list to describe how her mother, Verity Burnett, dedicated the statue with the sculptor, Bessie Onahotema Potter Vonnoh, and Mayor La Guardia, in 1927. I made a point of visiting the lovely fountain in New York the following spring, when it was surrounded by very Burnettian flowers, and placed a photograph in the list's photo section.

Book discussions continued, with *The Secret Garden* as the main subject for some time. There was a lively examination of Anglo Indian themes in the book, of the filmed versions and allusions in books like Noel Streatfeild's *The Painted Garden*; Burnett's love for flowers, and her ability to write Yorkshire dialect were discussed; and the sequel *Misselthwaite* was thoroughly disparaged (if not roasted). I brought up links between Burnett's writing and Jane Austen's, and Judy Geater in England and Cédric Barbé in France mentioned Dickens's influence on Burnett; Cédric posted his notes on the topic in French! *The Lost Prince* was discussed next, followed by *Little Lord Fauntleroy*, which involved a minute examination of fashions in boys' clothing of the era, to which Angelica Carpenter contributed, with quotes from Alison Lurie. *T. Tembarom* was read and discussed with a feeling of excitement and discovery by many members who had not encountered this stirring tale before, and as many were delighted by *The Making of a Marchioness* and its sequel, *The Methods of Lady Walderhurst*, published in a single volume by Persephone Press, for which Gretchen Gerzina wrote the afterword.

At Christmas 2003, Cédric gave us a wonderful gift from Paris—a series of photographs of 16, rue Christophe Colomb, the house in which Burnett lived in 1890 when she was in Paris, and where, sadly, her son Lionel died. News was posted on the list in February 2004 of the liquidation of the Country House Association, that meant that Great Maytham Hall, the fine Sir Edwin Lutyens house which Burnett once owned, was to be sold. *That Lass o' Lowrie's* was discussed and *Memoirs of a London Doll* described. The next great event was the Children's Literature Association conference organized by Angelica and held in Fresno June 10–12, 2004. Many speakers and attendees from the Burnett conference of a little more than a year before, were at this one too, including Gretchen Gerzina, Sally Stokes (speaking on Noel Streatfeild), and Peter Hanff of the Bancroft Library at Berkeley (speaking on Lewis Carroll), and myself, a happy spectator. This was quite a reunion of the first Burnett event, and there was much discussion of the conference on the list. Gretchen Gerzina's book, *Frances Hodgson Burnett: The Unexpected Life of the Author of* The Secret Garden, was published at about the time of the conference, and members of the list eagerly obtained their copies and happily buried their noses in it, thoroughly relishing Gretchen's scholarship and insight, with the eyes of connoisseurs and the pleasant feeling that inside knowledge brings.

Throughout the life of this online group, people's paths have kept crossing, information has been exchanged, and friends made. For example, Ellen Jordan of the University of Newcastle in Australia posted on the Girls Own list reflections on Mrs. Craven's possible pregnancy, and the similarity of her death to that of a character in a book by Charlotte Yonge, *The Clever Woman of the Family*. This material made its way to our list, with its description of Burnett as a literary magpie. And, only this September, Ellen passed through Los Angeles en route between Washington and Australia, and she and I spent a happy day like magpies ourselves, picking over my books, particularly my precious pile of Burnetts, discussing Burnett, Yonge, Austen, Gaskell, Delafield, Gissing, and others of our favorite writers, "con amore" indeed (as was once said about Yonge talking about Austen).

A list high point was reached when members read and discussed *The Shuttle*, clearly a strong favorite, which might possibly be reissued by Persephone, having been proposed to an editor there by list member Elaine Simpson-Long. There were side discussions of authors such as Jean Webster and Gene Stratton Porter, of "middlebrow" authors and the categorization of Burnett as such. Elaine and Lynne Hatwell reported on the Persephone Weekend held at Newnham College, Cambridge, in September 2004, which sounded little short of divine. Updates on Great Maytham Hall; Burnett books for sale on eBay; reports on visits to Burnett sites; discussions of tea, servants, sequels, movie reviews; and the feelings of children in Victorian times have all been topics addressed in lively if somewhat scattered and periodic fashion on this list.

Recently, the list helped forge the way to an exciting discovery. I had known that my grandmother, Onoto Watanna, the first Asian American novelist,[1] was a guest at Mark Twain's seventieth birthday party at the Delmonico in New York, a glittering event attended by 170 celebrities, mostly of the literary world—including Frances Hodgson Burnett. I had read the description of the dinner in *Harper's Weekly* for December 23, 1905, but it was brought to my attention by a friend in Montreal, Professor Greg Robinson, that there was a supplement containing photos of each of the tables. That meant if the very rare supplement could be located, we might gaze upon photos of both my grandmother and Burnett, in addition to a cornucopia of fascinating celebrities. Enter Peter Hanff and the Bancroft Library,

15.1   Frances Hodgson Burnett (far left) at Mark Twain's seventieth birthday party with Carolyn Wells (center) and Robert Louis Stevenson's stepson Lloyd Osbourne (far right). This photograph was originally published in the "Mark Twain's 70th Birthday/Souvenir of Its Celebration" Supplement to Harper's Weekly *49, no. 2557 (December 23, 1905), p. 1900. Courtesy of the Mark Twain Papers, the Bancroft Li-*

with its famous collection of Mark Twain Papers. I had only to ask, and have: Peter and Robert Hirst, Curator of the Papers, found the supplement and scanned beautiful prints of the pertinent photographs. I have now seen my grandmother, age thirty, radiantly lovely and hiding a nine-month pregnancy under the table while wearing an elaborate period gown—and, in a different picture (see figure 15.1) Burnett, then fifty-six, laced into an elaborate frou-frou ruffled gown herself, sitting somberly, a little apart from the elegant personages at her table. These pictures and others are a marvelous glimpse into the past, for which I am very grateful to Peter and Robert. And so the list continues its useful, diverting, semi-scholarly and enormously entertaining Internet existence, for the pleasure and use of all discerning readers who love the works of Frances Hodgson Burnett.

The list can be reached by going to www.yahoogroups.com, typing in "FrancesHodgsonBurnett" as one word, and then clicking the option to join.

NOTE

1. Amy Ling, "Teaching Asian American Literature," *The Heath Anthology of American Literature Newsletter Online*, no. IX, (Spring 1993), www.georgetown.edu/tamlit/newsletter/9/Ling.htm (accessed September 29, 2005).

· 16 ·

Keeper of the Keys

Gretchen Holbrook Gerzina Interviews Penny Deupree

Editor's note: The interview took place on April 21, 2003, at a garden party, the final event of a conference organized by Angelica Carpenter, "Frances Hodgson Burnett: Beyond the Secret Garden," at California State University, Fresno.

Gretchen Holbrook Gerzina [to the audience]: This is such a treat for us to be able to stand up together. Before we came, we were trying to plan how we would give a talk at a brunch in a garden, and we decided that the best way would be an interview format, so that's what we're going to do. I will ask Penny some questions that I'm sure all of you would like to ask of Frances Hodgson Burnett's great-granddaughter.

Before I do that, we have some thanks, too. I particularly want to thank not only the organizers of this wonderful weekend but also those who have been the seminal people working on Frances's work, whose work really inspired all of us to do the kind of work we've been able to do. I'd particularly like to thank Ann Thwaite for her marvelous and ground-breaking biography of Frances Hodgson Burnett, *Waiting for the Party*. Her work was the foundation for so many of us. Thanks to Phyllis Bixler, too, whose critical work on Frances has inspired so many of us, judging by the number of people who quoted her in their presentations, and I know Penny has some people she'd like to thank as well.

Penny Deupree: Well, first of all I want to thank Angelica for including Tom [Penny's husband] and me in this conference and for inviting us non-scholars to join you. My Secret Garden is overflowing with new buds and sprouts that I'm excited to explore. Thank you for including us.

Gerzina: Penny, you are in the incredible position of being the repository of all things Frances Hodgson Burnett, I think, in the world, and I certainly would not have been unable to write my biography without your help and without the family materials you shared. I wonder, what was your first encounter with Frances and how did you come to know about her works and her life?

Deupree: The first thing I remember was having my parents read me *Little Lord Fauntleroy*. Not much else was mentioned about her—I know that's hard for you to understand—but Frances was really never talked about in my home, and so it took me a lot of research to figure out who she was and why she was part of our life. I did know that she wrote three books: *The Secret Garden, Little Lord Fauntleroy,* and *A Little Princess.* And when I was a child, that was basically all I knew.

Gerzina: Why? Why didn't your family talk about her?

Deupree: Well, mostly because she lived such an accelerated life. She did things that weren't really normal for the time, and I think that she just had to stay in the closet, so to speak, for a couple of generations. In 1975 I received Frances in a box—about four or five boxes, actually—of letters, papers, books, newspaper articles, and photographs that came from my mother's house. When my parents got divorced, Mother sent me all this stuff and it came as a total surprise—I had no concept that it had been in our home as I was growing up. I do recall as a young child being dressed in a velvet suit. My hair was long then, and I remember a photograph, but I have never been able to find it in the family pictures, and since I have all of those now, I think it is lost.

Gerzina: You discovered all of those materials and you are still in the process of discovering them, but I wonder what it has meant to you to be the person who knew very little about Frances, but who has become the keeper of the legacy of Frances—not just in the way of the memories but in material objects, in the repository, and in keeping her legacy alive. What has that meant to you and how do you go about doing that?

Deupree: I think over the years I've realized what a big responsibility it is. I didn't understand at first. When the boxes were delivered, we happened to have guests that night, and one of them was a librarian who referred me to an elementary school librarian in our area. When I met him, he could not believe that I had received all these historical items and he said, "My third-grade teacher read us *The Secret Garden!* Would you come and give a lecture about Frances Hodgson Burnett?" I said that I would but that I didn't know much about her.

I did give a short lecture for his group and then another friend of mine belonged to an antique club that needed a speaker for their fall meeting. My daughter was in the seventh grade at this time. She and I spent the summer, one day a week, at the public library, doing research on Frances. I knew nothing about computers then but my daughter was just learning, so she did all the computer work. We found any information that we could and I know that all of you who have done research know that whatever you find gives you five more places to look, and those five send you to five more and those five send you to . . . it's endless, absolutely endless.

So eventually I worked up a lecture that I do in our area. I share it all the time. Every time a schoolteacher calls I say, "Yes, I'll be there," but first I have some requirements: the children have to have read the stories, either *The Secret Garden* or *Little Lord Fauntleroy*. I love going into the schools and I speak for a lot of women's groups, too.

My daughter and I even went to New York, to Long Island, where Frances lived, and I gave a lecture there when they dedicated a statue to her at the Manhasset Public Library. We've done research at the New York Public Library and we saw the statue in Central Park. We went to the archive at Princeton and they brought out three boxes full of stuff on carts. I went through one, my daughter went through the second, and Tom went through the third. I love sharing the information I've found—I feel like that's what I'm here for; and I do have a daughter who is about to have her first child. She could give the lectures as well as I do and I do believe that my husband could, too!

Gerzina: Could you please tell us a bit about the copyright issue? Of course Frances's books are out of copyright and the royalties are gone, but Frances herself was responsible for changing copyright law in England.

Deupree: Actually I still get the occasional royalty check for $2.50 from the Gloria Loomis agency! But to answer your question, at home I have a certificate that was given to Frances by a group of British authors after she won a landmark copyright case. This certificate is framed and it is too large to bring on a plane, but I do share it with the children in my local lectures.

Frances gave a gift to all authors by getting the British copyright law changed to a law that is still in effect today. This came about when she heard from a friend that someone had made a play out of *Little Lord Fauntleroy* and was about to open it in London. The news did not sit well with her, so she got on the train (because she was in Florence at the time), wrote her own version of *Little Lord Fauntleroy* on the trip, rented the hall across the street from this man, and sued him for copyright infringement. In the beginning he thought that he could handle her by cutting her in for a share of his profits, but she was outraged and she would not let the matter slide. Up until this time, British copyright laws were very vague about how books could be adapted into plays and they were also not well enforced. When Frances won her complaint against this man; his play had to close—she ran him out of town! This case gave judges a more specific set of rules to refer to in the future. The end result was that the copyright laws were, for the first time, enforceable, and after that, authors' works were protected.

Gerzina: It was really a legacy to all authors, and speaking of legacies, that bracelet really has a nice glint in the sunshine!

Deupree: Frances received this diamond bracelet as a thank you, along with the plaque, and I think that what she did is something that we for generations should be very grateful to her for doing.

Gerzina [to the audience]: At this point we have time for you to ask Penny questions about Frances and anything that you might like to know about, and this is our last chance to be together so why don't we open it up to questions from all of you?

Deborah Bellew: Did you ever get to know your grandfather at all?

Deupree: No, he died in 1937 and I'm not that old—but I'm getting there! Vivian was my grandfather. My mother was Verity, one of Vivian's two daughters, and Dorinda was the other. My Aunt Dorinda had no children and I am really the only one left in my family, so I have all the family heirlooms.

Angelica Carpenter: Are you planning to publish any of the letters, and did you find any unfinished manuscripts?

Deupree: I'm going to let other people tend to the publishing. One of my good friends was with me the night before I came here and she asked me, "When are you gong to write your book?" and I said "Not going to happen." Other people can do that. I don't have the resources. I do have a lot of the letters—I don't know, I hadn't even thought about that. As for unfinished manuscripts . . .

Gerzina: Frances knew the value of her work and she rarely wrote things that didn't get published. About a year ago I encountered a book dealer who had found three of her handwritten early stories. These have been bound and preserved with gilt lettering on the spine and the dealer wants $18,000 for them. Two of those stories have been published; one we have not yet been able to track down. As for the letters, of which there are many, many, many—these have not yet been published. Frances did have diaries and journals, and Vivian typed those up and attempted to publish her letters at one point, but he did not succeed. Who knows, maybe there will be more interest in this someday, especially if we can get a Burnett Society going.

Question from the audience: Penny, could you please tell us a bit about your personal life?

Deupree: My personal life . . . oh, my gosh! Okay, I am a mother of three. I've been married to a wonderful man for thirty-nine years this year. We are expecting grandchild number five any moment—if that had happened, Gretchen would have had to give this talk by herself! I have a home-based business as a Creative Memories consultant. These products help to preserve family memories in safe albums, and I have put my family photos into those albums that you have been looking at for the past two days.

I stay very busy with my grandchildren. I love children and I also love roses and gardens. I have a fabulous garden at home, not this fabulous, but I love it. Ann Thwaite talked about the cabinet that she saw at my grandmother's house in Boston—does anybody remember the cabinet that she talked about the other day? I have that cabinet at my home. It was my great grandmother's; it was Frances's. It's all hand-hewed, made in the 1500s is basically what the experts say. Frances used it in her parlor and actually my mother talked about seeing it there as a child. The bottom part was a dollhouse. I've had it refurbished and now it is filled with toys so it's back being used for grandchildren. So that's what I do. I love kids and I'm available for them any time.

Bellew: What is your favorite Burnett book?

Deupree: Oh, *A Little Princess*. The other ones are great but I just love *A Little Princess*.

Bellew: Why? Why is it your favorite?

Deupree: I don't know. I don't read consistently like all these scholars here, but it just took my interest and I could not put it down. I love *The Secret Garden*, too, because I'm such a gardener and I love the Earth and the dirt and—but I just was very enamored with that book. Ann?

Ann Thwaite: You said when you go into schools you make sure they've read *Little Lord Fauntleroy* or *The Secret Garden*—why not *A Little Princess*?

Deupree: Because normally the teachers don't have time to do all three, and I have so little on *A Little Princess* and so many visual things for the other two books that I recommend them first. I cover it at the end of my talk if I have time. My children's speech is very brief and by the end I can tell whether I have time to add more. The teachers have so little time to read one, let alone two, books so I also say to the teacher that if she doesn't have time to read both, to be sure to get the video and have the children see that because she can do that in a shorter amount of time. Then the children are at least familiar with Frances's work. When I speak for women's groups, I make sure that it is advertised that they need to re-read one of the books because I really think that my lectures are better if you know what I'm talking about.

Carpenter: What are some of the visual things you have for those books that you didn't bring here today?

Deupree: That was the hardest part—bringing or not bringing. I made one stack of things to bring and another of things I could not. I have lots of books in other languages, including a Japanese one that is absolutely fabulous, but I just didn't have room to bring those. My daughter and her husband spent three months in Turkey and I told her that the only thing she had to bring back was one book and she did—*Little Lord Fauntleroy* in Turkish.

The book that I brought that I love the most is a copy of *Little Lord Fauntleroy* that some of you saw at the library reception. The story on that book is cute: a man in our church came up to Tom and me at coffee hour and said, "Penny, you've got to come with me this afternoon. I was at a flea market over in Fort Worth and I found something that I know you will like." So I went. At this point I was just beginning to try to collect all the copies I possibly could of Frances's books. When I saw this *Little Lord Fauntleroy*, I realized that it was a first edition, first date, first issue, which is incredible to find, and it was also a signed copy, one of a thousand copies. The price tag on it was $750, which was not in my budget at that time. But I left my name and number and I did end up getting the book—from a flea market! I mean it was an antique flea market in the middle of nowhere, so I thought it was pretty amazing to find it there.

Keeper of the Keys 229

16.1 Artist Frank Ver Beck's drawing in Frances's guest book from Maytham Hall. Courtesy of the private collection of Penny Deupree.

Most of my collection came in those boxes from my mother. I didn't know what some of the stuff was, so my research has helped me to figure out why certain things had been saved, like a wooden book with leather straps to hold it together. This was the guest book that was at Maytham Hall during the years that Frances lived there. (See figure 16.1.) So if you were a visiting artist, you signed it, but you also did a piece of artwork in the book. If you were a musician or songwriter, then you wrote a sheet of music and then wrote the words for it on the other side. It's the most amazing artifact, all produced during the dates when she was there. One man did little caricatures of people who were there for the weekend. It's just amazing, absolutely amazing. But it's too fragile—I just couldn't bring it. What else?

Tom Deupree: What else is in the book?

Deupree: Oh, what else was in the book? Thank you, Tom. In it there was also a little sheet of paper that says, "Maytham Hall, Rolvendens," so it is nice to have the name of Maytham Hall on this. There is also a picture of a robin—I'm going to say it's a robin—a little bird, sitting on a branch and the caption says, "Thinking of his tea." This is from Henry James, so we immediately took that page out and framed it.

Gerzina: Well, we are just about out of time, so I'd like to close with a final question. Penny, what does a conference like this do for you? You have talked to scholars over the years and you have been so generous with people like me. [To the audience] When I thought that I was done with my research, I contacted Penny. Of course then there were three more years of work to come after that. Then I thought I was done again, and she called me up one day and said she'd found four more boxes of letters and was that going to be a problem. I said, "No, that's not a problem." But a conference like this has opened up the whole world of Frances, and I'd love to hear your response to what it has been like for you to see all these people who are studying her and caring so much about her work—not just her books for children but the work for adults, and the widening of the field now with the formation of a Frances Hodgson Burnett Society. You have been the keeper of the keys and the legend and the legacy—what does all of this do for you?

Deupree: Well, of course, I'm absolutely ecstatic. I just can't believe it, and I'm pinching myself that we have gotten to meet all the wonderful people whose work I have read. I am a nonscholar, so it has been fun just to communicate and hear their thoughts on things and everything that you have shared—I will say it again: my garden, my personal garden, is overflowing with ideas and I'm thrilled that we're all going to stay connected—that's what I'm excited about, because I did sit there thinking, "Why can't we have a Society?" so now it seems that we are going to have one and I think that will be the main way to keep everybody connected. Then the things that you find, things that you want to share, will be sent around to everybody so I'm no longer the only keeper. I get the physical things but then other people can get the other parts of it, too.

A Filmography of Motion Picture Adaptations of Frances Hodgson Burnett's Stories

Paul H. Frobose

This filmography of motion pictures derived from the novels, short stories, and plays of Frances Hodgson Burnett contains all of the known films and televison movies made through 1995. Information about the silent film productions has been gleaned from contemporary motion picture trade journals, reviews, biographies, and other accounts of the early period of American film making. The year given is the year the film was released, which may not necessarily be the year in which the film was produced. Cast lists and production credits may be incomplete, especially for the early movies. This survey was intended to be comprehensive, but it does not include foreign language films.

1914   *A Lady of Quality*
Famous Players Film Co.
Distribution: State Rights. Opened January 1, 1914
Producer: Daniel Frohman
Cast: Cecelia Loftus, Geraldine O'Brien, House Peters, Peter Lang, Hal Clarendon, Edna Weick, Roy Pilser, Dave Wall, Alexander Gaden, Henrietta Goodman
This picture marked the film debut of stage actress Cecelia Loftus, who continued to appear in silent films. House Peters went on to have a lengthy motion picture career, extending into the sound era. Famous Players Film Company was founded by Adolph Zukor, who provided the financial backing for its films. During the early years of the company, Zukor's name was conspicuously absent from film credits. Theatrical impresario Daniel Frohman

was given sole credit for the production of *A Lady of Quality*.

1914   *Little Lord Fauntleroy*
Kinemacolour [British]
Distribution: American opening, June 23, 1914
Producer: F. Martin Thornton
Cast: H. Agar Lyons, Fred Eustace, B. Murray, Edward Viner, Master Gerald Royston, Miss Jane Wells, Bernard Vaughan, Miss V. Osmond, Frank Strather, Master D. Callam, Harry Edwards
Most of the cast were veterans of the English stage. Bernard Vaughan enjoyed a long career as a film character actor. Gerald Royston appeared in only six films. This was Edward Viner's last film. The *New York Times* noted that the film "followed very closely the original story." Although released in June 1914 in the United States, this film may have been shot prior to Famous Players' *A Lady of Quality*, perhaps in late 1913.

1915   *The Pretty Sister of José*
Famous Players Film Co.
Distribution: Paramount Pictures. Opened May 31, 1915
Producer: Daniel Frohman
Cast: Marguerite Clark, Jack Pickford, Edythe Chapman, Gertrude Norman, William Lloyd, Rupert Julian, Teddy Simpson, Dick Rosson
Jack (Mary's brother) Pickford starred in many silent films in which he played juvenile leads. In the mid-1920s his career faltered and he became a victim of drugs and alcohol at an early age. Rupert Julian also wrote and directed films during the silent era. Stage-trained Marguerite Clark went on to considerable success as a motion picture actress.

1915   *The Dawn of a Tomorrow*
Famous Players Film Co.
Distribution: Paramount Pictures. Opened June 7, 1915
Producer: Daniel Frohman
Director: James Kirkwood

Scenario: Eve Unsell
Cast: Mary Pickford, David Powell, Forrest Robinson, Robert Cain, Margaret Seddon, Blanche Craig, Ogden Childe
Critics and audiences loved Mary Pickford as Glad, the optimistic London slum child. The film proved so popular that Paramount actually re released in 1919. James Kirkwood directed Mary Pickford in several films for Famous Players including *Mistress Nell, Cinderella, Little Pal, Esmeralda,* and *Rags.*

1915 *Esmeralda*
Famous Players Film Co.
Distribution: Paramount Pictures. Opened September 6, 1915
Producer: Daniel Frohman
Director: James Kirkwood
Camera: Emmett A. Williams
Cast: Mary Pickford, Ida Waterman, Fuller Mellish, Arthur Hoops, William Buckley, Charles Waldron
This is one of Hollywood's many "lost films," and perhaps it is better this way. Critics found little merit in this production, which some considered beneath Mary Pickford's talents.

1916 *Secret Love* [**Adapted from** *That Lass o' Lowrie's*]
Bluebird Photoplays [Universal]
Distribution: Universal. Opened in January 1916
Producer: Carl Laemmle
Director: Robert Leonard
Scenario: Robert Leonard
Cast: Jack Curtis, Helen Ware, Dixey Carr, Harry Carey, Harry Carter, Marc Robbins, Harry Southard, Warren Ellsworth, Ella Hall, Willis Marks, Lule Warrenton
Rugged Harry Carey was a contract player for Universal when tapped for the part of Fergus Derrick, the future husband of Joan Lowrie (Helen Ware).

1917 *A Little Princess*
Mary Pickford Film Corp.
Distribution: Artcraft Pictures. Opened November 5, 1917

Producer: Mary Pickford
Director: Marshall Neilan
Assistant Directors: Nat Deverich and Howard Hawks [uncredited]
Scenario: Frances Marion
Camera: Walter Strading
Cast: Mary Pickford, Norman Kerry, Katherine Griffith, Ann Schaefer, Zasu Pitts, William E. Lawrence, Theodore Roberts, Gertrude Short, Gustav Von Seyffertitz, Loretta Blake, George McDaniel

Mary Pickford was in her twenties when she played Sara Crewe, but her public suspended disbelief once again to witness her portrayal of the indomitable child of wealth who falls to the bottom of the heap. The major complaint about the film by contemporary critics was the over-long "Ali Baba" sequence. Mary Pickford personally chose teenager Zasu Pitts for the role of Becky, and she retained the services of her good friend Frances Marion for the scenario.

1917 *The Fair Barbarian*
Pallas Pictures
Distribution: Paramount Pictures. Opened December 17, 1917
Producer: Jesse L. Laski
Director: Robert Thornby
Scenario: Edith M. Kennedy
Camera: James C. Van Trees
Cast: Vivian Martin, C. H. Geldert, Josephine Crowell, Mae Busch, William Hutchinson, Al Paget, Ruth Handforth, Elinor Hancock, Charlie Gerard, Helen Jerome Eddy, John Burton

Pallas Pictures was an independent studio that was absorbed into Famous Players/Lasky shortly after production was completed on this film. Vivian Martin was Pallas Pictures' principal leading lady, appearing in forty films between 1915 and 1920. Mae Busch had appeared in films for five years when she left Triangle/Keystone Film Company to join Lasky. She is best known for her starring role in Erich von Stroheim's *Foolish Wives* (1922). Stage-trained Marguerite Clark was a popular silent screen actress until her retirement from the movies in 1921.

1918 *The Shuttle*
Select Pictures Corporation
Distribution: Select Pictures Corp. Opened February 1918
Producer: Louis J. Selznick
Director: Rollin Sturgeon
Scenario: Margaret Turnbull and Harvey Thew
Camera: James C. Van Trees
Cast: Constance Talmadge, Albert Roscoe, Edith Johnson, E. B. Tilton, Helen Dunbar, George McDaniel, Thomas Persse, Edward Peil, Casson Ferguson

1919 *Louisana*
Famous Players/Lasky Corp
Distribution: Paramount Pictures. Opened July 20, 1919
Producer: Jesse L. Lasky
Director: Robert G. Vignola
Scenario: Alice Eyton
Camera: Frank E. Garbutt
Cast: Vivian Martin, Robert Ellis, Noah Beery, Arthur Allardt, Lillian West, Lillian Leighton

1919 *The Secret Garden*
Famous Players/Lasky Corp.
Distribution: Paramount Pictures. Opened January 12, 1919
Producer: Jesse L. Lasky
Director: G. Butler Clonebough
Assistant Director: Lou Howland
Scenario: Marion Fairfax
Camera: Henry Kotani
Cast: Lila Lee, Spottiswoode Aitken, Clarence H. Geldart, Dick Rosson, Fay Holderness, Ann Malone, Paul Willis,

Lucille Ward, Mae Wilson, James Neill, Seymore Hastings, Rose Dione, Larry Steers, Forrest Seabury, Miss Guwha

1921   *Little Lord Fauntleroy*
Mary Pickford Film Corp.
Distribution: United Artists. Opened November 13, 1917
Producer: Mary Pickford
Directors: Alfred E. Green and Jack Pickford
Scenario: Bernard McConville
Photography: Charles Rosher
Music: Louis F. Gottschalk
Cast: Mary Pickford (dual role), Claude Gillingwater, Joseph Dowling, James Marcus, Kate Price, Fred Malatesta, Rose Dione, Frances Marion, Arthur Thalasso, Colin Kenny, Emmett King, Madame de Bodamere
I have only seen a very poor quality tape of this film, but Pickford's exuberance shines through. The film received considerable praise from the critics and did very well at the box office. Charles Roshner's cinematography was superb, and the technical excellence of his double exposures such as when Mary as "Fauntleroy" kisses Mary as "Dearest" rivals any computer-generated images of contemporary film-makers.

1924   *The Dawn of a Tomorrow*
Famous Players/Lasky
Distribution: Paramount Pictures. April 14, 1924
Producers: Jesse L. Lasky and Adolph Zukor
Director: George Melford
Scenario: Harvey Thew
Photography: Charles G. Clarke
Cast: Jacqueline Logan, David Torrence, Raymond Griffith, Roland Bottomley, Harris Gordon, Guy Oliver, Tempe Piggot, Mabel Van Buren, Marguerite Clayton, Alma Bennett, Warren Rogers

1924   *A Lady of Quality*
Universal-Jewel
Distribution: Universal Pictures. Opened January 14, 1924

Producer/Director: Hobart Henley
Scenario: Arthur Ripley and Marian Ainslee
Photography: John Stumar
Continuity: Marion Fairfax
Cast: Virginia Valli, Lionel Belmore, Margaret Seddon, Peggy Cartwright, Milton Sills, Florence Gibson, Dorothea Wolbert, Bert Roach, Earle Foxe, Leo White, George B. Williams, Willard Louis, Patterson Dial, Yvonne Armstrong, Bobby Mack

Fine direction by Hobart Henley elevated this film, which became one of Universal's most successful offerings of 1924. Virginia Valli's acting was especially noteworthy. Milton Sills continued to demonstrate why he was one of the best leading men of the twenties. His premature death of a heart attack in 1930 cut short an outstanding film career.

1936 *Little Lord Fauntleroy*
Selznick International
Distribution: United Artists Corp. Opened March 6, 1936
Producer: David O. Selznick
Director: John Cromwell
Screenplay: Hugh Walpole
Photography: Charles Rosher
Music: Max Steiner
Art Director: Sturges Carne
Cast: Freddie Bartholomew, Dolores Costello Barrymore, C. Aubrey Smith, Guy Kibbee, Henry Stephenson, Mickey Rooney, Constance Collier, E. E. Clive, Una O'Connor, Jessie Ralph, Ivan Simpson, Helen Flint, Mae Beatty, Virginia Field, Reginald Barlow, Lionel Belmore, Tempe Piggott, Gilbert Emery, Lawrence Grant, Walter Kingsford, Eily Malyon, Fred Walton, Robert Emmett O'Connor, Elsa Buchanan

John Cromwell crafted a warm, sentimental, and humorous adaptation of Burnett's story under the watchful eye of David O. Selznick. Freddie Bartholomew and Mickey Rooney create lasting impressions in their characterizations of Fauntleroy and Dick Tipton, respectively. A fine example of studio film-making during Hollywood's golden era, with excellent production values. Dolores Costello Barrymore was particularly noteworthy in her portrayal of Dearest.

1939   *The Little Princess*
Twentieth Century-Fox Film Corp.
Distribution: Twentieth Century-Fox Film Corp. Opened March 17, 1939
Producer: Darryl F. Zanuck
Director: Walter Lang
Screenplay: Ethel Hill and Walter Ferris
Photography: Arthur Miller and William Skall
Cast: Shirley Temple, Richard Greene, Anita Louise, Ian Hunter, Cesar Romero, Arthur Treacher, Mary Nash, Sybil Jason, Miles Mander, Marcia Mae Jones, Beryl Mercer, Deidre Gale, Ira Stevens, E. E. Clive, Eily Maylon, Clyde Cook, Keith Kenneth, Will Stanton, Harry Allen, Holmes Herbert, Guy Bellis, Evan Thomas, Kenneth Hunter, Lionel Braham

The year 1939 was one of Hollywood's greatest years, with an astonishing list of classic films having been released that year including *Gone with the Wind*, *Stagecoach*, *Wuthering Heights*, *The Wizard of Oz*, *Gunga Din*, and many others. While not in league with such screen greats, Twentieth Century-Fox's version is characterized by first-class production values. Typical of such star vehicles, the writers took considerable liberties with Burnett's story to adapt it to fit Temple's talent and persona. Shirley Temple's first color film. Available on DVD and videocassette.

1949   *The Secret Garden*
Metro-Goldwyn-Mayer
Distribution: MGM/Loews, Inc.
Producer: Clarence Brown
Director: Fred M. Wilcox
Screenplay: Robert Ardrey
Cinematography: Ray June

Music: André Previn
Art Design: Cedric Gibbons and Urie McCleary
Set Design: Edwin B. Willis and Richard Pefferle
Cast: Margaret O'Brien, Herbert Marshall, Dean Stockwell, Gladys Cooper, Elsa Lanchester, Reginald Owen, Brian Roper, Aubrey Mather, George Zucco, Lowell Gilmore, Billy Bevan, Dennis Hoey, Matthew Boulton, Isobel Elsom, Norma Varden

Released one hundred years after the birth of Frances Hodgson Burnett, Clarence Brown's production of *The Secret Garden* still holds up well, and certainly is one of the best adaptations of a Burnett story on film. It is rich in atmosphere and characterization, and the performances of Margaret O'Brien, Herbert Marshall, Elsa Lanchester, Reginald Owen, Brian Roper, and Dean Stockwell are excellent. The "surprise" color film sequences in the garden add to the magical elements of the film.

1980 *Little Lord Fauntleroy*
Made-for-televison
Screenplay: Blanche Hanalis
Photography: Arthur Ibbetson
Cast: Ricky Schroder, Victoria Tennant, Alec Guinness, Eric Porter, Colin Blakely, Connie Booth, Rachel Kempson

As TV productions go, this one was reasonably well done. Photography by Arthur Ibbetson won an Emmy award. Available on videocassete, but it is hard to find.

1984 *The Secret Garden*
BBC
Distribution: BBC Worldwide; CBS/FOX First Showing 1984
Producer: Dorothea Brooking
Director: Katrina Murray
Teleplay: Dorothea Brooking
Camera: John Baker

Film Editor: Monica Mead
Cast: Sarah Hollis Andrews, David Patterson, Andrew Harrison, Hope Johnson, Jacqueline Hoyle, Tom Harrison, John Woodnutt, William Marsh, Lorraine Peters, Jenny Goossens, Richard Warner, Clifford Cox, Charles Collingwood, Allison Lowdes, Basil Clark, Biny Balini, John Linstrum, Ray Dunbobbin, Lisa Kendrick, Jonathon Wall
This version was well done throughout, with fine acting performances from the cast. It is available on videocassette.

1986 *A Little Princess*
London Weekend Television (LWT)
Distribution: WonderWorks Video; first televised 1986
Producer: Colin Shindler
Director: Carol Wiseman
TV Adaptation: Jeremy Burnham
Director of Photography: Dave Taylor
Film Editor: Clayton Park
Designer: Gordon Melhuish
Cast: Amelia Shankley, Nigel Havers, Maureen Lipman, Miriam Margolyes, David Yelland, Annette Badland, Natalie Abbott, John Bird, Annie Lambert, Patsy Rowlands, Dikon Ashworth, Tariq Alibai, Johanna Hargreaves, Alison Reynolds, Katrina Heath, Joanna Dukes, Jessica Simpson, Christopher Haley, Zoe Mair, Alessia Gwyther, Mia Fothergill, Jake Wood
This British production is a straightforward adaptation of Burnett's story, flawed by the performance of Shankley as Mary Lennox. First seen in the United States on PBS, this British production is distributed by WonderWorks and available on videocassette. Somewhat "stagey" for my taste, but young children can easily follow the story. Doesn't hold a candle to the 1996 Alfonso Cuarón film.

1987 *The Secret Garden*
Hallmark (made-for-TV movie)
Producer: Hallmark
Director: Alan Grint

Cast: Gennie James, Barret Oliver, Michael Hordem, Jadrien Steele, Derek Jacobi, Billie Whitelaw, Lucy Gutteridge, Julian Glover, Colin Firth, Alan Grint
Well-received adaptation with outstanding acting from the whole cast. Gennie James is especially noteworthy in the role of Mary Lennox. Available on videocassette.

1993 *The Secret Garden*
American Zeotrope
Distribution: Warner Brothers
Producer: F. F. Coppola
Director: Agnieszka Holland
Screenplay: Caroline Thompson
Film Editor: Isabelle Lorente
Photography: Roger Deakins
Cast: Kate Maberly, Heydon Prowse, Andrew Knott, Maggie Smith, Laura Crossley, John Lynch, Walter Sparrow, Irene Jacob, Frank Baker, Valerie Hill, Andrea Pickering, Peter Moreton, Arthur Spreckley, Colin Bruce, Parsan Singh
This is the only production which tops MGM's 1949 *The Secret Garden*. Director Holland combines deft and subtle direction with textured story-telling that appeals to viewers of all ages. Holland preserves the sense of wonder and magic in Burnett's story. Maggie Smith as Mrs. Medlock could have stolen the film had not Holland elicited such moving performances from Kate Maberly and Heydon Prouse. Available on videocassette.

1995 *A Little Princess*
Warner Brothers (WB)
Distribution: WB
Producer: Mark Johnson
Director: Alfonso Cuarón
Screenplay: Elizabeth Chandle and Richard LaGravenese
Film Editor: Steve Weisberg
Art Director: Bo Welch
Cinematography: Emmanuel Lubezki

Cast: Liesel Matthews, Eleanor Bron, Liam Cunningham, Rusty Schwimmer, Arthur Malet, Vanessa Lee Chester, Errol Sitahal, Vincent Schiavelli

A four-star film on virtually every critic's list, this stunning film captures the child-like sense of wonder and magic which characterized Burnett's original story. Outstanding direction by Mexican-born Alfonso Cuarón, production by Mark Johnson, and cinematography by Emmanuel Lubezki evoke the precious gift of wonder so missing from today's "family" films. I can't help but believe that were she alive today, Frances Hodgson Burnett would have enthusiastically endorsed this delightful rendering of her classic children's story.

Index

Note: Page numbers that appear in italic indicate that a figure or image appears on that page.

A. A. *Milne* (Thwaite), 23, 27
Abeles, Edward, 144n18
Africa, as "Darkest England," 68
Aiken, Joan, 18
Ainslee, Marian, 138, 141
Aitken, Spottiswoode, 141
Alcott, Louisa May, 34; *Little Women*, 142, 148
Alice's Adventures in Wonderland (Carroll), 34
Allen, Thomas B., 164
American Library Association, 159
The American Magazine, 30, 154, 158
American Writers of To-Day, 114
anti-miscegenation laws, 48n21
Appel, Augusta, 173
Applebaum, Susan, 190
Archer, William, 122
Ardrey, Robert, 174, 178, 180
Association of Junior Leagues of America, 176
Athenaeum, 159
Atherton, Getrude, 138
Atlantic (magazine), 116
At the Children's Matinée (Meadowcroft), *127*

Austen, Jane, 219
The Awkward Age (James), 101

Ballet Shoes (Streatfield), 169, 171
Barbé, Cédric, 219
Barrie, J. M., 24
Barrymore, Dolores Costello, 142
Barrymore, John, 135–36
Bartholomew, Freddie, 142
Barton, Mary, 31
Baum, L. Frank, 213
Beach, Rex, 138
Bechtel, Louise Seaman, 161; *Books in Search of Children*, 161
Belasco, David, 135
Belmont, Eleanor Robson, 2
Ben Hur (film), 143n6
Bernhardt, Sarah, 135
Beery, Noah, Sr., 137, 141
Bigelow, Poultney, *100*
Birch, Reginald, 3–4, *36*, *46–47*, *69*, *75*, *83*, *119*
The Birth of a Nation (film), 140
Bixler, Phyllis, 45, 51–52, 164, 223
Blackwell, Carlyle, 144n18
Bodger, Joan, 162

243

Bok, Edward, 3
Booklist, 159
The Bookman, 158–59
Book Shelf for Boys and Girls, 160
Books in Search of Children (Bechtel), 161
Boond, William, 8
Booth, Edwin, 117, 118
Bosmajiian, Hamida, "Nightmares of History: the Outer Limits of Children's Literature," 189
Boucicault, Dion, 117
Bower, Maurice Lincoln, *73*
"The Boy Who Became a Socialist" (Burnett, F. H.), 69–70, 76
Brennan, Alfred, *151*
Briggs, Asa, 68
Bronte, Emily, *Wuthering Heights*, 29
Brownell, Kitty Hall, 2, 13, 113
Bull, Angela, 171
Burgess, B. G., 106
Burgess, Nelson, 107
Burnett, Constance Buel, 5, 19; *Happily Ever After*, 26
Burnett, Frances Hodgson, *221*; biography of, 17–31; "The Boy Who Became a Socialist," 69–70, 76; Burnett, S., and, 8–9; complete works of, availability, 206–14, *207*; *The Dawn of a Tomorrow*, 2, 13, 105, 155, 157, 208; early days of, 7–8; early writings, 8–9; education of, 114–15; *Emily Fox-Seton*, 208; *Esmeralda*, 4, 118–20, 135, 208; *A Fair Barbarian*, 137, 140–41, 208; feminism and, 18; film adaptations, for books, 121–43; *Giovanni and the Other: Children Who Have Made Stories*, *119*; *The Head of the House of Coombe*, 208; health issues for, 10; *His Grace of Osmonde*, 208; *In the Closed Room*, 208; inspirational source for, 114; Jacobean cupboard, 19–20, 27; James and, 24–25, 94, 101, 103; *Jarl's Daughters and Other Stories*, 209; *A Lady of Quality*, 13, 208; *The Land of the Blue Flower*, 73, 208; last days of, 1; *A Little Princess*, 2, 12, 23, *57*, 89, 105, 123–25, 205, 208; *Little Lord Fauntleroy*, 2, 4–5, 9, 12, 21, 31, 33–45, *36*, *44*, 57, *83*, 89, 190, 205, 208, 219; *Little Saint Elizabeth*, 208; *The Little Flower Book*, 155, 157; *The Little Hunchback Zia*, 208; "Lodusky," 208; *The Lost Prince*, 71–74, *73*, 208, 219; *Louisiana*, 137, 141; magazine stories of, 115; *The Making of a Marchioness*, 12, 79–90, *80*, 103, 209, 219; maternal themes for, 54–55; at Maytham Hall, 10–11, 94, 96–99, 104–10; *Memoirs of a London Doll*, 219; memorial for, 1–5, *6*, 14, 113, 218; mental health issues for, 104–5; "Mère Giraud's Little Daughter," 208; *The Methods of Lady Walderhurst*, 12, 219; "Le Monsieur De La Petite Dame," 208; as mother, 9–10; *My Robin*, 105, 208; "nervous exhaustion" of, 9; "One Day at Arle," 208; *The One I Knew the Best of All: A Memory of the Mind of a Child*, 67, 75, 113–14; online discussion groups about, 217–21; philanthropy of, 10; "The Plain Miss Burnie," 208; *The Pretty Sister of José*, 137; as prolific, 11;

pseudonyms for, 213; "The Quite True Story of an Old Hawthorn Tree," 74; *Racketty-Packetty House*, 19, 113, 125, *126–27*, 208; *The Real Little Lord Fauntleroy*, 113, 121; residences of, 10–11, 19, 93–94, 94, *96*, 96–99, 101–10, 104–10, 219; reversal of fortune as plot device for, 81; romantic fiction of, 205; *Sara Crewe, or What Happened at Miss Minchin's*, 69, 105, 123, 208; *The Secret Garden*, 2, 19, 23–24, 28–29, *62*, 85, 89, 105, 107, 149, 152, *156*, 205, 208; sentimentality of, 30–31; *The Shuttle*, 7, 13, 94, *95*, 96–98, 101–3, 105, 109, 159, 208, 220; "Smethurstses," 208; social life of, 5; stage adaptations by, 175–77; "Surly Tim's Trouble," 208; "That Lass o' Lowries," 9, 23–24, 74, 121, 219; theater productions, 113, 117, 118–25, 127; Townesend and, 10–11, 13, 25, 28, 86–87, 93–94, 97–98, 102–4; *T. Tembarom*, 13, 208, 219; on urban poor, 67–72, *73*, 75–76; "What the Pug Knew," 208; *The White People*, 208; "The Woman Who Saved Me," 208. See also *A Little Princess*; *Little Lord Fauntleroy*; *The Making of a Marchioness*; *The Secret Garden*; *That Lass o' Lowries*

Burnett, Swan, 8–9, 117

Burnett, Verity, 218

Burnett, Vivian, 21, 26, 28; *The Romantick Lady: The Life Story of an Imagination*, 19, 21, *22*, 26–27, 114, 214

Busch, Mae, 137, 140

Cable, George Washington, 31

Cady, Harrison, *126*

The Camelthorn Papers (Thwaite), 18–19

Campbell, Rosamond, 97, 109

Canadian Magazine, 159

Carey, Harry, 137, 140

Carpenter, Angelica, 28, 219; *Frances Hodgson Burnett: Beyond the Secret Garden*, 106

Carpenter, Humphrey, 163

Carroll, Lewis, 169, 219; *Alice's Adventures in Wonderland*, 34

Carrots (Mrs. Molesworth), 34

The Carved Lions (Mrs. Molesworth), 67

Central Park, New York, Frances Hodgson Burnett memorial in, 1–5, *6*, 14, 113, 218

Century (magazine), 19, 31, 105

Chapman, Edythe, 140

children's literature. *See* literature, children's

Children's Literature, 164

Children's Literature Association, 219

Children's Literature in Education, 164

children's theater. *See* theater, children's

Children's Theater of Evanston, Illinois, 176

Children's Theater of New York, 175

Children's Theatre, 125, 127

The Children's Catalog, 160

The Children's Literature Association Quarterly, 164

The Children's Magazine, 213

A Christmas Carol (Dickens), 142

Cinderella: *Little Lord Fauntleroy* and, 71; *A Little Princess* and, 56; *The Making of a Marchioness* and, 81

Civil War (U.S.), national identity after, 35
Clark, Marguerite, 137, 140, 144n18, 145n30
The Clever Woman of the Family (Yonge), 220
Clynes, J. R., 68
Coffee, Lenore, 138
Collins Magazine for Boys and Girls, 175
Colomb, Christoph, 219
"Colonial Discourse and 'Post'-Colonial Negotiations: *A Little Princess* and Its Adaptations" (Mirchandani), 190
Comer, Virginia Lee, 185n41
Communism, 76; Socialism v., 71
The Communist Manifesto (Engels/Marx), 71
Contagious Diseases Acts, 40
Cooper, Gladys, 175
Cooper, James Fenimore, *Last of the Mohicans*, 142
Coppola, Francis Ford, 142
Country Houses Association, 106, 108, 219
Crane, William H., 144n18
Crews, Laura Hope, 136
A Critical History of Children's Literature (Meigs), 161
Crouch, Marcus: *The Nesbit Tradition*, 182n3; *Treasure Seekers and Borrowers*, 163
Cuarón, Alfonso, xvi, 142, 190, 191, 194–95, 199–200
Cult of Beautiful Child, 37; in *Little Lord Fauntleroy* (book), 33–35, 43
Curwood, James Oliver, 138

Davis, Richard Harding, 138
Dawn, Hazel, 144n18

The Dawn of a To-morrow (Burnett, F. H.), 2, 13, 105, 155, 157, 208; film versions of, 132–33, 137–38, 140–41
de Kay, Helena, 19
De Mille, Cecil B., 136
The Dial, 158
Dickens, Charles, 138; *A Christmas Carol*, 142; *The Old Curiosity Shop*, 33
Dickinson, Emily, 165
Dixon, Ella Hepworth, 101, 105
Dodge, Mary Mapes, 120
Doro, Marie, 144n18
Drabble, Margaret, 18
Dunbar, Janet, 24
Deupree, Penny, 218; Gerzina interview of, 223–30

Edeson, Robert, 136
Edison, Thomas, 132, 136
Educational Alliance of New York, 124–25
Eliot, George, *Silas Marner*, 33
Elizabeth and her German Garden (von Arnim), 110n9, 157
Ellis, Robert, 141
Ellis, Sarah, *The Women of England: Their Social Duties and Domestic Habits*, 39
Emerson, John, 144n18
Emery, Mary Lou, "Refiguring the Postcolonial Imagination: Tropes of Visuality in Writing by Rhys, Kincaid, and Cliff," 190
Emily Fox-Seton (Burnett, F. H.), 208
Engels, Friedrich, *The Communist Manifesto*, 71
Enright, Elizabeth, 169
Erikson, Erik, 149

Esmeralda (Burnett, F. H.), 4, 118–20, 135, 208; film version of, 133, 137–38, 140
The Evanston Review, 177
Eyton, Alice, 138, 141

A Fair Barbarian (book/film), 137, 140–41, 208
Fairfax, Marion, 138, 141, 173, 180
fallen woman, 40
Farnum, Dustin, 136
Farnum, William, 136, 144n18
"Feminine Language and the Politics of Children's Literature" (Thacker), 51
feminism: Burnett, F. H., and, 18; *The Making of a Marchioness* and, 90
Ferrier, Paddy, 108
Field, R. M., 122
Fisk, Minnie Maddern, 135
Foxe, Earle, 141
Frances Hodgson Burnett: Beyond the Secret Garden (Carpenter/Shirley), 106
Frances Hodgson Burnett Society, 217
Frances Hodgson Burnett: The Unexpected Life of the Author of The Secret Garden (Gerzina), 153, 206, 219
Frederick, Pauline, 136
French, T. H., 123
Frohman, Charles, 135
Frohman, Daniel, 118, 135–37, 140

Gamble, Michael, 176
Garland, Judy, 174
Garver, John A., 3
Gaskell, Elizabeth, 31
Geater, Judy, 219
Gemma (Streatfield), 182

Gerzina, Gretchen Holbrook, 34, 104, 110, 153, 218; Deupree interview by, 223–30; *Frances Hodgson Burnett: The Unexpected Life of the Author of The Secret Garden*, 153, 206, 219
Gilder, Richard Watson, 4, 19, 116
Gilder, Rodman, 4
Gillette, William, 118
Giovanni and the Other: Children Who Have Made Stories (Burnett, F. H.), *119*
Girl of the Ozarks (film), 174
Gladstone, William, 33–34
Glimpses of the Wonderful (Thwaite), 24
Godey's Lady's Book, 115–16, 212–13
Goldfish, Samuel, 136
Gosse, Edmund, 25
Gosse, Philip Henry, 24
Grahame, Kenneth, *The Wind in the Willows*, 147–48
The Great Train Robbery (film), 135
Green, Alfred E., 141
Green, Roger Lancelyn: *Only Connect*, 163; *Tellers of Tales*, 163
Griffith, D. W., 136
Griffith, Katherine, 140
Griswold, Jerry, 35
Gross, John, *The Rise and Fall of the Man of Letters*, 25

Hackett, James K., 135
Haggard, H. Rider, *King Solomon's Mines*, 34
Hague, Michael, 164
Hanff, Peter, 219–20
Happily Ever After (Constance Buel Burnett), 26
Harper's (magazine), 101, 115–16, 212

Harper's Bazaar, 1
Harper's Weekly, 220
Hatwell, Elaine, 220
Hatwell, Lynne, 220
Havers, Nigel, 201
The Head of the House of Coombe (Burnett, F. H.), 208
Heidi (Spyri), 148
Heinemann, William, 105
Heins, Paul, 161
Hepburn Katherine, 174
Herrick, Walter, 4–5
Herts, A. Minnie, 124
Hill Cutler, Martha, 3
Hirst, Peter, 221
Hirst, Robert, 221
His Grace of Osmonde (Burnett, F. H.), 208
Hodgkin, Marni, 19, 27
Hodgson, Eliza, 8
Hodgson, Frances. *See* Burnett, Frances Hodgson
Hoffman, Daniel, 4
Holland, Agnieszka, 142
Holmes, Oliver Wendell, 122
Homer, *Odyssey*, 38
Hopper, Hedda, 178–79
The Horn Book, 160–61, 164
The House of Mirth (Wharton), 89
Howard, Elizabeth Jane, 26
Howells, John Mead, 2
Howells, William Dean, 31
Huckleberry Finn (Twain), 142
Humble, Nicola, *Victorian Heroines*, 43
Hunt, Clara, 160
Hunter, Ian, 193–94
Hurst, Fannie, 4
Huse, Nancy, 171

The Independent, 157
Industrial Revolution, 68–69

Inglis, Fred, *The Promise of Happiness*, 163
Internet, literary sources on, 207–8, 210
Internet Movie Database, 193; *A Little Princess* commentary, for film versions, 198–202
In The Closed Room (Burnett, F. H.), 208
In the Garden, 14; imagery in, 14

Jacobean cupboard, 19–20, *20*, 27
James, Henry, 1, 31, 101, 120; *The Awkward Age*, 101; Burnett, F. H., and, 24–25, 94, 101, 103
Japan, *Little Lord Fauntleroy* popularity in, 48n4
Jarl's Daughters and Other Stories (Burnett, F. H.), 209
Jarman, Claude, Jr., 178–79
Jennewein C. Paul, 2
Jogaku-Zasshi, 48n4
Jordan, Alice, 161
Jordan, Edith, 4, 93
Jordan, Elizabeth Garver, 1, 11–12
Jordan, Ellen, 220
Julian, Rupert, 140

Keene, Laura, 117
Kennedy, Edith M., 138
Kenyon, Ley, *181*
Kerry, Norman, 140
Keyser, Elizabeth Lennox, 190
Kinemacolor Film Company, 133, 143n8
King Solomon's Mines (Haggard), 34
Kipling, Rudyard, 99, 101
Kirk, Maria L., *62*, 154, *156*
Kirkwood, James, 137, 140
Kyne, Peter B., 138

Ladies' Home Journal, 3
A Lady of Quality (Burnett, F. H.), 13, 208; film version of, 132, 137, 138, 141
La Guardia, Fiorello, 5, 218
Lanchester, Elsa, 175
The Land of the Blue Flower (Burnett, F. H.), 74, 208
Langtry, Lily, 135
Lang, Walter, 190
Laski, Marghanita, 87, 89; *Mrs. Molesworth, Mrs. Ewing, and Mrs. Hodgson Burnett*, 20–21, 162
Lasky, Jessie L., 136
Last of the Mohicans (Cooper), 142
Laurette Messimy roses, 110n9; at Maytham Hall, *96*, 97, 107
Le Clair, Dorinda, 26–27
Lee, F. Marshall, 143n8
Lee, Lila, 141, 173–74, 182
Leonard, Robert, 140
Leslie's (magazine), 116
The Lion and the Unicorn, 164
The Listener, 17–18
literacy rates, 121
Literary Digest, 157–58
literature: adventure novels, 120; domestic novels, 120; fallen woman in, 40; non-Anglo prejudice as theme in, 40–41, 45; the "Other" in, 37, 41, 45; scar/birthmark cliche in, 38; Victorian heroines in, 43. *See also* melodrama; realism
literature, children's: *A Critical History of Children's Literature*, 161; Cult of Beautiful Child in, 33–34; maternal themes in, 51–57, 58–61, 63–64; morality in, 43; "Nightmares of History—The Outer Limits of Children's Literature," 189; snugness in, 147–50, 152; stage productions of, 125; Victorian repression in, 51
A Little Princess (Burnett, F. H.), 2, 12, 23, *57*, 89, 105, 205, 208; Cinderella story as influence on, 56; film versions of, 131–32, 137–38, *139*, 140, 142, 146n36, 189–202; Internet Movie Database commentary on, for film versions of, 198–202; mothering role in, 52, 54–56, 58; non-Anglo prejudice in, 68; stage productions of, 123–25; urban poor in, 68
Little House on the Prairie (Wilder), 148
Little, Jean, 162
Little Lord Fauntleroy (Burnett, F. H.), 2, 4–5, 9, 12, 21, 31, 33–45, *36*, *44*, 57, *83*, 89, 190, 205, 208, 219; as Cinderella story, 71; Cult of Beautiful Child in, 33–35, 43; fallen woman in, 40; false mother in, 45; film versions of, 2, 131–33, 141–42, 143n2; innocence as theme in, 42–43; in Japan, 48n4; mothering role in, 52–54; non-Anglo prejudice as theme in, 40–41, 45; the "Other" in, 37, 41, 45; serialization of, 34, 120, 123, 154; Socialism in, 70; worldwide popularity of, 23, 30, 34, 121, 155, 160
Little Saint Elizabeth and Other Stories (Burnett, F. H.), 208
The Little Flower Book (Burnett, F. H.), 155, 157
The Little Hunchback Zia (Burnett, F. H.), 208
Little Women (Alcott), 142, 148; stage productions of, 175
Loftus, Cecilia, 144n18

Logan, Jacqueline, 141
London, Jack, 138; *White Fang*, 142
Loos, Anita, 138
The Lost Prince (Burnett, F. H.), 71–74, *73*, 208, 219; urban poor in, 72–76
The Lost World (film), 173
Louisiana (film), 137, 141
Lowell, James Russell, 34
Lowry, Lois, 162
Lurie, Alison, 219
Luytens, Edwin, Maytham Hall and, 106, 108, 219
The Lying Truth (film), 173

Maberly, Kate, 142
MacPhearson, Jeanie, 138
Magic and the Magician (Streatfield), 182n3
Magnus, Julian, 117
Mahony, Bertha, 160; *Realms of Gold*, 160
Major, Clare Tree, 175, 177, 182
"Making Princesses, Re-Making *A Little Princess*" (Reimer), 190
The Making of a Marchioness (Burnett, F. H.), 12, 79–90, *80*, 103, 209, 219; autobiographical elements in, 85–87; as Cinderella story, 81; evolution of, 84; feminism and, 90; realism in, 87–88; as Victorian melodrama, 79, 84–85
Marchalonis, Shirley, 184
Marion, Frances, 138, 140, 146n36
Marshall, Herbert, 142
Martin, Vivian, 141
Marx, Karl, *The Communist Manifesto*, 71
Masten, Helen Adams, 161
Maternal Thinking: Toward a Politics of Peace (Ruddick), 63

Mathis, June, 138
Matthews, Liesel, 201
Maytham Hall (home), 10–11, 94, 96–99, *100*, 104–10, 219, *229*; construction of, 94, 96; gardens at, 97, 107–8; government use of, 106; Laurette Messimy roses at, 97, 107; Luytens and, 106, 108; sale of, 109; as *The Secret Garden* inspiration, 10, 28, 93; social life at, 99–100, *100*, 101
McCall's Magazine, 3
McCreary, William, 177
McElderry, Margaret, 18
McNulty, Faith, 164
Meadowcroft, Clara Pratt, *At the Children's Matinée*, 127
Meigs, Cornelia, *A Critical History of Children's Literature*, 161
Melbourne (Lord), 68
melodrama, *The Making of a Marchioness* as, 79, 84–85
Memoirs of a London Doll (Burnett, F. H.), 219
Meredyth, Bess, 138
"Mère Giraud's Little Daughter" (Burnett, F. H.), 208
Merington, Marguerite, 1, 3
The Methods of Lady Walderhurst (Burnett, F. H.), 12, 219
Millum, Harry, 29
Milne, A. A., 25–26; *Winnie-the-Pooh*, 34
Milne, Christopher, 26
Minneapolis Journal, 155
Mirchandani, Manisha, "Colonial Discourse and 'Post'-Colonial Negotiations: *A Little Princess* and Its Adaptations," 190, 197
Misselthwaite (Moody and O'Brien), 219

Mitchell, William, 117
"Le Monsieur De La Petite Dame" (Burnett, F. H.), 208
Montgomery, Florence, *Transformed*, 34
Moore, Anne Carroll, 161–62, 164
Moore, Clement, "The Night Before Christmas," 148
mothering roles: false mother, in *Little Lord Fauntleroy*, 45; gender variability in, 52, 63
Motion Picture Patents Company, 136, 144n20
motion pictures: of Burnett, F. H. works, 131–43, 173–75; industry development, 132–38, 140–42; one-reel films, 144n10; screen rights for, 133; star system in, 133
Motion Picture World, 144n12
Movie-Made America: A Social History of American Movies (Sklar), 144n20
Mrs. Molesworth: *Carrots*, 34; *The Carved Lions*, 67
Mrs. Molesworth, Mrs. Ewing, and Mrs. Hodgson Burnett (Laski), 20–21, 162
Mrs. Wiggs of the Cabbage Patch (film), 174
Murdoch, Iris, 18
Murray, David, 97
Mutual Households Association, 106
My Roads to Childhood (Moore, A. C.), 161
My Robin (Burnett, F. H.), 105, *151*, 208

The Nation, 158
Neilan, Marshall, 137, 140, 146n36
Nesbitt, Elizabeth, 161
The Nesbit Tradition (Crouch), 182n3

New Statesman, 17
The New Yorker, 164
New York Herald, 116
New York Public Library, 18, 161–62
New York Times, 116–17, 118, 123–24, 141, 157–58, 160, 174
"Nightmares of History: The Outer Limits of Children's Literature" (Bosmajiian), 189
"The Night Before Christmas" (Moore, A. C.), 148
Norton, Mary, 169
Nugent, Frank, 142

O'Brien, Margaret, 131, 142, 174–75, 178–79
Odyssey (Homer), 38
The Old Curiosity Shop (Dickens), 33
"One Day at Arle" (Burnett, F. H.), 208
O'Neill, James, 135
The One I Knew the Best of All: A Memory of the Mind of a Child (Burnett, F. H.), 67, *75*, 113–14; Small Person in, 114
Only Connect (Green, R. L.), 163
Osbourne, Lloyd, *221*
the "Other," 37, 41, 45; urban poor as, 68
Outlook, 158, 160

The Painted Garden (Streatfield), 170, 177–82, *181*, 219
Pasley, A. Du Gard, 106
Paterson, Katherine, 162
Pearce, Philipa, 162
People (magazine), 90
Peters, House, 137
Peterson's Magazine, 116, 212–14
Phillips, Eric, 169, 182
Pickford, Jack, 137, 140–41

Pickford, Mary, 2, 136–38, *139*, 140–41, 146n36, 190; film salary of, 145n32
Piffard, Harold, 57
Pitts, Zasu, 140, 146n36
"The Plain Miss Burnie" (Burnett, F. H.), 208
Plandome (home), 19
Porter, Edwin S., 135
Porter, Gene Stratton, 220
Potter, Beatrix, 30
poverty. *See* urban poor
Power, Tyrone, 144n18
Pratt, Florence E., "Wishes," *46–47*
The Pretty Sister of José (film), 137, 140
Project Gutenberg, 207
The Promise of Happiness (Inglis), 163
Prowse, Hayden, 142
Publisher's Weekly, 154–55

Queen Elizabeth (film), 134–35
"The Quite True Story of an Old Hawthorn Tree" (Burnett, F. H.), 74

racial prejudice: anti-miscegenation laws and, 48n21; in literature, 40–41, 45; in *A Little Princess*, 68
Racketty-Packetty House (Burnett, F. H.), 19, 113, 125, *126–27*, 208
Ransome, Arthur, 169
Reade, Charles, 117
realism: in *The Making of a Marchioness*, 87–88; in *The Secret Garden*, 191
Realms of Gold (Mahony), 160
The Real Little Lord Fauntleroy (play) (Burnett, F. H.), 113, 122
"Refiguring the Postcolonial Imagination: Tropes of Visuality in Writing by Rhys, Kincaid, and Cliff" (Emery), 190

Reimer, Mavis, "Making Princesses, Re-Making *A Little Princess*," 190
Reynolds, Kimberley, *Victorian Heroines*, 43
Rice, Charlie, 12
Rinehart, Mary Roberts, 138
Ripley, Arthur, 141
The Rise and Fall of the Man of Letters (Gross), 25
Roberts, Theodore, 140
Robinson, Charles, 159
Robinson, Greg, 220
Rolvenden (village), 29–30, 94
The Romantick Lady: The Life Story of an Imagination (Burnett, Vivian), 19, 21, *22*, 26–27, 114, 214; source material for, 28
Rooney, Mickey, 142, 174
Roper, Brian, 179
Rose, Jacqueline, 43
Rosher, Charles, 137, 141
Rousseau, Jean Jacques, 33
Rowling, J. K., 9
Ruddick, Sara, *Maternal Thinking: Toward a Politics of Peace*, 63
Russell, Annie, 4
Rust, Graham, 164

St. Nicholas Magazine, 9, 120–21, 123, 154, 160, 213
Sara Crewe, or, What Happened at Miss Minchin's (Burnett, F. H.), 69, 105, 123, 208
The Saturday Review, 162
Sayers, Frances Clarke, 162; *Summoned by Books*, 162
Scott, Cyril, 144n18
Scribner's Magazine, 113, 115–16, 212
Secret Love (film), 140

The Secret Garden, 2, 19, 23–24, 28–29, *62*, 85, 89, 105, 107, 149, 152, *156*, 205, 208; Anglo-Indian themes in, 218–19; child abuse as theme in, 192; commercial success of, 154–55, 160–61, 164–65; critical reception toward, 153, 155, 157–65; early versions of, 30; female writers influenced by, 164; film versions of, 131–32, 137, 141–42, 165, 173–75; influence of, 12; inspiration for, 7; literary neglect of, 20; Maytham Hall as inspiration for, 10, 28, 93; mothering role in, 52, 58–61, 63–64; realism in, 191; serialization of, 154; snugness in, 147; stage productions of, 175–77, 185n41; Streatfield influenced by, 169–71, 173; worldwide popularity of, 23
Seebohm E. V., 121–23; suicide of, 122
Selznick, David O., 141–42
Sensational Designs: The Cultural Work of American Fiction, 1790–1860 (Tompkins), 153
Shakespeare, William, *The Tempest*, 125
Shankley, Amelia, 200–201
Shipman, Nell, 138
Shirley, Jean, *Frances Hodgson Burnett: Beyond the Secret Garden*, 106
The Shuttle (Burnett, F. H.), 7, 13, 94, *95*, 96–98, 101–3, 105, 109, 159, 208, 220; film version of, 141
Signal, 164
Silas Marner (Eliot), 33
Sills, Milton, 141
Silver, Anna, 63

Simpson-Long, Elaine, 220
Sklar, Robert, *Movie-Made America: A Social History of American Movies*, 144n20
"Smethurstses" (Burnett, F. H.), 208
Smith, Barbara Hernstein, 154
Smith, C. Aubrey, 142
Smith, G. Albert, 143n8
Smith, Maggie, 142
snugness: Basic Trust and, 149; in children's literature, 147–50, 152
Socialism, 76; Communism v., 71; in *Little Lord Fauntleroy*, 70
Society of British Authors, 122
Song of Solomon, 172
Spyri, Johanna, *Heidi*, 148
Stevenson, Robert Louis, 138
Stockwell, Dean, 131, 142, 175, 178–79
Stokes, Frederick, 2
Stokes, Sally, 219
Streatfield, Noel, 169, 174–75; *Ballet Shoes*, 169, 171; *Gemma*, 182; *Magic and the Magician*, 182n3; nature as restorative for, 171–73; *The Painted Garden*, 170, 177–82, *181*, 183n21, 184n36, 219; *The Secret Garden* as influence on, 169–71, 173; *Thursday's Child*, 187n71; *The Whicharts*, 171; *The Winter Is Past*, 172
Sturgeon, Rollin, 137, 141
Summoned by Books (Sayers), 162
"Surly Tim's Trouble" (Burnett, F. H.), 208
Sutcliffe, Rosemary, 169

Talmadge, Constance, 137, 141
Tellers of Tales (Green, R. L.), 163
The Tempest (Shakespeare), 125

Temple, Shirley, 142, 190, 193–94, 201–2
Terry, Ellen, 105
Thacker, Deborah, "Feminine Language and the Politics of Children's Literature," 51
That Lass o' Lowries (Burnett, F. H.), 9, 23–24, 72, 74, 75, 121, 219; army metaphor in, 72; film version of, 140; serialization of, 116; urban poor in, 72
theater, children's, 125, 175–77; Association of Junior Leagues of America and, 176; Burnett, F. H., and, 123–25, 175–77, 185n41
theaters: children's literature productions in, 125, 175–77; in New York City, expansion of, 117, 118
The Theatre Magazine, 124–25
Thew, Harvey, 141
The Women of England: Their Social Duties and Domestic Habits (Ellis), 39
Thomas, Bob, 178
Thompson, Caroline, 142
A Thoroughbred Mongrel (Townesend), 104
Through One Administration (Burnett, F. H.), 12
Thursday's Child (Streatfield), 187n71
Thwaite, Anne, 28, 76, 153; *A. A. Milne*, 23, 27; *The Camelthorn Papers*, 18–19; *Waiting for the Party*, 17, 21, 25, 153, 163–64, 206, 223
Times of London, 160, 163, 174
Tolstoy, Leo, *War and Peace*, 30, 34
Tompkins, Jane, 154; *Sensational Designs: The Cultural Work of American Fiction, 1790–1860*, 153
Tom Sawyer (Twain), 142

Tops and Bottoms (Streatfield), 171–72
Torrence, David, 141
Townesend, Stephen, 29; Burnett, F. H., and, 10–11, 13, 25, 28, 86–87, 93–94, 97–98, 102–4; *A Thoroughbred Mongrel*, 104
Townsend, John Rowe, 20, 23; *Written for Children*, 20, 163
Transformed (Montgomery), 34
Treasure Seekers and Borrowers (Crouch), 163
T. Tembarom (Burnett, F. H.), 13, 208, 219
Tudor, Tasha, 164
Turnbull, Margaret, 138, 141
Turner, Edward R., 143n8
Twain, Mark, 1, 138, 220; *Huckleberry Finn*, 142; *Tom Sawyer*, 142
Tyler, George, 127
Tynan, Katherine, 159

Ulmer, John, 194, 198
Underwood, Clarence F., *95*
Unsell, Eve, 138, 140
Unwin, Nora S., 164
Urban, Charles, 143n8
urban poor: Burnett, F. H., on, 67–72, 75–76; as the "Other," 68; in *That Lass o' Lowries*, 72

Vagabondia (home), 8
Vanderbilt, William K., 127
Van Trees, James C., 137, 140–41
Ver Beck, Frank, *229*
Victoria (Queen), 68
Victorian Heroines (Humble/Reynolds), 43
Victorian melodrama. *See The Making of a Marchioness*; melodrama

von Arnim, Elizabeth, *Elizabeth and Her German Garden*, 110n9, 157
Vonnoh, Bessie Potter, 4, *6*
von Seyffertitz, Gustav, 173

Waiting for the Party (Thwaite), 17, 21, 25, 153, 163–64, 206, 223
Wakamatsu, Sizuko, 48n4
Wallace, Lew, 143n6
Wallack, Lester, 117
War and Peace (Tolstoy), 30, 34
Ward, Winifred, 176, 182
Ware, Helen, 140
Warner, H. B., 136, 144n18
Washington Post, 178
Watanna, Onoto, 220
Weber, Lois, 138
Webster, Jean, 220
Weidler, Virginia, 174
Wells, Carolyn, *221*
Wharton, Edith, *The House of Mirth*, 89
"What the Pug Knew" (Burnett, F. H.), 208
Whay, R. A., 158
The Whicharts (Streatfield), 171
White Fang (London), 142
The White People (Burnett, F. H.), 208
Wilder, Laura Ingalls, *Little House on the Prairie*, 148
Williams, C. D., *80*
Williams, Malcolm, 144n18
Wilson, Anna, 43
The Wind in the Willows (Grahame), 147–48
Winnie-the-Pooh (Milne), 34
The Winter Is Past (Streatfield), 172
Wiseman, Carol, 190, 196–97
"Wishes" (Pratt), *46–47*
"The Woman Who Saved Me" (Burnett, F. H.), 208
Woolson, Constance Fenimore, 31
World, 122
The Writer (magazine), 169
Written for Children (Townsend), 20, 163
Wuthering Heights (Bronte), 29

The Yearling (film), 178
Yonge, Charlotte, *The Clever Woman of the Family*, 220
Young Folks' Way (Burnett, F. H.), 120. *See also Esmeralda*
Youth's Companion, 161

Zukor, Adolph, 134–38, 145n32

About the Editor and Contributors

Deborah Fox Bellew works as an IT project manager in West Chester, Pennsylvania. She holds degrees in computer science from the University of Pennsylvania and economics from the Wharton School. Bellew has been an avid collector of Frances Hodgson Burnett books, articles, and ephemera for more than fifteen years. She maintains an ever-growing online bibliography of Burnett's rediscovered magazine stories.

Diana Birchall has written several Jane Austen sequels and reads novels for Warner Bros. Studios, where she is a story analyst. She is list owner of the Frances Hodgson Burnett online discussion group and the author of *Onoto Watanna*, the biography of her grandmother.

Angelica Shirley Carpenter is the founding curator of the Arne Nixon Center for the Study of Children's Literature at California State University, Fresno, and the author or coauthor of four biographies for young people, *Frances Hodgson Burnett*, *L. Frank Baum*, *Robert Louis Stevenson*, and *Lewis Carroll*. She is president of the International Wizard of Oz Club and a board member of the Lewis Carroll Society of North America.

Michael Cart is a columnist and reviewer for the American Library Association's *Booklist* magazine. A nationally known expert in the fields of children's and young adult literature, he is the founding editor of the literary journal *RUSH HOUR* and is the author of nearly a dozen books. Cart is also a founding board member of the Arne Nixon Center.

About the Editor and Contributors

Penny Deupree is the great-granddaughter of Frances Hodgson Burnett and owner of the Burnett family archive. She is passing down family traditions to her three grown children and seven grandchildren. She works as a home-based Creative Memories consultant in the Dallas area, where she lives with her husband Tom.

Deborah Druley received her M.A. in English from California State University, Fresno. She is an adjunct instructor at the Madera Center of Reedley College in California's Central Valley, where she teaches composition and critical thinking. Druley has loved Victorian children's stories since she was a little girl. As a teenager, she began to perceive Victorian children's literature as a force for positive social change, a theme she continues to develop in her research. She lives in rural Madera County, California, with her husband, son, and three cats.

Carole Dunbar was born and brought up in Manchester, England, but has spent her adult life in Ireland. She graduated with a degree in English from the New University of Ulster in Ulster, Ireland, and in 2001 was awarded a Ph.D. by Dublin City University in Dublin, Ireland, for her thesis, "The Other Nation," which examines the portrayal of the working classes in the works of four nineteenth-century children's novelists, including Frances Hodgson Burnett. She regularly reviews children's books for periodicals in both Ireland and England and has contributed essays to several publications dealing with children's literature, her latest being a study of the so-called Wild Irish Girl in the fiction of L. T. Meade and Mrs. George De Horne Vaizey in *Studies in Children's Literature 1500–2000*. Dunbar teaches at St. Patrick's College in Dublin, where she lectures in the M.A. course in children's literature.

Paul H. Frobose is a cultural and social historian specializing in the silent film era. He received his M.A. in history from California State University in Sacramento, in 1999. His thesis, "The United States Feature Film Company: A History of the First Motion Picture Studio in the Sacramento Valley," is an examination of the formation and development of one of the earliest motion picture production companies in California. He has lectured extensively on California history and the formative years of the motion picture industry. His published work includes "Sacramento's Golden Decade of Film Making" and "Buster

Keaton's Last Hurrah." Now a resident of Vermont, Frobose continues to write about the early motion picture industry and its social, cultural, and economic impact on local history. He is working on a book that examines the history of filmmaking in the Sacramento Valley.

Gretchen Holbrook Gerzina was a professor of English at Vassar College and Barnard College, Columbia University, and is now head of the English Department at Dartmouth College. She is the author of the biographies *Frances Hodgson Burnett: The Unexpected Life of the Author of The Secret Garden* and *Carrington: A Life* and of the social history *Black London: Life Before Emancipation*. She is also the editor of *Black Victorians/Black Victoriana* and the Norton Critical Edition of *The Secret Garden*.

Jerry Griswold is a professor in the Department of English and Comparative Literature at San Diego State University, where he is also director of the National Center for the Study of Children's Literature. He is the author of several books, including the prize-winning *Audacious Kids* (in paperback, *The Classic American Children's Story*), where he examines well-known American children's books, among them *Little Lord Fauntleroy* and *The Secret Garden*. He also writes occasionally for the *Los Angeles Times* and other publications.

Ariko Kawabata is an associate professor at Aichi Prefectural University in Japan, where she teaches English, children's literature, and English literature and culture. She recently submitted her Ph.D. thesis, "The Border-Crossings of Frances Hodgson Burnett: Children's Literature and Romance in Fin de Siècle Britain," to Roehampton University in England. She is an editorial member of the *Bookbird* (journal of the International Board on Books for Youth) and another research journal in Japan and has contributed essays to several publications dealing with children's literature. Her latest coauthored publication is *How to Make an English Lady* (written in Japanese), an illustrated book that demonstrates the culture and lifestyle of Victorian women and children.

Anne Lundin is a professor in the School of Library and Information Studies at the University of Wisconsin–Madison, where she teaches children's literature and storytelling. With research interests in the cultural reception to children's literature/librarianship, she has published

Victorian Horizons: the Reception of the Picture Books of Walter Crane, Randolph Caldecott, and Kate Greenaway and most recently *Constructing the Canon of Children's Literature: Beyond Library Walls and Ivory Towers.* Proud to proclaim *The Secret Garden* as her most formative book, she draws on her own passion for the book as a touchstone for the mythic lifelong power of childhood reading that inspires her life's work.

Alison Lurie is a professor of English at Cornell University, where she teaches courses in children's literature, folklore, humor, and writing. She is the author of nine novels, including *Foreign Affairs* (Pulitzer Prize, 1985), and her latest, *Truth and Consequences*. She has also published *Women and Ghosts*, a collection of supernatural stories; two collections of essays on children's literature, *Don't Tell the Grownups* and *Boys and Girls Forever*; and three books of traditional folktales for children. She is married to writer Edward Hower and has three grown sons and three growing grandchildren.

Barbara Jo Maier is an assistant professor in the Department of Theatre at Northern Arizona University, where she heads the Theatre Education Degree Emphasis and directs plays for youth. Her Ph.D. is in theatre for youth from Arizona State University, and she earned a M.A. in theatre with an emphasis in directing from Western Washington University. She was a Winifred Ward Scholar winner in 1999. Prior to NAU she taught at California State University, Fresno. Maier has vivid memories of reading *The Secret Garden* as a child. Her favorite reading spot was in the room her dad created just for her in the attic. She says that she and Fluffy share vivid imaginations.

Sally Sims Stokes is a librarian and historian who lives and works in the Washington, D.C., area. She is also the research specialist for the White House Historical Association. From 1987 to 2003, Sally was the curator of the National Trust for Historic Preservation Library Collection at the University of Maryland. In 2004 she received the Helene Gladstone Williams Scholarship from the D.C. branch of the English-Speaking Union to support her study in England of the work of Noel Streatfeild. Growing up in the Philadelphia suburbs, she read and reread *The Secret Garden*, as well as many Noel Streatfeild novels.

About the Editor and Contributors

Ann Thwaite is the author of *Waiting for the Party: The Life of Frances Hodgson Burnett, 1849–1924*, which was first published in 1974. It was her first biography, followed by four more on A. A. Milne, Emily Tennyson, and both Edmund and Philip Henry Gosse—son and father. Thwaite is a fellow of the Royal Society of Literature and has a doctorate in literature from Oxford University. *A. A. Milne, His Life* won the Whitbread prize for the best biography of 1990.

Lance Weldy is a visiting assistant professor at Western Michigan University, where he teaches classes in children's literature and the Bible as literature. He moved to Western Michigan University after successfully defending his dissertation at Texas A&M University–Commerce in the summer of 2004. He holds a lifelong passion for literary adaptations into film and recalls as a child memorizing passages from such BBC classics as *The Lion, the Witch, and the Wardrobe* and *A Little Princess*. He has recently written his first book, *Seeking a Felicitous Space: The Dialectics of Women and Frontier Space in* Giants in the Earth, Little House on the Prairie, *and* My Ántonia.